Praise for *Learning Go*

"Go is unique and even experienced programmers have to unlearn a few things and think differently about software. *Learning Go* does a good job of working through the big features of the language while pointing out idiomatic code, pitfalls, and design patterns along the way."

—*Aaron Schlesinger, Sr. Engineer, Microsoft*

"Jon has been a critical voice in the Go community for many years and we have been strongly benefitted from his talks and articles. With *Learning Go*, Jon has written the programmers' guide to learning Go. It strikes just the right balance of giving a good overview of what you need to know without rehashing well understood concepts from other languages."

—*Steve Francia, Go language product lead, Google, and author of Hugo, Cobra, and Viper*

"Bodner gets Go. In clear, lively prose, he teaches the language from its basics to advanced topics like reflection and C interop. He demonstrates through numerous examples how to write *idiomatic* Go, with its emphasis on clarity and simplicity. He also takes the time to explain the underlying concepts that can affect your program's behavior, like the effects of pointers on memory layout and garbage collection. Beginners who read this book will come up to speed quickly, and even experienced Go programmers are likely to learn something."

—*Jonathan Amsterdam, Software Engineer on the Go team at Google*

FIRST EDITION

Learning Go

*An Idiomatic Approach to
Real-World Go Programming*

Jon Bodner

Beijing · Boston · Farnham · Sebastopol · Tokyo

Learning Go

by Jon Bodner

Copyright © 2021 Jon Bodner. All rights reserved.

Published by O'Reilly Media, Inc., 1005 Gravenstein Highway North, Sebastopol, CA 95472.

O'Reilly books may be purchased for educational, business, or sales promotional use. Online editions are also available for most titles (*http://oreilly.com*). For more information, contact our corporate/institutional sales department: 800-998-9938 or *corporate@oreilly.com*.

Acquisitions Editor: Suzanne McQuade
Developmental Editor: Michele Cronin
Production Editor: Beth Kelly
Copyeditor: Piper Editorial Consulting, LLC
Proofreader: Piper Editorial Consulting, LLC

Indexer: Judith McConville
Interior Designer: David Futato
Cover Designer: Karen Montgomery
Illustrator: Kate Dullea

March 2021:   First Edition

Revision History for the First Edition
2021-03-02:   First Release
2021-05-14:   Second Release
2022-05-13:   Third Release

See *http://oreilly.com/catalog/errata.csp?isbn=9781492077213* for release details.

978-1-492-07721-3

[LSI]

Table of Contents

Preface

My first choice for a book title was *Boring Go* because, properly written, Go is boring.

It might seem a bit weird to write a book on a boring topic, so I should explain. Go has a small feature set that is out of step with most other modern programming languages. Well-written Go programs tend to be straightforward and sometimes a bit repetitive. There's no inheritance, no generics (yet), no aspect-oriented programming, no function overloading, and certainly no operator overloading. There's no pattern matching, no named parameters, no exceptions. To the horror of many, there are *pointers*. Go's concurrency model is unlike other languages, but it's based on ideas from the 1970s, as is the algorithm used for its garbage collector. In short, Go feels like a throwback. And that's the point.

Boring does not mean *trivial*. Using Go correctly requires an understanding of how its features are intended to fit together. While you can write Go code that looks like Java or Python, you're going to be unhappy with the result and wonder what all the fuss is about. That's where this book comes in. It walks through the features of Go, explaining how to best use them to write idiomatic code that can grow.

When it comes to building things that last, being boring is great. No one wants to be the first person to drive their car over a bridge built with untested techniques that the engineer thought were cool. The modern world depends on software as much as it depends on bridges, perhaps more so. Yet many programming languages add features without thinking about their impact on the maintainability of the codebase. Go is intended for building programs that last, programs that are modified by dozens of developers over dozens of years.

Go is boring and that's fantastic. I hope this book teaches you how to build exciting projects with boring code.

Who Should Read This Book

This book is targeted at developers who are looking to pick up a second (or fifth) language. The focus is on people who are new to Go. This ranges from those who don't know anything about Go other than it has a cute mascot, to those who have already worked through a Go tutorial or even written some Go code. The focus for *Learning Go* isn't just how to write programs in Go; it's how to write Go *idiomatically*. More experienced Go developers can find advice on how to best use the newer features of the language. The most important thing is that the reader wants to learn how to write Go code that looks like Go.

Experience is assumed with the tools of the developer trade, such as version control (preferably Git) and IDEs. Readers should be familiar with basic computer science concepts like concurrency and abstraction, as the book explains how they work in Go. Some of the code examples are downloadable from GitHub and dozens more can be tried out online on The Go Playground. While an internet connection isn't required, it is helpful when reviewing executable examples. Since Go is often used to build and call HTTP servers, some examples assume familiarity with basic HTTP concepts.

While most of Go's features are found in other languages, Go makes different trade-offs, so programs written in it have a different structure. *Learning Go* starts by looking at how to set up a Go development environment, and then covers variables, types, control structures, and functions. If you are tempted to skip over this material, resist the urge and take a look. It is often the details that make your Go code idiomatic. Some of what seems obvious at first glance might actually be subtly surprising when you think about it in depth.

Conventions Used in This Book

The following typographical conventions are used in this book:

Italic
: Indicates new terms, URLs, email addresses, filenames, and file extensions.

`Constant width`
: Used for program listings, as well as within paragraphs to refer to program elements such as variable or function names, databases, data types, environment variables, statements, and keywords.

`Constant width bold`
: Shows commands or other text that should be typed literally by the user.

Constant width italic

Shows text that should be replaced with user-supplied values or by values determined by context.

 This element signifies a tip or suggestion.

 This element signifies a general note.

 This element indicates a warning or caution.

Using Code Examples

Supplemental material (code examples, exercises, etc.) is available for download at *https://github.com/learning-go-book*.

If you have a technical question or a problem using the code examples, please send email to *bookquestions@oreilly.com*.

This book is here to help you get your job done. In general, if example code is offered with this book, you may use it in your programs and documentation. You do not need to contact us for permission unless you're reproducing a significant portion of the code. For example, writing a program that uses several chunks of code from this book does not require permission. Selling or distributing examples from O'Reilly books does require permission. Answering a question by citing this book and quoting example code does not require permission. Incorporating a significant amount of example code from this book into your product's documentation does require permission.

We appreciate, but do not require, attribution. An attribution usually includes the title, author, publisher, and ISBN. For example: *"Learning Go* by Jon Bodner (O'Reilly). Copyright 2021 Jon Bodner, 978-1-492-07721-3."

If you feel your use of code examples falls outside fair use or the permission given above, feel free to contact us at *permissions@oreilly.com*.

O'Reilly Online Learning

O'REILLY® For more than 40 years, *O'Reilly Media* has provided technology and business training, knowledge, and insight to help companies succeed.

Our unique network of experts and innovators share their knowledge and expertise through books, articles, and our online learning platform. O'Reilly's online learning platform gives you on-demand access to live training courses, in-depth learning paths, interactive coding environments, and a vast collection of text and video from O'Reilly and 200+ other publishers. For more information, visit *http://oreilly.com*.

How to Contact Us

Please address comments and questions concerning this book to the publisher:

O'Reilly Media, Inc.
1005 Gravenstein Highway North
Sebastopol, CA 95472
800-998-9938 (in the United States or Canada)
707-829-0515 (international or local)
707-829-0104 (fax)

We have a web page for this book, where we list errata, examples, and any additional information. You can access this page at *https://oreil.ly/learn-go*.

Email *bookquestions@oreilly.com* to comment or ask technical questions about this book.

For news and information about our books and courses, visit *http://oreilly.com*.

Find us on Facebook: *http://facebook.com/oreilly*

Follow us on Twitter: *http://twitter.com/oreillymedia*

Watch us on YouTube: *http://youtube.com/oreillymedia*

Acknowledgments

Writing a book seems like a solitary task, but it doesn't happen without the help of a great number of people. I mentioned to Carmen Andoh that I wanted to write a book on Go and at GopherCon 2019, and she introduced me to Zan McQuade at O'Reilly. Zan guided me through the acquisition process and continued to provide me advice while I was writing *Learning Go*. Michele Cronin edited the text, gave feedback, and listened during the inevitable rough patches. Tonya Trybula's copy editing and Beth Kelly's production editing made my draft production-quality.

While writing, I received critical feedback (and encouragement) from many people including Jonathan Altman, Jonathan Amsterdam, Johnny Ray Austin, Chris Fauerbach, Chris Hines, Bill Kennedy, Tony Nelson, Phil Pearl, Liz Rice, Aaron Schlesinger, Chris Stout, Kapil Thangavelu, Claire Trivisonno, Volker Uhrig, Jeff Wendling, and Kris Zaragoza. I'd especially like to recognize Rob Liebowitz, whose detailed notes and rapid responses made this book far better than it would have been without his efforts.

My family put up with me spending nights and weekends at the computer instead of with them. In particular, my wife Laura graciously pretended that I didn't wake her up when I'd come to bed at 1 A.M. or later.

Finally, I want to remember the two people who started me on this path four decades ago. The first is Paul Goldstein, the father of a childhood friend. In 1982, Paul showed us a Commodore PET, typed PRINT 2 + 2, and hit the enter key. I was amazed when the screen said 4 and was instantly hooked. He later taught me how to program and even let me borrow the PET for a few weeks. Second, I'd like to thank my mother for encouraging my interest in programming and computers, despite having no idea what any of it was for. She bought me the BASIC programming cartridge for the Atari 2600, a VIC-20 and then a Commodore 64, along with the programming books that inspired me to want to write my own someday.

Thank you all for helping make this dream of mine come true.

CHAPTER 1

Setting Up Your Go Environment

Every programming language needs a development environment, and Go is no exception. If you've already written a Go program or two, you should have a working environment, but you might have missed out on some of the newer techniques and tools. If this is your first time setting up Go on your computer, don't worry; installing Go and its supporting tools is easy. After we set up our environment and verify it, we'll build a simple program, learn about the different ways to build and run Go code, and then explore some tools and techniques that make Go development easier.

Installing the Go Tools

To write Go code, you first need to download and install the Go development tools. The latest version of the tools can be found at the downloads page on the Go website (*https://golang.org/dl*). Choose the download for your platform and install it. The *.pkg* installer for Mac and the *.msi* installer for Windows automatically install Go in the correct location, remove any old installations, and put the Go binary in the default executable path.

 If you are a Mac developer, you can install Go using Homebrew (*https://brew.sh*) with the command `brew install go`. Windows developers who use Chocolatey (*https://chocolatey.org*) can install Go with the command `choco install golang`.

The various Linux and FreeBSD installers are gzipped tar files and expand to a directory named *go*. Copy this directory to */usr/local* and add */usr/local/go/bin* to your $PATH so that the go command is accessible:

```
$ tar -C /usr/local -xzf go1.15.2.linux-amd64.tar.gz
$ echo 'export PATH=$PATH:/usr/local/go/bin' >> $HOME/.profile
$ source $HOME/.profile
```

Go programs compile to a single binary and do not require any additional software to be installed in order to run them. Install the Go development tools only on computers that build Go programs.

You can validate that your environment is set up correctly by opening up a terminal or command prompt and typing:

```
$ go version
```

If everything is set up correctly, you should see something like this printed:

```
go version go1.15.2 darwin/amd64
```

This tells you that this is Go version 1.15.2 on Mac OS. (Darwin is the name of the kernel for Mac OS and amd64 is the name for the 64-bit CPU architecture from both AMD and Intel.)

If you get an error instead of the version message, it's likely that you don't have go in your executable path, or you have another program named go in your path. On Mac OS and other Unix-like systems, use which go to see the go command being executed, if any. If it isn't the go command at */usr/local/go/bin/go*, you need to fix your executable path.

If you're on Linux or FreeBSD, it's possible you installed the 64-bit Go development tools on a 32-bit system or the development tools for the wrong chip architecture.

The Go Workspace

Since the introduction of Go in 2009, there have been several changes in how Go developers organize their code and their dependencies. Because of this churn, there's lots of conflicting advice, and most of it is obsolete.

For modern Go development, the rule is simple: you are free to organize your projects as you see fit.

However, Go still expects there to be a single workspace for third-party Go tools installed via go install (see "Getting Third-Party Go Tools" on page 5). By default, this workspace is located in *$HOME/go*, with source code for these tools stored in *$HOME/go/src* and the compiled binaries in *$HOME/go/bin*. You can use this default or specify a different workspace by setting the $GOPATH environment variable.

Whether or not you use the default location, it's a good idea to explicitly define GOPATH and to put the *$GOPATH/bin* directory in your executable path. Explicitly defining GOPATH makes it clear where your Go workspace is located and adding *$GOPATH/bin* to your executable path makes it easier to run third-party tools installed via go install, which we'll talk about in a bit.

If you are on a Unix-like system using bash, add the following lines to your *.profile*. (If you are using zsh, add these lines to *.zshrc* instead):

```
export GOPATH=$HOME/go
export PATH=$PATH:$GOPATH/bin
```

You'll need to source *$HOME/.profile* to make these changes take effect in your current terminal window.

On Windows, run the following commands at the command prompt:

```
setx GOPATH %USERPROFILE%\go
setx path "%path%;%GOPATH%\bin"
```

After running these commands, you must close your current command prompt and open a new one for these changes to take effect.

There are other environment variables that are recognized by the go tool. You can get a complete list, along with a brief description of each variable, using the go env command. Many of them control low-level behavior that can be safely ignored, but we cover some of these variables when discussing modules and cross-compilation.

 Some online resources tell you to set the GOROOT environment variable. This variable specifies the location where your Go development environment is installed. This is no longer necessary; the go tool figures this out automatically.

The go Command

Out of the box, Go ships with many development tools. You access these tools via the go command. They include a compiler, code formatter, linter, dependency manager, test runner, and more. As we learn how to build high-quality idiomatic Go, we'll explore many of these tools throughout the book. Let's start with the ones that we use to build Go code and use the go command to build a simple application.

go run and go build

There are two similar commands available via go: go run and go build. Each takes either a single Go file, a list of Go files, or the name of a package. We are going to create a simple program and see what happens when we use these commands.

go run

We'll start with go run. Create a directory called *ch1*, open up a text editor, enter the following text, and save it inside *ch1* to a file named *hello.go*:

```
package main

import "fmt"

func main() {
    fmt.Println("Hello, world!")
}
```

After the file is saved, open up a terminal or command prompt and type:

```
go run hello.go
```

You should see Hello, world! printed in the console. If you look inside the directory after running the go run command, you see that no binary has been saved there; the only file in the directory is the *hello.go* file we just created. You might be thinking: I thought Go was a compiled language. What's going on?

The go run command does in fact compile your code into a binary. However, the binary is built in a temporary directory. The go run command builds the binary, executes the binary from that temporary directory, and then deletes the binary after your program finishes. This makes the go run command useful for testing out small programs or using Go like a scripting language.

Use go run when you want to treat a Go program like a script and run the source code immediately.

go build

Most of the time you want to build a binary for later use. That's where you use the go build command. On the next line in your terminal, type:

```
go build hello.go
```

This creates an executable called hello (or *hello.exe* on Windows) in the current directory. Run it and you unsurprisingly see Hello, world! printed on the screen.

The name of the binary matches the name of the file or package that you passed in. If you want a different name for your application, or if you want to store it in a different location, use the -o flag. For example, if we wanted to compile our code to a binary called "hello_world," we would use:

```
go build -o hello_world hello.go
```

Use `go build` to create a binary that is distributed for other people to use. Most of the time, this is what you want to do. Use the `-o` flag to give the binary a different name or location.

Getting Third-Party Go Tools

While some people choose to distribute their Go programs as pre-compiled binaries, tools written in Go can also be built from source and installed into your Go workspace via the `go install` command.

Go's method for publishing code is a bit different than most other languages. Go developers don't rely on a centrally hosted service, like Maven Central for Java or the NPM registry for JavaScript. Instead, they share projects via their source code repositories. The `go install` command takes an argument, which is the location of the source code repository of the project you want to install, followed by an @ and the version of the tool you want (if you just want to get the latest version, use `@latest`). It then downloads, compiles, and installs the tool into your *$GOPATH/bin* directory.

Let's look at a quick example. There's a great Go tool called hey that load tests HTTP servers. You can point it at the website of your choosing or an application that you've written. Here's how to install hey with the `go install` command:

```
$ go install github.com/rakyll/hey@latest
go: downloading github.com/rakyll/hey v0.1.4
go: downloading golang.org/x/net v0.0.0-20181017193950-04a2e542c03f
go: downloading golang.org/x/text v0.3.0
```

This downloads hey and all of its dependencies, builds the program, and installs the binary in your *$GOPATH/bin* directory.

As we'll talk about in "Module Proxy Servers" on page 200, the contents of Go repositories are cached in proxy servers. Depending on the repository and the values in your GOPROXY environment variable, `go install` may download from a proxy or directly from a repository. If `go install` downloads directly from a repository, it relies on command-line tools being installed on your computer. For example, you must have Git installed to download from GitHub.

Now that we have built and installed *hey*, we can run it with:

```
$ hey https://www.golang.org

Summary:
  Total:        0.6864 secs
  Slowest:      0.3148 secs
```

```
Fastest:        0.0696 secs
Average:        0.1198 secs
Requests/sec: 291.3862
```

If you have already installed a tool and want to update it to a newer version, rerun go install with the newer version specified or with @latest:

```
go install github.com/rakyll/hey@latest
```

Of course, you don't need to leave tools written in Go in your Go workspace; they are regular executable binaries and can be stored anywhere on your computer. Likewise, you don't have to distribute programs written in Go using go install; you can put a binary up for download. However, go install is a very convenient way to distribute Go programs to other Go developers.

Formatting Your Code

One of the chief design goals for Go was to create a language that allowed you to write code efficiently. This meant having simple syntax and a fast compiler. It also led Go's authors to reconsider code formatting. Most languages allow a great deal of flexibility on how code is laid out. Go does not. Enforcing a standard format makes it a great deal easier to write tools that manipulate source code. This simplifies the compiler and allows the creation of some clever tools for generating code.

There is a secondary benefit as well. Developers have historically wasted extraordinary amounts of time on format wars. Since Go defines a standard way of formatting code, Go developers avoid arguments over One True Brace Style and Tabs vs. Spaces, For example, Go programs use tabs to indent, and it is a syntax error if the opening brace is not on the same line as the declaration or command that begins the block.

 Many Go developers think the Go team defined a standard format as a way to avoid developer arguments and discovered the tooling advantages later. However, Russ Cox has publicly stated (*https://oreil.ly/rZEUv*) that better tooling was his original motivation.

The Go development tools include a command, go fmt, which automatically reformats your code to match the standard format. It does things like fixing up the whitespace for indentation, lining up the fields in a struct, and making sure there is proper spacing around operators.

There's an enhanced version of go fmt available called goimports that also cleans up your import statements. It puts them in alphabetical order, removes unused imports, and attempts to guess any unspecified imports. Its guesses are sometimes inaccurate, so you should insert imports yourself.

You can download `goimports` with the command `go install golang.org/x/tools/cmd/goimports@latest`. You run it across your project with the command:

```
goimports -l -w .
```

The `-l` flag tells `goimports` to print the files with incorrect formatting to the console. The `-w` flag tells `goimports` to modify the files in-place. The `.` specifies the files to be scanned: everything in the current directory and all of its subdirectories.

The Semicolon Insertion Rule

The `go fmt` command won't fix braces on the wrong line, because of the *semicolon insertion rule*. Like C or Java, Go requires a semicolon at the end of every statement. However, Go developers never put the semicolons in themselves; the Go compiler does it for them following a very simple rule described in Effective Go (*https://oreil.ly/hTOHU*):

If the last token before a newline is any of the following, the lexer inserts a semicolon after the token:

- An identifier (which includes words like int and float64)
- A basic literal such as a number or string constant
- One of the tokens: "break," "continue," "fallthrough," "return," "++," "--," ")," or "}"

With this simple rule in place, you can see why putting a brace in the wrong place breaks. If you write your code like this:

```
func main()
{
    fmt.Println("Hello, world!")
}
```

the semicolon insertion rule sees the ")" at the end of the `func main()` line and turns that into:

```
func main();
{
    fmt.Println("Hello, world!");
};
```

and that's not valid Go.

The semicolon insertion rule is one of the things that makes the Go compiler simpler and faster, while at the same time enforcing a coding style. That's clever.

Always run go fmt or goimports before compiling your code!

Linting and Vetting

While go fmt ensures your code is formatted correctly, it's just the first step in ensuring that your code is idiomatic and of high quality. All Go developers should read through Effective Go (*https://oreil.ly/GBRut*) and the Code Review Comments page on Go's wiki (*https://oreil.ly/FHi_h*) to understand what idiomatic Go code looks like.

There are tools that help to enforce this style. The first is called golint. (The term "linter" comes from the Unix team at Bell Labs; the first linter was written in 1978.) It tries to ensure your code follows style guidelines. Some of the changes it suggests include properly naming variables, formatting error messages, and placing comments on public methods and types. These aren't errors; they don't keep your programs from compiling or make your program run incorrectly. Also, you cannot automatically assume that golint is 100% accurate: because the kinds of issues that golint finds are more fuzzy, it sometimes has false positives and false negatives. This means that you don't *have* to make the changes that golint suggests. But you should take the suggestions from golint seriously. Go developers expect code to look a certain way and follow certain rules, and if your code does not, it sticks out.

 2022 Update: golint has been deprecated. In addition to golangci-lint, other recommended replacements are staticcheck (*https://staticcheck.io*) and revive (*https://revive.run*). This section will be updated in future editions.

Install golint with the following command:

```
go install golang.org/x/lint/golint@latest
```

And run it with:

```
golint ./...
```

That runs golint over your entire project.

There is another class of errors that developers run into. The code is syntactically valid, but there are mistakes that are not what you meant to do. This includes things like passing the wrong number of parameters to formatting methods or assigning values to variables that are never used. The go tool includes a command called go vet to detect these kinds of errors. Run go vet on your code with the command:

```
go vet ./...
```

There are additional third-party tools to check code style and scan for potential bugs. However, running multiple tools over your code slows down the build because each tool spends time scanning the source code for itself. Rather than use separate tools, you can run multiple tools together with `golangci-lint` (*https://oreil.ly/O15u-*). It combines `golint`, `go vet`, and an ever-increasing set of other code quality tools. Once it is installed (*https://oreil.ly/IKa_S*), you run `golangci-lint` with the command:

```
golangci-lint run
```

Because `golangci-lint` runs so many tools (as of this writing, it runs 10 different linters by default and allows you to enable another 50), it's inevitable that your team may disagree with some of its suggestions. You can configure which linters are enabled and which files they analyze by including a file named *.golangci.yml* at the root of your project. Check out the documentation (*https://oreil.ly/vufj1*) for the file format.

I recommend that you start off using `go vet` as a required part of your automated build process and `golint` as part of your code review process (since `golint` might have false positives and false negatives, you can't require your team to fix every issue it reports). Once you are used to their recommendations, try out `golangci-lint` and tweak its settings until it works for your team.

 Make `golint` and `go vet` (or `golangci-lint`) part of your development process to avoid common bugs and nonidiomatic code. But if you are using `golangci-lint`, make sure your team agrees on the rules that you want to enforce!

Choose Your Tools

While we wrote a small Go program using nothing more than a text editor and the `go` command, you'll probably want more advanced tools when working on larger projects. Luckily, there are excellent Go development tools (*https://oreil.ly/MwCWT*) for most text editors and IDEs. If you don't already have a favorite tool, two of the most popular Go development environments are Visual Studio Code and Goland.

Visual Studio Code

If you are looking for a free development environment, Visual Studio Code (*https://oreil.ly/zktT8*) from Microsoft is your best option. Since it was released in 2015, VS Code has become the most popular source code editor for developers. It does not ship with Go support, but you can make it a Go development environment by downloading the Go extension from the extensions gallery.

VS Code's Go support relies on third-party tools. This includes the Go Development tools, The Delve debugger (*https://oreil.ly/sosLu*), and gopls (*https://oreil.ly/TLapT*), a Go Language Server developed by the Go team. While you need to install the Go development kit yourself, the Go extension will install Delve and gopls for you.

 What is a language server? It's a standard specification for an API that enables editors to implement intelligent editing behavior, like code completion, linting, and finding usages. You can check out the language server protocol (*https://oreil.ly/2T2fw*).

Once your tools are set up, you can then open your project and work with it. Figure 1-1 shows you what your project window should look like. Getting Started with VS Code Go (*https://oreil.ly/XhoeB*) is a walkthrough that demonstrates the VS Code Go extension.

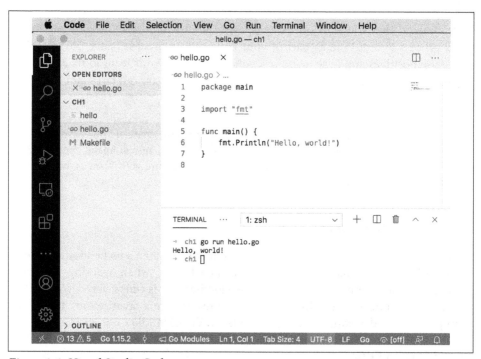

Figure 1-1. Visual Studio Code

GoLand

GoLand (*https://oreil.ly/6cXjL*) is the Go-specific IDE from JetBrains. While JetBrains is best known for Java-centric tools, GoLand is an excellent Go development environment. As you can see in Figure 1-2, GoLand's user interface looks similar to IntelliJ,

PyCharm, RubyMine, WebStorm, Android Studio, or any of the other JetBrains IDEs. Its Go support includes refactoring, syntax highlighting, code completion and navigation, documentation pop-ups, a debugger, code coverage, and more. In addition to Go support, GoLand includes JavaScript/HTML/CSS and SQL database tools. Unlike VS Code, GoLand doesn't require you to download any additional tools to get it to work.

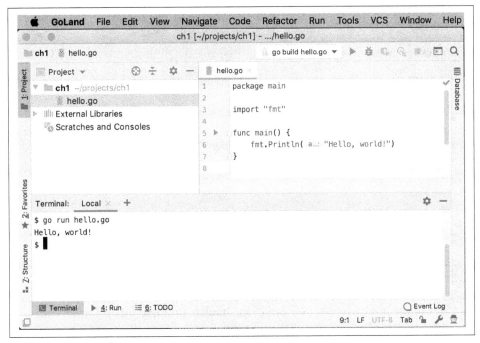

Figure 1-2. GoLand

If you already subscribe to IntelliJ Ultimate (or qualify for a free license), you can add Go support via a plug-in. Otherwise, you have to pay for GoLand; there is no free version available.

The Go Playground

There's one more important tool for Go development, but this is one that you don't install. Visit The Go Playground (*http://play.golang.org*) and you'll see a window that resembles Figure 1-3. If you have used a command-line environment like irb, node, or python, you'll find The Go Playground has a very similar feel. It gives you a place to try out and share small programs. Enter your program into the window and click the Run button to execute the code. The Format button runs go fmt on your program, and checking the Imports checkbox cleans up your imports like goimports. The Share button creates a unique URL that you can send to someone else to take a look at your program or to come back to your code at a future date (the URLs have been persistent for a long time, but I wouldn't use the playground as your source code repository).

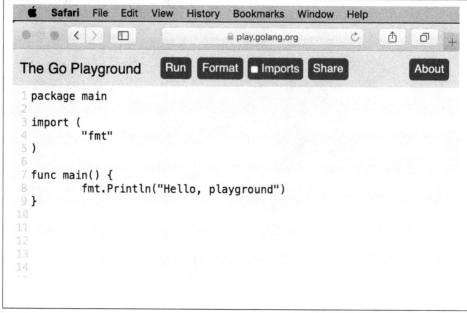

Figure 1-3. The Go Playground

As you can see in Figure 1-4, you can even simulate multiple files by separating each file with a line that looks like `-- filename.go --`.

Be aware that The Go Playground is someone else's computer (in particular, it is Google's computer), so you don't have completely free rein. It always runs the latest stable version of Go. You cannot make network connections, and processes that run for too long or use too much memory are stopped. If your program depends on time, be aware that the clock is set to November 10, 2009, 23:00:00 UTC (the date of the initial announcement of Go). But even with these limitations, The Go Playground is a very useful way to try out new ideas without creating a new project locally. Throughout this book, you'll find links to The Go Playground so you can run code examples without copying them onto your computer.

Do not put sensitive information (such as personally identifiable information, passwords, or private keys) into your playground! If you click the Share button, the information is saved on Google's servers and is accessible to anyone who has the associated Share URL. If you do this by accident, contact Google at *security@golang.org* with the URL and the reason the content needs to be removed.

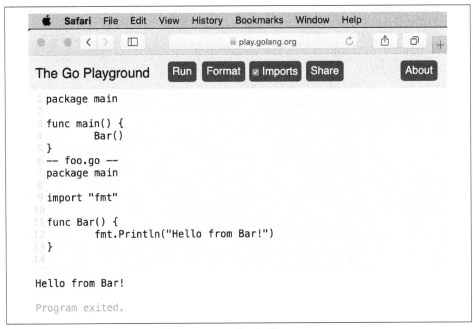

Figure 1-4. The Go Playground supports multiple files

Makefiles

An IDE is nice to use, but it's hard to automate. Modern software development relies on repeatable, automatable builds that can be run by anyone, anywhere, at any time. This avoids the age-old developer excuse of "It works on my machine!" The way to do this is to use some kind of script to specify your build steps. Go developers have adopted make as their solution. You may not be familiar with make, but it's been used to build programs on Unix systems since 1976.

Here's a sample Makefile to add to our very simple project:

```
.DEFAULT_GOAL := build

fmt:
        go fmt ./...
```

```
.PHONY:fmt

lint: fmt
        golint ./...
.PHONY:lint

vet: fmt
        go vet ./...
.PHONY:vet

build: vet
        go build hello.go
.PHONY:build
```

Even if you haven't seen a Makefile before, it's not too difficult to figure out what is going on. Each possible operation is called a *target*. The .DEFAULT_GOAL defines which target is run when no target is specified. In our case, we are going to run the build target. Next we have the target definitions. The word before the colon (:) is the name of the target. Any words after the target (like vet in the line build: vet) are the other targets that must be run before the specified target runs. The tasks that are performed by the target are on the indented lines after the target. (The .PHONY line keeps make from getting confused if you ever create a directory in your project with the same name as a target.)

Before you can use this Makefile, you need to make this project a Go module. We'll cover modules in Chapter 9, but for now, change to the *ch1* directory and type in the following command:

```
go mod init ch1
```

Now you can use the Makefile. Type:

```
make
```

You should see the following output:

```
go fmt ./...
go vet ./...
go build hello.go
```

By entering a single command, we make sure the code was formatted correctly, vet the code for nonobvious errors, and compile. We can also run the linter with make lint, vet the code with make vet, or just run the formatter with make fmt. This might not seem like a big improvement, but ensuring that formatting and vetting always happen before a developer (or a script running on a continuous integration build server) triggers a build means you won't miss any steps.

One drawback to Makefiles is that they are exceedingly picky. You *must* indent the steps in a target with a tab. They are also not supported out-of-the-box on Windows. If you are doing your Go development on a Windows computer, you need to install make first. The easiest way to do so is to first install a package manager like Chocolatey (*https://chocolatey.org*) and then use it to install make (for Chocolatey, the command is choco install make.)

Staying Up to Date

As with all programming languages, there are periodic updates to the Go development tools. Go programs are native binaries that don't rely on a separate runtime, so you don't need to worry that updating your development environment could cause your currently deployed programs to fail. You can have programs compiled with different versions of Go running simultaneously on the same computer or virtual machine.

Since Go 1.2, there has been a new major release roughly every six months. There are also minor releases with bug and security fixes released as needed. Given the rapid development cycles and the Go team's commitment to backward compatibility, Go releases tend to be incremental rather than expansive. The Go Compatibility Promise (*https://oreil.ly/p_NMY*) is a detailed description of how the Go team plans to avoid breaking Go code. It says that there won't be backward-breaking changes to the language or the standard library for any Go version that starts with 1, unless the change is required for a bug or security fix. However, there might be (and have been) backward-incompatible changes to the flags or functionality of the go commands.

Despite these backward compatibility guarantees, bugs do happen, so it's natural to want to make sure that a new release doesn't break your programs. One option is to install a secondary Go environment. For example, if you are currently running version 1.15.2 and wanted to try out version 1.15.6, you would use the following commands:

```
$ go get golang.org/dl/go.1.15.6
$ go1.15.6 download
```

You can then use the command go1.15.6 instead of the go command to see if version 1.15.6 works for your programs:

```
$ go1.15.6 build
```

Once you have validated that your code works, you can delete the secondary environment by finding its GOROOT, deleting it, and then deleting its binary from your *$GOPATH/bin* directory. Here's how to do that on Mac OS, Linux, and BSD:

```
$ go1.15.6 env GOROOT
/Users/gobook/sdk/go1.15.6
$ rm -rf $(go1.15.6 env GOROOT)
$ rm $(go env GOPATH)/bin/go1.15.6
```

When you are ready to update the Go development tools installed on your computer, Mac and Windows users have the easiest path. Those who installed with brew or chocolatey can use those tools to update. Those who used the installers on *https://golang.org/dl* can download the latest installer, which removes the old version when it installs the new one.

Linux and BSD users need to download the latest version, move the old version to a backup directory, expand the new version, and then delete the old version:

```
$ mv /usr/local/go /usr/local/old-go
$ tar -C /usr/local -xzf go1.15.2.linux-amd64.tar.gz
$ rm -rf /usr/local/old-go
```

Wrapping Up

In this chapter, we learned how to install and configure our Go development environment. We also talked about tools for building Go programs and ensuring code quality. Now that our environment is ready, we're on to our next chapter, where we explore the built-in types in Go and how to declare variables.

CHAPTER 2

Primitive Types and Declarations

Now that we have our development environment set up, it's time to start looking at Go's language features and how to best use them. When trying to figure out what "best" means, there is one overriding principle: write your programs in a way that makes your intentions clear. As we go through features, we'll look at the options and I'll explain why I find a particular approach produces clearer code.

We'll start by looking at primitive types and variables. While every programmer has experience with these concepts, Go does some things differently, and there are subtle differences between Go and other languages.

Built-in Types

Go has many of the same built-in types as other languages: booleans, integers, floats, and strings. Using these types idiomatically is sometimes a challenge for developers who are transitioning from another language. We are going to look at these types and see how they work best in Go. Before we review the types, let's cover some of the concepts that apply to all types.

The Zero Value

Go, like most modern languages, assigns a default *zero value* to any variable that is declared but not assigned a value. Having an explicit zero value makes code clearer and removes a source of bugs found in C and C++ programs. As we talk about each type, we will also cover the zero value for the type.

Literals

A *literal* in Go refers to writing out a number, character, or string. There are four common kinds of literals that you'll find in Go programs. (There's a rare fifth kind of literal that we'll cover when discussing complex numbers.)

Integer literals are sequences of numbers; they are normally base ten, but different prefixes are used to indicate other bases: 0b for binary (base two), 0o for octal (base eight), or 0x for hexadecimal (base sixteen). You can use either or upper- or lowercase letters for the prefix. A leading 0 with no letter after it is another way to represent an octal literal. Do not use it, as it is very confusing.

To make it easier to read longer integer literals, Go allows you to put underscores in the middle of your literal. This allows you to, for example, group by thousands in base ten (1_234). These underscores have no effect on the value of the number. The only limitations on underscores are that they can't be at the beginning or end of numbers, and you can't have them next to each other. You could put an underscore between every digit in your literal (1_2_3_4), but don't. Use them to improve readability by breaking up base ten numbers at the thousands place or to break up binary, octal, or hexadecimal numbers at one-, two-, or four-byte boundaries.

Floating point literals have decimal points to indicate the fractional portion of the value. They can also have an exponent specified with the letter e and a positive or negative number (such as 6.03e23). You also have the option to write them in hexadecimal by using the 0x prefix and the letter p for indicating any exponent. Like integer literals, you can use underscores to format your floating point literals.

Rune literals represent characters and are surrounded by single quotes. Unlike many other languages, in Go single quotes and double quotes are *not* interchangeable. Rune literals can be written as single Unicode characters ('a'), 8-bit octal numbers ('\141'), 8-bit hexadecimal numbers ('\x61'), 16-bit hexadecimal numbers ('\u0061'), or 32-bit Unicode numbers ('\U00000061'). There are also several backslash escaped rune literals, with the most useful ones being newline ('\n'), tab ('\t'), single quote ('\''), double quote ('\"'), and backslash ('\\').

Practically speaking, use base ten to represent your number literals and, unless the context makes your code clearer, try to avoid using any of the hexadecimal escapes for rune literals. Octal representations are rare, mostly used to represent POSIX permission flag values (such as 0o777 for rwxrwxrwx). Hexadecimal and binary are sometimes used for bit filters or networking and infrastructure applications.

There are two different ways to indicate *string literals*. Most of the time, you should use double quotes to create an *interpreted string literal* (e.g., type **"Greetings and Salutations"**). These contain zero or more rune literals, in any of the forms allowed. The only characters that cannot appear are unescaped backslashes, unescaped newlines, and unescaped double quotes. If you use an interpreted string literal and want your greetings on a different line from your salutations and you want "Salutations" to appear in quotes, you need to type **"Greetings and\n\"Salutations\""**.

If you need to include backslashes, double quotes, or newlines in your string, use a *raw string literal*. These are delimited with backquotes (`` ` ``) and can contain any literal character except a backquote. When using a raw string literal, we write our multiline greeting like so:

```
`Greetings and
"Salutations"`
```

As we'll see in "Explicit Type Conversion" on page 26 you can't even add two integer variables together if they are declared to be of different sizes. However, Go lets you use an integer literal in floating point expressions or even assign an integer literal to a floating point variable. This is because literals in Go are untyped; they can interact with any variable that's compatible with the literal. When we look at user-defined types in Chapter 7, we'll see that we can even use literals with user-defined types based on primitive types. Being untyped only goes so far; you can't assign a literal string to a variable with a numeric type or a literal number to a string variable, nor can you assign a float literal to an int. These are all flagged by the compiler as errors.

Literals are untyped because Go is a practical language. It makes sense to avoid forcing a type until the developer specifies one. There are size limitations; while you can write numeric literals that are larger than any integer can hold, it is a compile-time error to try to assign a literal whose value overflows the specified variable, such as trying to assign the literal 1000 to a variable of type `byte`.

As you will see in the section on variable assignment, there are situations in Go where the type isn't explicitly declared. In those cases, Go uses the *default type* for a literal; if there's nothing in the expression that makes clear what the type of the literal is, the literal defaults to a type. We will mention the default type for literals as we look at the different built-in types.

Booleans

The `bool` type represents Boolean variables. Variables of `bool` type can have one of two values: `true` or `false`. The zero value for a `bool` is `false`:

```
var flag bool // no value assigned, set to false
var isAwesome = true
```

It's hard to talk about variable types without showing a variable declaration, and vice versa. We'll use variable declarations first and describe them in "var Versus :=" on page 27.

Numeric Types

Go has a large number of numeric types: 12 different types (and a few special names) that are grouped into three categories. If you are coming from a language like Java-Script that gets along with only a single numeric type, this might seem like a lot. And in fact, some types are used frequently while others are more esoteric. We'll start by looking at integer types before moving on to floating point types and the very unusual complex type.

Integer types

Go provides both signed and unsigned integers in a variety of sizes, from one to eight bytes. They are shown in Table 2-1.

Table 2-1. The integer types in Go

Type name	Value range
int8	−128 to 127
int16	−32768 to 32767
int32	−2147483648 to 2147483647
int64	−9223372036854775808 to 9223372036854775807
uint8	0 to 255
uint16	0 to 65535
uint32	0 to 4294967295
uint64	0 to 18446744073709551615

It might be obvious from the name, but the zero value for all of the integer types is 0.

The special integer types

Go does have some special names for integer types. A byte is an alias for uint8; it is legal to assign, compare, or perform mathematical operations between a byte and a uint8. However, you rarely see uint8 used in Go code; just call it a byte.

The second special name is int. On a 32-bit CPU, int is a 32-bit signed integer like an int32. On most 64-bit CPUs, int is a 64-bit signed integer, just like an int64. Because int isn't consistent from platform to platform, it is a compile-time error to assign, compare, or perform mathematical operations between an int and an int32 or int64 without a type conversion (see "Explicit Type Conversion" on page 26 for more details). Integer literals default to being of int type.

There are some uncommon 64-bit CPU architectures that use a 32-bit signed integer for the int type. Go supports three of them: amd64p32, mips64p32, and mips64p32le.

The third special name is uint. It follows the same rules as int, only it is unsigned (the values are always 0 or positive).

There are two other special names for integer types, rune and uintptr. We looked at rune literals earlier and discuss the rune type in "A Taste of Strings and Runes" on page 26 and uintptr in Chapter 14.

Choosing which integer to use

Go provides more integer types than some other languages. Given all of these choices, you might wonder when you should use each of them. There are three simple rules to follow:

- If you are working with a binary file format or network protocol that has an integer of a specific size or sign, use the corresponding integer type.
- If you are writing a library function that should work with any integer type, write a pair of functions, one with int64 for the parameters and variables and the other with uint64. (We talk more about functions and their parameters in Chapter 5.)

The reason why int64 and uint64 are the idiomatic choice in this situation is that Go doesn't have generics (yet) and doesn't have function overloading. Without these features, you'd need to write many functions with slightly different names to implement your algorithm. Using int64 and uint64 means that you can write the code once and let your callers use type conversions to pass values in and convert data that's returned.

You can see this pattern in the Go standard library with the functions FormatInt/FormatUint and ParseInt/ParseUint in the strconv package. There are other situations, like in the math/bits package, where the size of the integer matters. In those cases, you need to write a separate function for every integer type.

- In all other cases, just use int.

Unless you *need* to be explicit about the size or sign of an integer for performance or integration purposes, use the int type. Consider any other type to be a premature optimization until proven otherwise.

Integer operators

Go integers support the usual arithmetic operators: +, -, *, /, with % for modulus. The result of an integer division is an integer; if you want to get a floating point result, you need to use a type conversion to make your integers into floating point numbers. Also, be careful not to divide an integer by 0; this causes a panic (we talk more about panics in "panic and recover" on page 174).

Integer division in Go follows truncation toward zero; see the Go spec's section on arithmetic operators (*https://oreil.ly/zp3OJ*) for the full details.

You can combine any of the arithmetic operators with = to modify a variable: +=, -=, *=, /=, and %=. For example, the following code results in x having the value 20:

```
var x int = 10
x *= 2
```

You compare integers with ==, !=, >, >=, <, and <=.

Go also has bit-manipulation operators for integers. You can bit shift left and right with << and >>, or do bit masks with & (logical AND), | (logical OR), ^ (logical XOR), and &^ (logical AND NOT). Just like the arithmetic operators, you can also combine all of the logical operators with = to modify a variable: &=, |=, ^=, &^=, <<=, and >>=.

Floating point types

There are two floating point types in Go, as shown in Table 2-2.

Table 2-2. The floating point types in Go

Type name	Largest absolute value	Smallest (nonzero) absolute value
float32	3.40282346638528859811704183484516925440e+38	1.401298464324817070923729583289916131280e-45
float64	1.797693134862315708145274237317043567981e+308	4.940656458412465441765687928682213723651e-324

Like the integer types, the zero value for the floating point types is 0.

Floating point in Go is similar to floating point math in other languages. Go uses the IEEE 754 specification, giving a large range and limited precision. Picking which floating point type to use is straightforward: unless you have to be compatible with an existing format, use float64. Floating point literals have a default type of float64, so always using float64 is the simplest option. It also helps mitigate floating point accuracy issues since a float32 only has six- or seven-decimal digits of precision. Don't worry about the difference in memory size unless you have used the profiler to determine that it is a significant source of problems. (We'll learn all about testing and profiling in Chapter 13.)

The bigger question is whether you should be using a floating point number at all. In most cases, the answer is no. Just like other languages, Go floating point numbers have a huge range, but they cannot store every value in that range; they store the nearest approximation. Because floats aren't exact, they can only be used in situations where inexact values are acceptable or the rules of floating point are well understood. That limits them to things like graphics and scientific operations.

A floating point number cannot represent a decimal value exactly. Do not use them to represent money or any other value that must have an exact decimal representation!

IEEE 754

As mentioned earlier, Go (and most other programming languages) stores floating point numbers using a specification called IEEE 754.

The actual rules are outside the scope of this book, and they aren't straightforward. For example, if you store the number –3.1415 in a float64, the 64-bit representation in memory looks like:

    1100000000001001001000011100101011000000100000110001001001101111

which is exactly equal to –3.141500000000000181118839761883.

Many programmers learn at some point how integers are represented in binary (rightmost position is 1, next is 2, next is 4, and so on). Floating point numbers are very different. Out of the 64 bits above, one is used to represent the sign (positive or negative), 11 are used to represent a base two exponent, and 52 bits are used to represent the number in a normalized format (called the *mantissa*).

You can learn more about IEEE 754 on its Wikipedia page (*https://oreil.ly/Gc05u*).

You can use all the standard mathematical and comparison operators with floats, except %. Floating point division has a couple of interesting properties. Dividing a nonzero floating point variable by 0 returns +Inf or -Inf (positive or negative infinity), depending on the sign of the number. Dividing a floating point variable set to 0 by 0 returns NaN (Not a Number).

While Go lets you use == and != to compare floats, don't do it. Due to the inexact nature of floats, two floating point values might not be equal when you think they should be. Instead, define a maximum allowed variance and see if the difference between two floats is less than that. This value (sometimes called *epsilon*) depends on what your accuracy needs are; I can't give you a simple rule. If you aren't sure, consult your friendly local mathematician for advice.

Complex types (you're probably not going to use these)

There is one more numeric type and it is pretty unusual. Go has first-class support for complex numbers. If you don't know what complex numbers are, you are not the target audience for this feature; feel free to skip ahead.

There isn't a lot to the complex number support in Go. Go defines two complex number types. complex64 uses float32 values to represent the real and imaginary part, and complex128 uses float64 values. Both are declared with the complex built-in function. Go uses a few rules to determine what the type of the function output is:

- If you use untyped constants or literals for both function parameters, you'll create an untyped complex literal, which has a default type of complex128.
- If both of the values passed into complex are of float32 type, you'll create a complex64.
- If one value is a float32 and the other value is an untyped constant or literal that can fit within a float32, you'll create a complex64.
- Otherwise, you'll create a complex128.

All of the standard arithmetic operators work on complex numbers. Just like floats, you can use == or != to compare them, but they have the same precision limitations, so it's best to use the epsilon technique. You can extract the real and imaginary portions of a complex number with the real and imag built-in functions, respectively. There are also some additional functions in the math/cmplx package for manipulating complex128 values.

The zero value for both types of complex numbers has 0 assigned to both the real and imaginary portions of the number.

Example 2-1 shows a simple program that demonstrates how complex numbers work. You can run it for yourself on The Go Playground (*https://oreil.ly/fuyIu*).

Example 2-1. Complex numbers

```go
func main() {
    x := complex(2.5, 3.1)
    y := complex(10.2, 2)
    fmt.Println(x + y)
    fmt.Println(x - y)
    fmt.Println(x * y)
    fmt.Println(x / y)
    fmt.Println(real(x))
    fmt.Println(imag(x))
    fmt.Println(cmplx.Abs(x))
}
```

Running this code gives you:

```
(12.7+5.1i)
(-7.699999999999999+1.1i)
(19.3+36.62i)
(0.2934098482043688+0.24639022584228065i)
2.5
3.1
3.982461550347975
```

You can see floating point imprecision on display here, too.

In case you were wondering what the fifth kind of primitive literal was, Go supports imaginary literals to represent the imaginary portion of a complex number. They look just like floating point literals, but they have an i for a suffix.

Despite having complex numbers as a built-in type, Go is not a popular language for numerical computing. Adoption has been limited because other features (like matrix support) are not part of the language and libraries have to use inefficient replacements, like slices of slices. (We'll look at slices in Chapter 3 and how they are implemented in Chapter 6.) But if you need to calculate a Mandelbrot set as part of a larger program, or implement a quadratic equation solver, complex number support is there for you.

You might be wondering why Go includes complex numbers. The answer is simple: Ken Thompson, one of the creators of Go (and Unix), thought they would be interesting (*https://oreil.ly/eBmkq*). There has been discussion about removing complex numbers (*https://oreil.ly/Q76EV*) from a future version of Go, but it's easier to just ignore the feature.

If you do want to write numerical computing applications in Go, you can use the third-party Gonum (*https://www.gonum.org*) package. It takes advantage of complex numbers and provides useful libraries for things like linear algebra, matrices, integration, and statistics. But you should consider other languages first.

A Taste of Strings and Runes

This brings us to strings. Like most modern languages, Go includes strings as a built-in type. The zero value for a string is the empty string. Go supports Unicode; as we showed in the section on string literals, you can put any Unicode character into a string. Like integers and floats, strings are compared for equality using ==, difference with !=, or ordering with >, >=, <, or <=. They are concatenated by using the + operator.

Strings in Go are immutable; you can reassign the value of a string variable, but you cannot change the value of the string that is assigned to it.

Go also has a type that represents a single code point. The *rune* type is an alias for the int32 type, just like byte is an alias for uint8. As you could probably guess, a rune literal's default type is a rune, and a string literal's default type is a string.

If you are referring to a character, use the rune type, not the int32 type. They might be the same to the compiler, but you want to use the type that clarifies the intent of your code.

We are going to talk a lot more about strings in the next chapter, covering some implementation details, relationship with bytes and runes, as well as advanced features and pitfalls.

Explicit Type Conversion

Most languages that have multiple numeric types automatically convert from one to another when needed. This is called *automatic type promotion,* and while it seems very convenient, it turns out that the rules to properly convert one type to another can get complicated and produce unexpected results. As a language that values clarity of intent and readability, Go doesn't allow automatic type promotion between variables. You must use a *type conversion* when variable types do not match. Even different-sized integers and floats must be converted to the same type to interact. This makes it clear exactly what type you want without having to memorize any type conversion rules (see Example 2-2).

Example 2-2. Type conversions

```
var x int = 10
var y float64 = 30.2
var z float64 = float64(x) + y
var d int = x + int(y)
fmt.Println(z, d)
```

In this sample code we define four variables. x is an int with the value 10, and y is a float64 with the value 30.2. Since these are not identical types, we need to convert them to add them together. For z, we convert x to a float64 using a float64 type conversion, and for d, we convert y to an int using an int type conversion. When you run this code, it prints out 40.2 40.

This strictness around types has other implications. Since all type conversions in Go are explicit, you cannot treat another Go type as a boolean. In many languages, a nonzero number or a nonempty string can be interpreted as a boolean true. Just like automatic type promotion, the rules for "truthy" values vary from language to language and can be confusing. Unsurprisingly, Go doesn't allow truthiness. In fact, _no other type can be converted to a bool, implicitly or explicitly_. If you want to convert from another data type to boolean, you must use one of the comparison operators (==, !=, >, <, <=, or >=). For example, to check if variable x is equal to 0, the code would be x == 0. If you want to check if string s is empty, use s == "".

> Type conversions are one of the places where Go chooses to add a little verbosity in exchange for a great deal of simplicity and clarity. You'll see this trade-off multiple times. Idiomatic Go values comprehensibility over conciseness.

var Versus :=

For a small language, Go has a lot of ways to declare variables. There's a reason for this: each declaration style communicates something about how the variable is used. Let's go through the ways you can declare a variable in Go and see when each is appropriate.

The most verbose way to declare a variable in Go uses the var keyword, an explicit type, and an assignment. It looks like this:

```
var x int = 10
```

If the type on the righthand side of the = is the expected type of your variable, you can leave off the type from the left side of the =. Since the default type of an integer literal is int, the following declares x to be a variable of type int:

```
var x = 10
```

Conversely, if you want to declare a variable and assign it the zero value, you can keep the type and drop the = on the righthand side:

```
var x int
```

You can declare multiple variables at once with var, and they can be of the same type:

```
var x, y int = 10, 20
```

all zero values of the same type:

```
var x, y int
```

or of different types:

```
var x, y = 10, "hello"
```

There's one more way to use var. If you are declaring multiple variables at once, you can wrap them in a *declaration list*:

```
var (
    x     int
    y           = 20
    z     int = 30
    d, e       = 40, "hello"
    f, g string
)
```

Go also supports a short declaration format. When you are within a function, you can use the := operator to replace a var declaration that uses type inference. The following two statements do exactly the same thing: they declare x to be an int with the value of 10:

```
var x = 10
x := 10
```

Like var, you can declare multiple variables at once using :=. These two lines both assign 10 to x and "hello" to y:

```
var x, y = 10, "hello"
x, y := 10, "hello"
```

The := operator can do one trick that you cannot do with var: it allows you to assign values to existing variables, too. As long as there is one new variable on the lefthand side of the :=, then any of the other variables can already exist:

```
x := 10
x, y := 30, "hello"
```

There is one limitation on :=. If you are declaring a variable at package level, you must use var because := is not legal outside of functions.

How do you know which style to use? As always, choose what makes your intent clearest. The most common declaration style within functions is :=. Outside of a function, use declaration lists on the rare occasions when you are declaring multiple package-level variables.

There are some situations within functions where you should avoid :=:

- When initializing a variable to its zero value, use `var x int`. This makes it clear that the zero value is intended.

- When assigning an untyped constant or a literal to a variable and the default type for the constant or literal isn't the type you want for the variable, use the long `var` form with the type specified. While it is legal to use a type conversion to specify the type of the value and use := to write `x := byte(20)`, it is idiomatic to write `var x byte = 20`.

- Because := allows you to assign to both new and existing variables, it sometimes creates new variables when you think you are reusing existing ones (see "Shadowing Variables" on page 62 for details). In those situations, explicitly declare all of your new variables with `var` to make it clear which variables are new, and then use the assignment operator (=) to assign values to both new and old variables.

While `var` and := allow you to declare multiple variables on the same line, only use this style when assigning multiple values returned from a function or the comma ok idiom (see Chapter 5 and "The comma ok Idiom" on page 54).

You should rarely declare variables outside of functions, in what's called the *package block* (see "Blocks" on page 61). Package-level variables whose values change are a bad idea. When you have a variable outside of a function, it can be difficult to track the changes made to it, which makes it hard to understand how data is flowing through your program. This can lead to subtle bugs. As a general rule, you should only declare variables in the package block that are effectively immutable.

Avoid declaring variables outside of functions because they complicate data flow analysis.

You might be wondering: does Go provide a way to *ensure* that a value is immutable? It does, but it is a bit different from what you may have seen in other programming languages. It's time to learn about `const`.

Using const

When developers learn a new programming language, they try to map familiar concepts. Many languages have a way to declare a value is immutable. In Go, this is done with the const keyword. At first glance, it seems to work exactly like other languages. Try out the code in Example 2-3 on The Go Playground (*https://oreil.ly/FdG-W*).

Example 2-3. const declarations

```
const x int64 = 10

const (
    idKey   = "id"
    nameKey = "name"
)

const z = 20 * 10

func main() {
    const y = "hello"

    fmt.Println(x)
    fmt.Println(y)

    x = x + 1
    y = "bye"

    fmt.Println(x)
    fmt.Println(y)
}
```

If you try to run this code, compilations fails with the following error messages:

```
./const.go:20:4: cannot assign to x
./const.go:21:4: cannot assign to y
```

As you see, you declare a constant at the package level or within a function. Just like var, you can (and should) declare a group of related constants within a set of parentheses.

However, const in Go is very limited. Constants in Go are a way to give names to literals. They can only hold values that the compiler can figure out at compile time. This means that they can be assigned:

- Numeric literals
- true and false
- Strings
- Runes
- The built-in functions complex, real, imag, len, and cap
- Expressions that consist of operators and the preceding values

We'll cover the len and cap functions in the next chapter. There's another value that can be used with const that's called iota. We'll talk about iota when we discuss creating your own types in Chapter 7.

Go doesn't provide a way to specify that a value calculated at runtime is immutable. As we'll see in the next chapter, there are no immutable arrays, slices, maps, or structs, and there's no way to declare that a field in a struct is immutable. This is less limiting than it sounds. Within a function, it is clear if a variable is being modified, so immutability is less important. In "Go Is Call By Value" on page 104, we'll see how Go prevents modifications to variables that are passed as parameters to functions.

Constants in Go are a way to give names to literals. There is *no* way in Go to declare that a variable is immutable.

Typed and Untyped Constants

Constants can be typed or untyped. An untyped constant works exactly like a literal; it has no type of its own, but does have a default type that is used when no other type can be inferred. A typed constant can only be directly assigned to a variable of that type.

Whether or not to make a constant typed depends on why the constant was declared. If you are giving a name to a mathematical constant that could be used with multiple numeric types, then keep the constant untyped. In general, leaving a constant untyped gives you more flexibility. There are situations where you want a constant to enforce a type. We'll use typed constants when we look at creating enumerations with iota in "iota Is for Enumerations—Sometimes" on page 137.

Here's what an untyped constant declaration looks like:

```
const x = 10
```

All of the following assignments are legal:

```
var y int = x
var z float64 = x
var d byte = x
```

Here's what a typed constant declaration looks like:

```
const typedX int = 10
```

This constant can only be assigned directly to an int. Assigning it to any other type produces a compile-time error like this:

```
cannot use typedX (type int) as type float64 in assignment
```

Unused Variables

One of the goals for Go is to make it easier for large teams to collaborate on programs. To do so, Go has some rules that are unique among programming languages. In Chapter 1, we saw that Go programs need to be formatted in a specific way with go fmt to make it easier to write code-manipulation tools and to provide coding standards. Another Go requirement is that *every declared local variable must be read*. It is a *compile-time error* to declare a local variable and to not read its value.

The compiler's unused variable check is not exhaustive. As long as a variable is read once, the compiler won't complain, even if there are writes to the variable that are never read. The following is a valid Go program that you can run on The Go Playground (*https://oreil.ly/8JLA6*):

```
func main() {
    x := 10
    x = 20
    fmt.Println(x)
    x = 30
}
```

While the compiler and go vet do not catch the unused assignments of 10 and 30 to x, golangci-lint detects them:

```
$ golangci-lint run
unused.go:6:2: ineffectual assignment to `x` (ineffassign)
    x := 10
    ^
unused.go:9:2: ineffectual assignment to `x` (ineffassign)
    x = 30
    ^
```

 The Go compiler won't stop you from creating unread package-level variables. This is one more reason why you should avoid creating package-level variables.

Unused Constants

Perhaps surprisingly, the Go compiler allows you to create unread constants with const. This is because constants in Go are calculated at compile time and cannot have any side effects. This makes them easy to eliminate: if a constant isn't used, it is simply not included in the compiled binary.

Naming Variables and Constants

There is a difference between Go's rules for naming variables and the patterns that Go developers follow when naming their variables and constants. Like most languages, Go requires identifier names to start with a letter or underscore, and the name can contain numbers, underscores, and letters. Go's definition of "letter" and "number" is a bit broader than many languages. Any Unicode character that is considered a letter or digit is allowed. This makes all of the variable definitions shown in Example 2-4 perfectly valid Go.

Example 2-4. Variable names you should never use

```
_0 := 0_0
_1 := 20
n := 3
a := "hello" // Unicode U+FF41
fmt.Println(_0)
fmt.Println(_1)
fmt.Println(n)
fmt.Println(a)
```

While this code works, *do not* name your variables like this. These names are considered nonidiomatic because they break the fundamental rule of making sure that your code communicates what it is doing. These names are confusing or difficult to type on many keyboards. Look-alike Unicode code points are the most insidious, because even if they appear to be the same character, they represent entirely different variables. You can run the code shown in Example 2-5 on The Go Playground (*https://oreil.ly/hrvb6*).

Example 2-5. Using look-alike code points for variable names

```
func main() {
    a := "hello"   // Unicode U+FF41
    a := "goodbye" // standard lowercase a (Unicode U+0061)
    fmt.Println(a)
    fmt.Println(a)
}
```

When you run this program, you get:

```
hello
goodbye
```

Even though underscore is a valid character in a variable name, it is rarely used, because idiomatic Go doesn't use snake case (names like index_counter or number_tries). Instead, Go uses camel case (names like indexCounter or numberTries) when an identifier name consists of multiple words.

An underscore by itself (_) is a special identifier name in Go; we'll talk more about it when we cover functions in Chapter 5.

In many languages, constants are always written in all uppercase letters, with words separated by underscores (names like INDEX_COUNTER or NUMBER_TRIES). Go does not follow this pattern. This is because Go uses the case of the first letter in the name of a package-level declaration to determine if the item is accessible outside the package. We will revisit this when we talk about packages in Chapter 9.

Within a function, favor short variable names. The smaller the scope for a variable, the shorter the name that's used for it. It is very common in Go to see single-letter variable names. For example, the names k and v (short for *key* and *value*) are used as the variable names in a for-range loop. If you are using a standard for loop, i and j are common names for the index variable. There are other idiomatic ways to name variables of common types; we will mention them as we cover more parts of the standard library.

Some languages with weaker type systems encourage developers to include the expected type of the variable in the variable's name. Since Go is strongly typed, you don't need to do this to keep track of the underlying type. However, there are still conventions around variable types and single-letter names. People will use the first letter of a type as the variable name (for example, i for integers, f for floats, b for booleans). When you define your own types, similar patterns apply.

These short names serve two purposes. The first is that they eliminate repetitive typing, keeping your code shorter. Second, they serve as a check on how complicated your code is. If you find it hard to keep track of your short-named variables, it's likely that your block of code is doing too much.

When naming variables and constants in the package block, use more descriptive names. The type should still be excluded from the name, but since the scope is wider, you need a more complete name to make it clear what the value represents.

Wrapping Up

We've covered a lot of ground here, understanding how to use the built-in types, declare variables, and work with assignments and operators. In the next chapter, we are going to look at the composite types in Go: arrays, slices, maps, and structs. We are also going to take another look at strings and runes and learn about encodings.

CHAPTER 3

Composite Types

In the last chapter, we looked at simple types: numbers, booleans, and strings. In this chapter, we'll learn about the composite types in Go, the built-in functions that support them, and the best practices for working with them.

Arrays—Too Rigid to Use Directly

Like most programming languages, Go has arrays. However, arrays are rarely used directly in Go. We'll learn why in a bit, but first we'll quickly cover array declaration syntax and use.

All of the elements in the array must be of the type that's specified (this doesn't mean they are always of the same type). There are a few different declaration styles. In the first, you specify the size of the array and the type of the elements in the array:

```
var x [3]int
```

This creates an array of three ints. Since no values were specified, all of the positions (x[0], x[1], and x[2]) are initialized to the zero value for an int, which is (of course) 0. If you have initial values for the array, you specify them with an *array literal*:

```
var x = [3]int{10, 20, 30}
```

If you have a *sparse array* (an array where most elements are set to their zero value), you can specify only the indices with values in the array literal:

```
var x = [12]int{1, 5: 4, 6, 10: 100, 15}
```

This creates an array of 12 ints with the following values: [1, 0, 0, 0, 0, 4, 6, 0, 0, 0, 100, 15].

When using an array literal to initialize an array, you can leave off the number and use ... instead:

```
var x = [...]int{10, 20, 30}
```

You can use == and != to compare arrays:

```
var x = [...]int{1, 2, 3}
var y = [3]int{1, 2, 3}
fmt.Println(x == y) // prints true
```

Go only has one-dimensional arrays, but you can simulate multidimensional arrays:

```
var x [2][3]int
```

This declares x to be an array of length 2 whose type is an array of ints of length 3. This sounds pedantic, but there are languages with true matrix support; Go isn't one of them.

Like most languages, arrays in Go are read and written using bracket syntax:

```
x[0] = 10
fmt.Println(x[2])
```

You cannot read or write past the end of an array or use a negative index. If you do this with a constant or literal index, it is a compile-time error. An out-of-bounds read or write with a variable index compiles but fails at runtime with a *panic* (we'll talk more about panics in "panic and recover" on page 174).

Finally, the built-in function len takes in an array and returns its length:

```
fmt.Println(len(x))
```

Earlier I said that arrays in Go are rarely used explicitly. This is because they come with an unusual limitation: Go considers the *size* of the array to be part of the *type* of the array. This makes an array that's declared to be [3]int a different type from an array that's declared to be [4]int. This also means that you cannot use a variable to specify the size of an array, because types must be resolved at compile time, not at runtime.

What's more, *you can't use a type conversion to convert arrays of different sizes to identical types.* Because you can't convert arrays of different sizes into each other, you can't write a function that works with arrays of any size and you can't assign arrays of different sizes to the same variable.

 We'll learn how arrays work behind the scenes when we discuss memory layout in Chapter 6.

Due to these restrictions, don't use arrays unless you know the exact length you need ahead of time. For example, some of the cryptographic functions in the standard library return arrays because the sizes of checksums are defined as part of the algorithm. This is the exception, not the rule.

This raises the question: why is such a limited feature in the language? The main reason why arrays exist in Go is to provide the backing store for *slices*, which are one of the most useful features of Go.

Slices

Most of the time, when you want a data structure that holds a sequence of values, a slice is what you should use. What makes slices so useful is that the length is *not* part of the type for a slice. This removes the limitations of arrays. We can write a single function that processes slices of any size (we'll cover function writing in Chapter 5), and we can grow slices as needed. After going over the basics of using slices in Go, we'll cover the best ways to use them.

Working with slices looks quite a bit like working with arrays, but there are subtle differences. The first thing to notice is that we don't specify the size of the slice when we declare it:

```
var x = []int{10, 20, 30}
```

 Using [...] makes an array. Using [ ] makes a slice.

This creates a slice of 3 `ints` using a *slice literal*. Just like arrays, we can also specify only the indices with values in the slice literal:

```
var x = []int{1, 5: 4, 6, 10: 100, 15}
```

This creates a slice of 12 `ints` with the following values: [1, 0, 0, 0, 0, 4, 6, 0, 0, 0, 100, 15].

You can simulate multidimensional slices and make a slice of slices:

```
var x [][]int
```

You read and write slices using bracket syntax, and, just like with arrays, you can't read or write past the end or use a negative index:

```
x[0] = 10
fmt.Println(x[2])
```

So far, slices have seemed identical to arrays. We start to see the differences between arrays and slices when we look at declaring slices without using a literal:

```
var x []int
```

This creates a slice of ints. Since no value is assigned, x is assigned the zero value for a slice, which is something we haven't seen before: nil. We'll talk more about nil in Chapter 6, but it is slightly different from the null that's found in other languages. In Go, nil is an identifier that represents the lack of a value for some types. Like the untyped numeric constants we saw in the previous chapter, nil has no type, so it can be assigned or compared against values of different types. A nil slice contains nothing.

A slice is the first type we've seen that isn't *comparable*. It is a compile-time error to use == to see if two slices are identical or != to see if they are different. The only thing you can compare a slice with is nil:

```
fmt.Println(x == nil) // prints true
```

 The reflect package contains a function called DeepEqual that can compare almost anything, including slices. It's primarily intended for testing, but you could use it to compare slices if you needed to. We'll look at it when we discuss reflection in Chapter 14.

len

Go provides several built-in functions to work with its built-in types. We already saw the complex, real, and imag built-in functions to build and take apart complex numbers. There are several built-in functions for slices, too. We've already seen the built-in len function when looking at arrays. It works for slices, too, and when you pass a nil slice to len, it returns 0.

 Functions like len are built in to Go because they can do things that can't be done by the functions that you can write. We've already seen that len's parameter can be any type of array or any type of slice. We'll soon see that it also works for strings and maps. In "Channels" on page 206, we'll see it working with channels. Trying to pass a variable of any other type to len is a compile-time error. As we'll see in Chapter 5, Go doesn't let developers write functions that behave this way.

append

The built-in append function is used to grow slices:

```
var x []int
x = append(x, 10)
```

The append function takes at least two parameters, a slice of any type and a value of that type. It returns a slice of the same type. The returned slice is assigned back to the slice that's passed in. In this example, we are appending to a nil slice, but you can append to a slice that already has elements:

```
var x = []int{1, 2, 3}
x = append(x, 4)
```

You can append more than one value at a time:

```
x = append(x, 5, 6, 7)
```

One slice is appended onto another by using the ... operator to expand the source slice into individual values (we'll learn more about the ... operator in "Variadic Input Parameters and Slices" on page 89):

```
y := []int{20, 30, 40}
x = append(x, y...)
```

It is a compile-time error if you forget to assign the value returned from append. You might be wondering why as it seems a bit repetitive. We will talk about this in greater detail in Chapter 5, but Go is a *call by value* language. Every time you pass a parameter to a function, Go makes a copy of the value that's passed in. Passing a slice to the append function actually passes a copy of the slice to the function. The function adds the values to the copy of the slice and returns the copy. You then assign the returned slice back to the variable in the calling function.

Capacity

As we've seen, a slice is a sequence of values. Each element in a slice is assigned to consecutive memory locations, which makes it quick to read or write these values. Every slice has a *capacity*, which is the number of consecutive memory locations reserved. This can be larger than the length. Each time you append to a slice, one or more values is added to the end of the slice. Each value added increases the length by one. When the length reaches the capacity, there's no more room to put values. If you try to add additional values when the length equals the capacity, the append function uses the Go runtime to allocate a new slice with a larger capacity. The values in the original slice are copied to the new slice, the new values are added to the end, and the new slice is returned.

The Go Runtime

Every high-level language relies on a set of libraries to enable programs written in that language to run, and Go is no exception. The Go runtime provides services like memory allocation and garbage collection, concurrency support, networking, and implementations of built-in types and functions.

The Go runtime is compiled into every Go binary. This is different from languages that use a virtual machine, which must be installed separately to allow programs written in those languages to function. Including the runtime in the binary makes it easier to distribute Go programs and avoids worries about compatibility issues between the runtime and the program.

When a slice grows via append, it takes time for the Go runtime to allocate new memory and copy the existing data from the old memory to the new. The old memory also needs to be garbage collected. For this reason, the Go runtime usually increases a slice by more than one each time it runs out of capacity. The rules as of Go 1.14 are to double the size of the slice when the capacity is less than 1,024 and then grow by at least 25% afterward.

Just as the built-in len function returns the current length of a slice, the built-in cap function returns the current capacity of a slice. It is used far less frequently than len. Most of the time, cap is used to check if a slice is large enough to hold new data, or if a call to make is needed to create a new slice.

You can also pass an array to the cap function, but cap always returns the same value as len for arrays. Don't put it in your code, but save this trick for Go trivia night.

Let's take a look at how adding elements to a slice changes the length and capacity. Run the code in Example 3-1 on The Go Playground (*https://oreil.ly/yiHu-*) or on your machine.

Example 3-1. Understanding capacity

```
var x []int
fmt.Println(x, len(x), cap(x))
x = append(x, 10)
fmt.Println(x, len(x), cap(x))
x = append(x, 20)
fmt.Println(x, len(x), cap(x))
x = append(x, 30)
fmt.Println(x, len(x), cap(x))
x = append(x, 40)
fmt.Println(x, len(x), cap(x))
x = append(x, 50)
fmt.Println(x, len(x), cap(x))
```

When you build and run the code, you'll see the following output. Notice how and when the capacity increases:

```
[] 0 0
[10] 1 1
[10 20] 2 2
[10 20 30] 3 4
[10 20 30 40] 4 4
[10 20 30 40 50] 5 8
```

While it's nice that slices grow automatically, it's far more efficient to size them once. If you know how many things you plan to put into a slice, create the slice with the correct initial capacity. We do that with the make function.

make

We've already seen two ways to declare a slice, using a slice literal or the nil zero value. While useful, neither way allows you to create an empty slice that already has a length or capacity specified. That's the job of the built-in make function. It allows us to specify the type, length, and, optionally, the capacity. Let's take a look:

```
x := make([]int, 5)
```

This creates an int slice with a length of 5 and a capacity of 5. Since it has a length of 5, x[0] through x[4] are valid elements, and they are all initialized to 0.

One common beginner mistake is to try to populate those initial elements using append:

```
x := make([]int, 5)
x = append(x, 10)
```

The 10 is placed at the end of the slice, *after* the zero values in positions 0–4 because append always increases the length of a slice. The value of x is now [0 0 0 0 0 10], with a length of 6 and a capacity of 10 (the capacity was doubled as soon as the sixth element was appended).

We can also specify an initial capacity with make:

```
x := make([]int, 5, 10)
```

This creates an int slice with a length of 5 and a capacity of 10.

You can also create a slice with zero length, but a capacity that's greater than zero:

```
x := make([]int, 0, 10)
```

In this case, we have a non-nil slice with a length of 0, but a capacity of 10. Since the length is 0, we can't directly index into it, but we can append values to it:

```
x := make([]int, 0, 10)
x = append(x, 5,6,7,8)
```

The value of x is now [5 6 7 8], with a length of 4 and a capacity of 10.

 Never specify a capacity that's less than the length! It is a compile-time error to do so with a constant or numeric literal. If you use a variable to specify a capacity that's smaller than the length, your program will panic at runtime.

Declaring Your Slice

Now that we've seen all these different ways to create slices, how do you choose which slice declaration style to use? The primary goal is to minimize the number of times the slice needs to grow. If it's possible that the slice won't need to grow at all (because your function might return nothing), use a var declaration with no assigned value to create a nil slice, as shown in Example 3-2.

Example 3-2. Declaring a slice that might stay nil

```
var data []int
```

 You can create a slice using an empty slice literal:

```
var x = []int{}
```

This creates a zero-length slice, which is non-nil (comparing it to nil returns false). Otherwise, a nil slice works identically to a zero-length slice. The only situation where a zero-length slice is useful is when converting a slice to JSON. We'll look at this more in "encoding/json" on page 241.

If you have some starting values, or if a slice's values aren't going to change, then a slice literal is a good choice (see Example 3-3).

Example 3-3. Declaring a slice with default values

```
data := []int{2, 4, 6, 8} // numbers we appreciate
```

If you have a good idea of how large your slice needs to be, but don't know what those values will be when you are writing the program, use make. The question then becomes whether you should specify a nonzero length in the call to make or specify a zero length and a nonzero capacity. There are three possibilities:

- If you are using a slice as a buffer (we'll see this in "io and Friends" on page 233), then specify a nonzero length.

- If you are *sure* you know the exact size you want, you can specify the length and index into the slice to set the values. This is often done when transforming values in one slice and storing them in a second. The downside to this approach is that if you have the size wrong, you'll end up with either zero values at the end of the slice or a panic from trying to access elements that don't exist.

- In other situations, use make with a zero length and a specified capacity. This allows you to use append to add items to the slice. If the number of items turns out to be smaller, you won't have an extraneous zero value at the end. If the number of items is larger, your code will not panic.

The Go community is split between the second and third approaches. I personally prefer using append with a slice initialized to a zero length. It might be slower in some situations, but it is less likely to introduce a bug.

 append always increases the length of a slice! If you have specified a slice's length using make, be sure that you mean to append to it before you do so, or you might end up with a bunch of surprise zero values at the beginning of your slice.

Slicing Slices

A *slice expression* creates a slice from a slice. It's written inside brackets and consists of a starting offset and an ending offset, separated by a colon (:). If you leave off the starting offset, 0 is assumed. Likewise, if you leave off the ending offset, the end of the slice is substituted. You can see how this works by running the code in Example 3-4 on The Go Playground (*https://oreil.ly/DW_FU*).

Example 3-4. Slicing slices

```
x := []int{1, 2, 3, 4}
y := x[:2]
z := x[1:]
d := x[1:3]
e := x[:]
fmt.Println("x:", x)
fmt.Println("y:", y)
fmt.Println("z:", z)
fmt.Println("d:", d)
fmt.Println("e:", e)
```

It gives the following output:

```
x: [1 2 3 4]
y: [1 2]
z: [2 3 4]
d: [2 3]
e: [1 2 3 4]
```

Slices share storage sometimes

When you take a slice from a slice, you are *not* making a copy of the data. Instead, you now have two variables that are sharing memory. This means that changes to an element in a slice affect all slices that share that element. Let's see what happens when we change values. You can run the code in Example 3-5 on The Go Playground (*https://oreil.ly/mHxe4*).

Example 3-5. Slices with overlapping storage

```
x := []int{1, 2, 3, 4}
y := x[:2]
z := x[1:]
x[1] = 20
y[0] = 10
z[1] = 30
fmt.Println("x:", x)
fmt.Println("y:", y)
fmt.Println("z:", z)
```

You get the following output:

```
x: [10 20 30 4]
y: [10 20]
z: [20 30 4]
```

Changing x modified both y and z, while changes to y and z modified x.

Slicing slices gets extra confusing when combined with append. Try out the code in Example 3-6 on The Go Playground (*https://oreil.ly/2mB59*).

Example 3-6. append makes overlapping slices more confusing

```
x := []int{1, 2, 3, 4}
y := x[:2]
fmt.Println(cap(x), cap(y))
y = append(y, 30)
fmt.Println("x:", x)
fmt.Println("y:", y)
```

Running this code gives the following output:

```
4 4
x: [1 2 30 4]
y: [1 2 30]
```

What's going on? Whenever you take a slice from another slice, the subslice's capacity is set to the capacity of the original slice, minus the offset of the subslice within the original slice. This means that any unused capacity in the original slice is also shared with any subslices.

When we make the y slice from x, the length is set to 2, but the capacity is set to 4, the same as x. Since the capacity is 4, appending onto the end of y puts the value in the third position of x.

This behavior creates some very odd scenarios, with multiple slices appending and overwriting each other's data. See if you can guess what the code in Example 3-7 prints out, then run it on The Go Playground (*https://oreil.ly/1u_tO*) to see if you guessed correctly.

Example 3-7. Even more confusing slices

```
x := make([]int, 0, 5)
x = append(x, 1, 2, 3, 4)
y := x[:2]
z := x[2:]
fmt.Println(cap(x), cap(y), cap(z))
y = append(y, 30, 40, 50)
x = append(x, 60)
z = append(z, 70)
fmt.Println("x:", x)
fmt.Println("y:", y)
fmt.Println("z:", z)
```

To avoid complicated slice situations, you should either never use append with a subslice or make sure that append doesn't cause an overwrite by using a *full slice expression*. This is a little weird, but it makes clear how much memory is shared between the parent slice and the subslice. The full slice expression includes a third part, which indicates the last position in the parent slice's capacity that's available for the subslice. Subtract the starting offset from this number to get the subslice's capacity. Example 3-8 shows lines three and four from the previous example, modified to use full slice expressions.

Example 3-8. The full slice expression protects against append

```
y := x[:2:2]
z := x[2:4:4]
```

You can try out this code on The Go Playground (*https://oreil.ly/Cn2cX*). Both y and z have a capacity of 2. Because we limited the capacity of the subslices to their lengths, appending additional elements onto y and z created new slices that didn't interact with the other slices. After this code runs, x is set to [1 2 3 4 60], y is set to [1 2 30 40 50], and z is set to [3 4 70].

 Be very careful when taking a slice of a slice! Both slices share the same memory and changes to one are reflected in the other. Avoid modifying slices after they have been sliced or if they were produced by slicing. Use a three-part slice expression to prevent append from sharing capacity between slices.

Converting Arrays to Slices

Slices aren't the only thing you can slice. If you have an array, you can take a slice from it using a slice expression. This is a useful way to bridge an array to a function that only takes slices. However, be aware that taking a slice from an array has the same memory-sharing properties as taking a slice from a slice. If you run the following code on The Go Playground (*https://oreil.ly/kliaJ*):

```
x := [4]int{5, 6, 7, 8}
y := x[:2]
z := x[2:]
x[0] = 10
fmt.Println("x:", x)
fmt.Println("y:", y)
fmt.Println("z:", z)
```

you get the output:

```
x: [10 6 7 8]
y: [10 6]
z: [7 8]
```

copy

If you need to create a slice that's independent of the original, use the built-in copy function. Let's take a look at a simple example, which you can run on The Go Playground (*https://oreil.ly/ilMNY*):

```
x := []int{1, 2, 3, 4}
y := make([]int, 4)
num := copy(y, x)
fmt.Println(y, num)
```

You get the output:

```
[1 2 3 4] 4
```

The copy function takes two parameters. The first is the destination slice and the second is the source slice. It copies as many values as it can from source to destination, limited by whichever slice is smaller, and returns the number of elements copied. The *capacity* of x and y doesn't matter; it's the length that's important.

You don't need to copy an entire slice. The following code copies the first two elements of a four-element slice into a two-element slice:

```
x := []int{1, 2, 3, 4}
y := make([]int, 2)
num = copy(y, x)
```

The variable y is set to [1 2] and num is set to 2.

You could also copy from the middle of the source slice:

```
x := []int{1, 2, 3, 4}
y := make([]int, 2)
copy(y, x[2:])
```

We are copying the third and fourth elements in x by taking a slice of the slice. Also note that we don't assign the output of copy to a variable. If you don't need the number of elements copied, you don't need to assign it.

The copy function allows you to copy between two slices that cover overlapping sections of an underlying slice:

```
x := []int{1, 2, 3, 4}
num = copy(x[:3], x[1:])
fmt.Println(x, num)
```

In this case, we are copying the last three values in x on top of the first three values of x. This prints out [2 3 4 4] 3.

You can use copy with arrays by taking a slice of the array. You can make the array either the source or the destination of the copy. You can try out the following code on The Go Playground (*https://oreil.ly/-mhRW*):

```
x := []int{1, 2, 3, 4}
d := [4]int{5, 6, 7, 8}
y := make([]int, 2)
copy(y, d[:])
fmt.Println(y)
copy(d[:], x)
fmt.Println(d)
```

The first call to copy copies the first two values in array d into slice y. The second copies all of the values in slice x into array d. This produces the output:

```
[5 6]
[1 2 3 4]
```

Strings and Runes and Bytes

Now that we've talked about slices, we can go back and look at strings again. You might think that a string in Go is made out of runes, but that's not the case. Under the covers, Go uses a sequence of bytes to represent a string. These bytes don't have to be in any particular character encoding, but several Go library functions (and the for-range loop that we discuss in the next chapter) assume that a string is composed of a sequence of UTF-8-encoded code points.

 According to the language specification, Go source code is always written in UTF-8. Unless you use hexadecimal escapes in a string literal, your string literals are written in UTF-8.

Just like you can extract a single value from an array or a slice, you can extract a single value from a string by using an *index expression*:

```
var s string = "Hello there"
var b byte = s[6]
```

Like arrays and slices, string indexes are zero-based; in this example, b is assigned the value of the seventh value in s, which is t.

The slice expression notation that we used with arrays and slices also works with strings:

```
var s string = "Hello there"
var s2 string = s[4:7]
var s3 string = s[:5]
var s4 string = s[6:]
```

This assigns "o t" to s2, "Hello" to s3, and "there" to s4.

While it's handy that Go allows us to use slicing notation to make substrings and use index notation to extract individual entries from a string, you should be very careful when doing so. Since strings are immutable, they don't have the modification problems that slices of slices do. There is a different problem, though. A string is composed of a sequence of bytes, while a code point in UTF-8 can be anywhere from one to four bytes long. Our previous example was entirely composed of code points that are one byte long in UTF-8, so everything worked out as expected. But when dealing with languages other than English or with emojis, you run into code points that are multiple bytes long in UTF-8:

```
var s string = "Hello 😀"
var s2 string = s[4:7]
var s3 string = s[:5]
var s4 string = s[6:]
```

In this example, s3 will still be equal to "Hello." The variable s4 is set to the sun emoji. But s2 is not set to "o ☀." Instead, you get "o ❖." That's because we only copied the first byte of the sun emoji's code point, which is invalid.

Go allows you to pass a string to the built-in len function to find the length of the string. Given that string index and slice expressions count positions in bytes, it's not surprising that the length returned is the length in bytes, not in code points:

```
var s string = "Hello ☀"
fmt.Println(len(s))
```

This code prints out 10, not 7, because it takes four bytes to represent the sun with smiling face emoji in UTF-8.

> Even though Go allows you to use slicing and indexing syntax with strings, you should only use it when you know that your string only contains characters that take up one byte.

Because of this complicated relationship between runes, strings, and bytes, Go has some interesting type conversions between these types. A single rune or byte can be converted to a string:

```
var a rune    = 'x'
var s string  = string(a)
var b byte    = 'y'
var s2 string = string(b)
```

> A common bug for new Go developers is to try to make an int into a string by using a type conversion:
>
> ```
> var x int = 65
> var y = string(x)
> fmt.Println(y)
> ```
>
> This results in y having the value "A," not "65." As of Go 1.15, go vet blocks a type conversion to string from any integer type other than rune or byte.

A string can be converted back and forth to a slice of bytes or a slice of runes. Try Example 3-9 out on The Go Playground (https://oreil.ly/N7fOB).

Example 3-9. Converting strings to slices

```
var s string = "Hello, ☀"
var bs []byte = []byte(s)
var rs []rune = []rune(s)
```

```
fmt.Println(bs)
fmt.Println(rs)
```

When you run this code, you see:

```
[72 101 108 108 111 44 32 240 159 140 158]
[72 101 108 108 111 44 32 127774]
```

The first output line has the string converted to UTF-8 bytes. The second has the string converted to runes.

Most data in Go is read and written as a sequence of bytes, so the most common string type conversions are back and forth with a slice of bytes. Slices of runes are uncommon.

UTF-8

UTF-8 is the most commonly used encoding for Unicode. Unicode uses four bytes (32 bits) to represent each *code point*, the technical name for each character and modifier. Given this, the simplest way to represent Unicode code points is to store four bytes for each code point. This is called UTF-32. It is mostly unused because it wastes so much space. Due to Unicode implementation details, 11 of the 32 bits are always zero. Another common encoding is UTF-16, which uses one or two 16-bit (2-byte) sequences to represent each code point. This is also wasteful; much of the content in the world is written using code points that fit into a single byte. And that's where UTF-8 comes in.

UTF-8 is very clever. It lets you use a single byte to represent the Unicode characters whose values are below 128 (which includes all of the letters, numbers, and punctuation commonly used in English), but expands to a maximum of four bytes to represent Unicode code points with larger values. The result is that the *worst* case for UTF-8 is the same as using UTF-32. UTF-8 has some other nice properties. Unlike UTF-32 and UTF-16, you don't have to worry about little-endian versus big-endian. It also allows you to look at any byte in a sequence and tell if you are at the start of a UTF-8 sequence, or somewhere in the middle. That means you can't accidentally read a character incorrectly.

The only downside is that you cannot randomly access a string encoded with UTF-8. While you can detect if you are in the middle of a character, you can't tell how many characters in you are. You need to start at the beginning of the string and count. Go doesn't require a string to be written in UTF-8, but it strongly encourages it. We'll see how to work with UTF-8 strings in upcoming chapters.

Fun fact: UTF-8 was invented in 1992 by Ken Thompson and Rob Pike, two of the creators of Go.

Rather than use the slice and index expressions with strings, you should extract substrings and code points from strings using the functions in the strings and unicode/utf8 packages in the standard library. In the next chapter, we'll see how to use a for-range loop to iterate over the code points in a string.

Maps

Slices are useful when you have sequential data. Like most languages, Go provides a built-in data type for situations where you want to associate one value to another. The map type is written as map[keyType]valueType. Let's take a look at a few ways to declare maps. First, you can use a var declaration to create a map variable that's set to its zero value:

```
var nilMap map[string]int
```

In this case, nilMap is declared to be a map with string keys and int values. The zero value for a map is nil. A nil map has a length of 0. Attempting to read a nil map always returns the zero value for the map's value type. However, attempting to write to a nil map variable causes a panic.

We can use a := declaration to create a map variable by assigning it a *map literal*:

```
totalWins := map[string]int{}
```

In this case, we are using an empty map literal. This is not the same as a nil map. It has a length of 0, but you can read and write to a map assigned an empty map literal. Here's what a nonempty map literal looks like:

```
teams := map[string][]string {
    "Orcas": []string{"Fred", "Ralph", "Bijou"},
    "Lions": []string{"Sarah", "Peter", "Billie"},
    "Kittens": []string{"Waldo", "Raul", "Ze"},
}
```

A map literal's body is written as the key, followed by a colon (:), then the value. There's a comma separating each key-value pair in the map, even on the last line. In this example, the value is a slice of strings. The type of the value in a map can be anything. There are some restrictions on the types of the keys that we'll discuss in a bit.

If you know how many key-value pairs you intend to put in the map, but don't know the exact values, you can use make to create a map with a default size:

```
ages := make(map[int][]string, 10)
```

Maps created with make still have a length of 0, and they can grow past the initially specified size.

Maps are like slices in several ways:

- Maps automatically grow as you add key-value pairs to them.
- If you know how many key-value pairs you plan to insert into a map, you can use make to create a map with a specific initial size.
- Passing a map to the len function tells you the number of key-value pairs in a map.
- The zero value for a map is nil.
- Maps are not comparable. You can check if they are equal to nil, but you cannot check if two maps have identical keys and values using == or differ using !=.

The key for a map can be any comparable type. This means you cannot use a slice or a map as the key for a map.

When should you use a map and when should you use a slice? Slices are for lists of data, especially for data that's processed sequentially. Maps are useful when you have data that's organized according to a value that's not a strictly increasing order.

Use a map when the order of elements doesn't matter. Use a slice when the order of elements is important.

What Is a Hash Map?

In computer science, a *map* is a data structure that associates (or maps) one value to another. Maps can be implemented several ways, each with their own trade-offs. The map that's built-in to Go is a *hash map*. In case you aren't familiar with the concept, here is a really quick overview.

A hash map does fast lookups of values based on a key. Internally, it's implemented as an array. When you insert a key and value, the key is turned into a number using a *hash algorithm*. These numbers are not unique for each key. The hash algorithm can turn different keys into the same number. That number is then used as an index into the array. Each element in that array is called a *bucket*. The key-value pair is then stored in the bucket. If there is already an identical key in the bucket, the previous value is replaced with the new value.

Each bucket is also an array; it can hold more than one value. When two keys map to the same bucket, that's called a *collision*, and the keys and values for both are stored in the bucket.

A read from a hash map works in the same way. You take the key, run the hash algorithm to turn it into a number, find the associated bucket, and then iterate over all the keys in the bucket to see if one of them is equal to the supplied key. If one is found, the value is returned.

You don't want to have too many collisions, because the more collisions, the slower the hash map gets, as you have to iterate over all the keys that mapped to the same bucket to find the one that you want. Clever hash algorithms are designed to keep collisions to a minimum. If enough elements are added, hash maps resize to rebalance the buckets and allow more entries.

Hash maps are really useful, but building your own is hard to get right. If you'd like to learn more about how Go does it, watch this talk from GopherCon 2016, Inside the Map Implementation (*https://oreil.ly/kIeJM*).

Go doesn't require (or even allow) you to define your own hash algorithm or equality definition. Instead, the Go runtime that's compiled into every Go program has code that implements hash algorithms for all types that are allowed to be keys.

Reading and Writing a Map

Let's look at a short program that declares, writes to, and reads from a map. You can run the program in Example 3-10 on The Go Playground (*https://oreil.ly/gBMvf*).

Example 3-10. Using a map

```
totalWins := map[string]int{}
totalWins["Orcas"] = 1
totalWins["Lions"] = 2
fmt.Println(totalWins["Orcas"])
fmt.Println(totalWins["Kittens"])
totalWins["Kittens"]++
fmt.Println(totalWins["Kittens"])
totalWins["Lions"] = 3
fmt.Println(totalWins["Lions"])
```

When you run this program, you'll see the following output:

```
1
0
1
3
```

We assign a value to a map key by putting the key within brackets and using = to specify the value, and we read the value assigned to a map key by putting the key within brackets. Note that you cannot use := to assign a value to a map key.

When we try to read the value assigned to a map key that was never set, the map returns the zero value for the map's value type. In this case, the value type is an int, so we get back a 0. You can use the ++ operator to increment the numeric value for a map key. Because a map returns its zero value by default, this works even when there's no existing value associated with the key.

The comma ok Idiom

As we've seen, a map returns the zero value if you ask for the value associated with a key that's not in the map. This is handy when implementing things like the counter we saw earlier. However, you sometimes do need to find out if a key is in a map. Go provides the *comma ok idiom* to tell the difference between a key that's associated with a zero value and a key that's not in the map:

```
m := map[string]int{
    "hello": 5,
    "world": 0,
}
v, ok := m["hello"]
fmt.Println(v, ok)

v, ok = m["world"]
fmt.Println(v, ok)

v, ok = m["goodbye"]
fmt.Println(v, ok)
```

Rather than assign the result of a map read to a single variable, with the comma ok idiom you assign the results of a map read to two variables. The first gets the value associated with the key. The second value returned is a bool. It is usually named ok. If ok is true, the key is present in the map. If ok is false, the key is not present. In this example, the code prints out 5 true, 0 true, and 0 false.

> The comma ok idiom is used in Go when we want to differentiate between reading a value and getting back the zero value. We'll see it again when we read from channels in Chapter 10 and when we use type assertions in Chapter 7.

Deleting from Maps

Key-value pairs are removed from a map via the built-in delete function:

```
m := map[string]int{
    "hello": 5,
    "world": 10,
}
delete(m, "hello")
```

The delete function takes a map and a key and then removes the key-value pair with the specified key. If the key isn't present in the map or if the map is nil, nothing happens. The delete function doesn't return a value.

Using Maps as Sets

Many languages include a *set* in their standard library. A set is a data type that ensures there is at most one of a value, but doesn't guarantee that the values are in any particular order. Checking to see if an element is in a set is fast, no matter how many elements are in the set. (Checking to see if an element is in a slice takes longer as you add more elements to the slice.)

Go doesn't include a set, but you can use a map to simulate some of its features. Use the key of the map for the type that you want to put into the set and use a bool for the value. The code in Example 3-11 demonstrates the concept. You can run it on The Go Playground (*https://oreil.ly/wC6XK*).

Example 3-11. Using a map as a set

```
intSet := map[int]bool{}
vals := []int{5, 10, 2, 5, 8, 7, 3, 9, 1, 2, 10}
for _, v := range vals {
    intSet[v] = true
}
fmt.Println(len(vals), len(intSet))
fmt.Println(intSet[5])
fmt.Println(intSet[500])
if intSet[100] {
    fmt.Println("100 is in the set")
}
```

We want a set of ints, so we create a map where the keys are of int type and the values are of bool type. We iterate over the values in vals using a for-range loop (which we discuss in "The for-range Statement" on page 71) to place them into intSet, associating each int with the boolean value true.

We wrote 11 values into intSet, but the length of intSet is 8, because you cannot have duplicate keys in a map. If we look for 5 in intSet, it returns true, because we have a key with the value 5. However, if we look for 500 or 100 in intSet, it returns false. This is because we haven't put either value into intSet, which causes the map to return the zero value for the map value, and the zero value for a bool is false.

If you need sets that provide operations like union, intersection, and subtraction, you can either write one yourself or use one of the many third-party libraries that provide the functionality. (We'll learn more about using third-party libraries in Chapter 9.)

Some people prefer to use struct{} for the value when a map is being used to implement a set. (We'll discuss structs in the next section.) The advantage is that an empty struct uses zero bytes, while a boolean uses one byte.

The disadvantage is that using a struct{} makes your code more clumsy. You have a less obvious assignment, and you need to use the comma ok idiom to check if a value is in the set:

```
intSet := map[int]struct{}{}
vals := []int{5, 10, 2, 5, 8, 7, 3, 9, 1, 2, 10}
for _, v := range vals {
    intSet[v] = struct{}{}
}
if _, ok := intSet[5]; ok {
    fmt.Println("5 is in the set")
}
```

Unless you have very large sets, it is unlikely that the difference in memory usage is significant enough to outweigh the disadvantages.

Structs

Maps are a convenient way to store some kinds of data, but they have limitations. They don't define an API since there's no way to constrain a map to only allow certain keys. Also, all of the values in a map must be of the same type. For these reasons, maps are not an ideal way to pass data from function to function. When you have related data that you want to group together, you should define a *struct*.

If you already know an object-oriented language, you might be wondering about the difference between classes and structs. The difference is simple: Go doesn't have classes, because it doesn't have inheritance. This doesn't mean that Go doesn't have some of the features of object-oriented languages, it just does things a little differently. We'll learn more about the object-oriented features of Go in Chapter 7.

Most languages have a concept that's similar to a struct, and the syntax that Go uses to read and write structs should look familiar:

```
type person struct {
    name string
    age  int
    pet  string
}
```

No commas

A struct type is defined with the keyword type, the name of the struct type, the keyword struct, and a pair of braces ({}). Within the braces, you list the fields in the struct. Just like we put the variable name first and the variable type second in a `var` declaration, we put the struct field name first and the struct field type second. Also note that unlike map literals, there are no commas separating the fields in a struct declaration. You can define a struct type inside or outside of a function. A struct type that's defined within a function can only be used within that function. (We'll learn more about functions in Chapter 5.)

 Technically, you can scope a struct definition to any block level. We'll learn more about blocks in Chapter 4.

Once a struct type is declared, we can define variables of that type:

```
var fred person
```

Here we are using a `var` declaration. Since no value is assigned to `fred`, it gets the zero value for the `person` struct type. A zero value struct has every field set to the field's zero value.

A *struct literal* can be assigned to a variable as well:

```
bob := person{}
```

Unlike maps, there is no difference between assigning an empty struct literal and not assigning a value at all. Both initialize all of the fields in the struct to their zero values. There are two different styles for a nonempty struct literal. A struct literal can be specified as a comma-separated list of values for the fields inside of braces:

```
julia := person{
    "Julia",
    40,
    "cat",
}
```

When using this struct literal format, a value for every field in the struct must be specified, and the values are assigned to the fields in the order they were declared in the struct definition.

The second struct literal style looks like the map literal style:

```
beth := person{
    age: 30,
    name: "Beth",
}
```

You use the names of the fields in the struct to specify the values. When you use this style, you can leave out keys and specify the fields in any order. Any field not specified is set to its zero value. You cannot mix the two struct literal styles: either all of the fields are specified with keys, or none of them are. For small structs where all fields are always specified, the simpler struct literal style is fine. In other cases, use the key names. It's more verbose, but it makes clear what value is being assigned to what field without having to reference the struct definition. It's also more maintainable. If you initialize a struct without using the field names and a future version of the struct adds additional fields, your code will no longer compile.

A field in a struct is accessed with dotted notation:

```
bob.name = "Bob"
fmt.Println(beth.name)
```

Just like we use brackets for both reading and writing to a map, we use dotted notation for reading and writing to struct fields.

Anonymous Structs

You can also declare that a variable implements a struct type without first giving the struct type a name. This is called an *anonymous struct*:

```
var person struct {
    name string
    age  int
    pet  string
}

person.name = "bob"
person.age = 50
person.pet = "dog"

pet := struct {
    name string
    kind string
}{
    name: "Fido",
    kind: "dog",
}
```

In this example, the types of the variables person and pet are anonymous structs. You assign (and read) fields in an anonymous struct just like you do for a named struct type. Just like you can initialize an instance of a named struct with a struct literal, you can do the same for an anonymous struct as well.

You might wonder when it's useful to have a data type that's only associated with a single instance. There are two common situations where anonymous structs are handy. The first is when you translate external data into a struct or a struct into external data (like JSON or protocol buffers). This is called *unmarshaling* and *marshaling* data. We'll learn how to do this in "encoding/json" on page 241.

Writing tests is another place where anonymous structs pop up. We'll use a slice of anonymous structs when writing table-driven tests in Chapter 13.

Comparing and Converting Structs

Whether or not a struct is comparable depends on the struct's fields. Structs that are entirely composed of comparable types are comparable; those with slice or map fields are not (as we will see in later chapters, function and channel fields also prevent a struct from being comparable).

Unlike in Python or Ruby, in Go there's no magic method that can be overridden to redefine equality and make == and != work for incomparable structs. You can, of course, write your own function that you use to compare structs.

Just like Go doesn't allow comparisons between variables of different primitive types, Go doesn't allow comparisons between variables that represent structs of different types. Go does allow you to perform a type conversion from one struct type to another *if the fields of both structs have the same names, order, and types*. Let's see what this means. Given this struct:

```
type firstPerson struct {
    name string
    age  int
}
```

We can use a type conversion to convert an instance of firstPerson to secondPerson, but we can't use == to compare an instance of firstPerson and an instance of secondPerson, because they are different types:

```
type secondPerson struct {
    name string
    age  int
}
```

We can't convert an instance of firstPerson to thirdPerson, because the fields are in a different order:

```
type thirdPerson struct {
    age  int
    name string
}
```

We can't convert an instance of firstPerson to fourthPerson because the field names don't match:

```
type fourthPerson struct {
    firstName string
    age       int
}
```

Finally, we can't convert an instance of `firstPerson` to `fifthPerson` because there's an additional field:

```
type fifthPerson struct {
    name          string
    age           int
    favoriteColor string
}
```

Anonymous structs add a small twist to this: if two struct variables are being compared and at least one of them has a type that's an anonymous struct, you can compare them without a type conversion if the fields of both structs have the same names, order, and types. You can also assign between named and anonymous struct types if the fields of both structs have the same names, order, and types:

```
type firstPerson struct {
    name string
    age  int
}
f := firstPerson{
    name: "Bob",
    age:  50,
}
var g struct {
    name string
    age  int
}

// compiles -- can use = and == between identical named and anonymous structs
g = f
fmt.Println(f == g)
```

Wrapping Up

We've learned a lot about container types in Go. In addition to learning more about strings, we now know how to use the built-in generic container types, slices and maps. We can also construct our own composite types via structs. In our next chapter, we're going to take a look at Go's control structures, `for`, `if/else`, and `switch`. We will also learn how Go organizes code into blocks, and how the different block levels can lead to surprising behavior.

CHAPTER 4

Blocks, Shadows, and Control Structures

Now that we have covered variables, constants, and built-in types, we are ready to look at programming logic and organization. We'll start by explaining blocks and how they control when an identifier is available. Then we'll look at Go's control structures: `if`, `for`, and `switch`. Finally, we will talk about `goto` and the one situation when you should use it.

Blocks

Go lets you declare variables in lots of places. You can declare them outside of functions, as the parameters to functions, and as local variables within functions.

So far, we've only written the `main` function, but we'll write functions with parameters in the next chapter.

Each place where a declaration occurs is called a *block.* Variables, constants, types, and functions declared outside of any functions are placed in the *package* block. We've used `import` statements in our programs to gain access to printing and math functions (and will talk about them in detail in Chapter 9). They define names for other packages that are valid for the file that contains the `import` statement. These names are in the *file* block. All of the variables defined at the top level of a function (including the parameters to a function) are in a block. Within a function, every set of braces (`{}`) defines another block, and in a bit we will see that the control structures in Go define blocks of their own.

You can access an identifier defined in any outer block from within any inner block. This raises the question: what happens when you have a declaration with the same name as an identifier in a containing block? If you do that, you *shadow* the identifier created in the outer block.

Shadowing Variables

Before explaining what shadowing is, let's take a look at some code (see Example 4-1). You can run it on The Go Playground (*https://oreil.ly/50t6b*).

Example 4-1. Shadowing variables

```
func main() {
    x := 10
    if x > 5 {
        fmt.Println(x)
        x := 5
        fmt.Println(x)
    }
    fmt.Println(x)
}
```

Before you run this code, try to guess what it's going to print out:

- Nothing prints; the code does not compile
- 10 on line one, 5 on line two, 5 on line three
- 10 on line one, 5 on line two, 10 on line three

Here's what happens:

```
10
5
10
```

A shadowing variable is a variable that has the same name as a variable in a containing block. For as long as the shadowing variable exists, you cannot access a shadowed variable.

In this case, we almost certainly didn't want to create a brand-new x inside the if statement. Instead, we probably wanted to assign 5 to the x declared at the top level of the function block. At the first fmt.Println inside the if statement, we are able to access the x declared at the top level of the function. On the next line, though, we *shadow* x by *declaring a new variable with the same name* inside the block created by the if statement's body. At the second fmt.Println, when we access the variable named x, we get the shadowing variable, which has the value of 5. The closing brace for the if statement's body ends the block where the shadowing x exists, and at the third fmt.Println, when we access the variable named x, we get the variable declared at the top level of the function, which has the value of 10. Notice that this x didn't disappear or get reassigned; there was just no way to access it once it was shadowed in the inner block.

I mentioned in the last chapter that there are situations where I avoid using := because it can make it unclear what variables are being used. That's because it is very easy to accidentally shadow a variable when using :=. Remember, we can use := to create and assign to multiple variables at once. Also, not all of the variables on the lefthand side have to be new for := to be legal. You can use := as long as there is at least one new variable on the lefthand side. Let's look at another program (see Example 4-2), which can be found on The Go Playground (*https://oreil.ly/U_m4B*).

Example 4-2. Shadowing with multiple assignment

```
func main() {
    x := 10
    if x > 5 {
        x, y := 5, 20
        fmt.Println(x, y)
    }
    fmt.Println(x)
}
```

Running this code gives you:

```
5 20
10
```

Although there was an existing definition of x in an outer block, x was still shadowed within the if statement. That's because := only reuses variables that are declared in the current block. When using :=, make sure that you don't have any variables from an outer scope on the lefthand side, unless you intend to shadow them.

You also need to be careful to ensure that you don't shadow a package import. We'll talk more about importing packages in Chapter 9, but we've been importing the fmt package to print out results of our programs. Let's see what happens when we declare a variable called fmt within our main function, as shown in Example 4-3. You can try to run it on The Go Playground (*https://oreil.ly/CKQvm*).

Example 4-3. Shadowing package names

```
func main() {
    x := 10
    fmt.Println(x)
    fmt := "oops"
    fmt.Println(fmt)
}
```

When we try to run this code, we get an error:

```
fmt.Println undefined (type string has no field or method Println)
```

Notice that the problem isn't that we named our variable fmt, it's that we tried to access something that the local variable fmt didn't have. Once the local variable fmt is declared, it shadows the package named fmt in the file block, making it impossible to use the fmt package for the rest of the main function.

Detecting Shadowed Variables

Given the subtle bugs that shadowing can introduce, it's a good idea to make sure that you don't have any shadowed variables in your programs. Neither go vet nor golangci-lint include a tool to detect shadowing, but you can add shadowing detection to your build process by installing the shadow linter on your machine:

```
$ go install golang.org/x/tools/go/analysis/passes/shadow/cmd/shadow@latest
```

If you are building with a Makefile, consider including shadow in the vet task:

```
vet:
        go vet ./...
        shadow ./...
.PHONY:vet
```

When you run make vet against the previous code, you'll see that the shadowed variable is now detected:

```
declaration of "x" shadows declaration at line 6
```

The Universe Block

There's actually one more block that is a little weird: the universe block. Remember, Go is a small language with only 25 keywords. What's interesting is that the built-in types (like int and string), constants (like true and false), and functions (like make or close) aren't included in that list. Neither is nil. So, where are they?

Rather than make them keywords, Go considers these *predeclared identifiers* and defines them in the universe block, which is the block that contains all other blocks.

Because these names are declared in the universe block, it means that they can be shadowed in other scopes. You can see this happen by running the code in Example 4-4 on The Go Playground (*https://oreil.ly/eoU2A*).

Example 4-4. Shadowing true

```
fmt.Println(true)
true := 10
fmt.Println(true)
```

When you run it, you'll see:

```
    true
    10
```

You must be very careful to never redefine any of the identifiers in the universe block. If you accidentally do so, you will get some very strange behavior. If you are lucky, you'll get compilation failures. If you are not, you'll have a harder time tracking down the source of your problems.

You might think that something this potentially destructive would be caught by linting tools. Amazingly, it isn't. Not even shadow detects shadowing of universe block identifiers.

if

The if statement in Go is much like the if statement in most programming languages. Because it is such a familiar construct, I've used it in early sample code without worrying that it'd be confusing. Example 4-5 shows a more complete sample.

Example 4-5. if and else

no parens (handwritten annotation)

```
n := rand.Intn(10)
if n == 0 {
    fmt.Println("That's too low")
} else if n > 5 {
    fmt.Println("That's too big:", n)
} else {
    fmt.Println("That's a good number:", n)
}
```

 If you run this code, you'll find that it always assigns 1 to n. This happens because the default random number seed in math/rand is hard-coded. In "Overriding a Package's Name" on page 183, we'll look at a way to ensure a good seed for random number generation while demonstrating how to handle package name collisions.

The most visible difference between if statements in Go and other languages is that you don't put parenthesis around the condition. But there's another feature that Go adds to if statements that helps you better manage your variables.

As we discussed in the section on shadowing variables, any variable declared within the braces of an if or else statement exists only within that block. This isn't that uncommon; it is true in most languages. What Go adds is the ability to declare variables that are scoped to the condition and to both the if and else blocks. Let's take a look by rewriting our previous example to use this scope, as shown in Example 4-6.

Example 4-6. Scoping a variable to an if statement

```
if n := rand.Intn(10); n == 0 {
    fmt.Println("That's too low")
} else if n > 5 {
    fmt.Println("That's too big:", n)
} else {
    fmt.Println("That's a good number:", n)
}
```

Having this special scope is very handy. It lets you create variables that are available only where they are needed. Once the series of if/else statements ends, n is undefined. You can test this by trying to run the code in Example 4-7 on The Go Playground (*https://oreil.ly/rz671*).

Example 4-7. Out of scope...

```
if n := rand.Intn(10); n == 0 {
    fmt.Println("That's too low")
} else if n > 5 {
    fmt.Println("That's too big:", n)
} else {
    fmt.Println("That's a good number:", n)
}
fmt.Println(n)
```

Attempting to run this code produces a compilation error:

```
undefined: n
```

 Technically, you can put any *simple statement* before the comparison in an if statement. This includes things like a function call that doesn't return a value or assigning a new value to an existing variable. But don't do this. Only use this feature to define new variables that are scoped to the if/else statements; anything else would be confusing.

Also be aware that just like any other block, a variable declared as part of an if statement will shadow variables with the same name that are declared in containing blocks.

for, Four Ways

As in other languages in the C family, Go uses a for statement to loop. What makes Go different from other languages is that for is the *only* looping keyword in the language. Go accomplishes this by using the for keyword in four different formats:

- A complete, C-style for
- A condition-only for
- An infinite for
- for-range

The Complete for Statement

The first one we'll look at is the complete for declaration you might be familiar with from C, Java, or JavaScript, as shown in Example 4-8.

Example 4-8. A complete for statement

```
for i := 0; i < 10; i++ {
    fmt.Println(i)
}
```

You would probably be unsurprised to find that this program prints out the numbers from 0 to 9, inclusive.

Just like the `if` statement, there are no parenthesis around the parts of the `for` statement. Otherwise, it should look very familiar. There are three parts, separated by semicolons. The first is an initialization that sets one or more variables before the loop begins. There are two important details to remember about the initialization section. First, you *must* use `:=` to initialize the variables; `var` is *not* legal here. Second, just like variable declarations in `if` statements, you can shadow a variable here.

The second part is the comparison. This must be an expression that evaluates to a `bool`. It is checked immediately *before* the loop body runs, after the initialization, and after the loop reaches the end. If the expression evaluates to `true`, the loop body is executed.

The last part of a standard `for` statement is the increment. You usually see something like i++ here, but any assignment is valid. It runs immediately after each iteration of the loop, before the condition is evaluated.

The Condition-Only for Statement

Go allows you to leave off both the initialization and the increment in a `for` statement. That leaves a `for` statement that functions like the `while` statement found in C, Java, JavaScript, Python, Ruby, and many other languages. It looks like Example 4-9.

Example 4-9. A condition-only for statement

```
i := 1
for i < 100 {
        fmt.Println(i)
        i = i * 2
}
```

The Infinite for Statement

The third `for` statement format does away with the condition, too. Go has a version of a `for` loop that loops forever. If you learned to program in the 1980s, your first program was probably an infinite loop in BASIC that printed HELLO to the screen forever:

```
10 PRINT "HELLO"
20 GOTO 10
```

Example 4-10 shows the Go version of this program. You can run it locally or try it out on The Go Playground (*https://oreil.ly/whOi-*).

Example 4-10. Infinite looping nostalgia

```
package main

import "fmt"

func main() {
    for {
        fmt.Println("Hello")
    }
}
```

Running this program gives you the same output that filled the screens of millions of Commodore 64s and Apple][s:

```
Hello
Hello
Hello
Hello
Hello
Hello
Hello
...
```

Press Ctrl-C when you are tired of walking down memory lane.

 If you run this on The Go Playground, you'll find that it will stop execution after a few seconds. As a shared resource, the playground doesn't allow any one program to run for too long.

break and continue

How do you get out of an infinite `for` loop without using the keyboard or turning off your computer? That's the job of the `break` statement. It exits the loop immediately, just like the `break` statement in other languages. Of course, you can use `break` with any `for` statement, not just the infinite `for` statement.

There is no Go equivalent of the do keyword in Java, C, and Java-Script. If you want to iterate at least once, the cleanest way is to use an infinite for loop that ends with an if statement. If you have some Java code, for example, that uses a do/while loop:

```
do {
    // things to do in the loop
} while (CONDITION);
```

The Go version looks like this:

```
for {
    // things to do in the loop
    if !CONDITION {
        break
    }
}
```

Note that the condition has a leading ! to *negate* the condition from the Java code. The Go code is specifying how to *exit* the loop, while the Java code specifies how to stay in it.

Go also includes the continue keyword, which skips over the rest of the body of a for loop and proceeds directly to the next iteration. Technically, you don't need a continue statement. You could write code like Example 4-11.

Example 4-11. Confusing code

```
for i := 1; i <= 100; i++ {
    if i%3 == 0 {
        if i%5 == 0 {
            fmt.Println("FizzBuzz")
        } else {
            fmt.Println("Fizz")
        }
    } else if i%5 == 0 {
        fmt.Println("Buzz")
    } else {
        fmt.Println(i)
    }
}
```

But this is not idiomatic. Go encourages short if statement bodies, as left-aligned as possible. Nested code is difficult to follow. Using a continue statement makes it easier to understand what's going on. Example 4-12 shows the code from the previous example, rewritten to use continue instead.

Example 4-12. Using continue to make code clearer

```
for i := 1; i <= 100; i++ {
    if i%3 == 0 && i%5 == 0 {
        fmt.Println("FizzBuzz")
        continue
    }
    if i%3 == 0 {
        fmt.Println("Fizz")
        continue
    }
    if i%5 == 0 {
        fmt.Println("Buzz")
        continue
    }
    fmt.Println(i)
}
```

As you can see, replacing chains of if/else statements with a series of if statements that use continue makes the conditions line up. This improves the layout of your conditions, which means your code is easier to read and understand.

The for-range Statement

The fourth for statement format is for iterating over elements in some of Go's built-in types. It is called a for-range loop and resembles the iterators found in other languages. In this section, we will look at how to use a for-range loop with strings, arrays, slices, and maps. When we cover channels in Chapter 10, we will talk about how to use them with for-range loops.

 You can only use a for-range loop to iterate over the built-in compound types and user-defined types that are based on them.

First, let's take a look at using a for-range loop with a slice. You can try out the code in Example 4-13 on The Go Playground (*https://oreil.ly/XwuTL*).

Example 4-13. The for-range loop

```
evenVals := []int{2, 4, 6, 8, 10, 12}
for i, v := range evenVals {
    fmt.Println(i, v)
}
```

Running this code produces the following output:

```
0 2
1 4
2 6
3 8
4 10
5 12
```

What makes a for-range loop interesting is that you get two loop variables. The first variable is the position in the data structure being iterated, while the second is the value at that position. The idiomatic names for the two loop variables depend on what is being looped over. When looping over an array, slice, or string, an i for *index* is commonly used. When iterating through a map, k (for *key*) is used instead.

The second variable is frequently called v for *value*, but is sometimes given a name based on the type of the values being iterated. Of course, you can give the variables any names that you like. If there are only a few statements in the body of the loop, single letter variable names work well. For longer (or nested) loops, you'll want to use more descriptive names.

What if you don't need to use the key within your for-range loop? Remember, Go requires you to access all declared variables, and this rule applies to the ones declared as part of a for loop, too. If you don't need to access the key, use an underscore (_) as the variable's name. This tells Go to ignore the value. Let's rewrite our slice ranging code to not print out the position. We can run the code in Example 4-14 on The Go Playground (*https://oreil.ly/2fO12*).

Example 4-14. Ignoring the key in a for-range loop

```
evenVals := []int{2, 4, 6, 8, 10, 12}
for _, v := range evenVals {
    fmt.Println(v)
}
```

Running this code produces the following output:

```
2
4
6
8
10
12
```

> Any time you are in a situation where there's a value returned, but you want to ignore it, use an underscore to hide the value. You'll see the underscore pattern again when we talk about functions in Chapter 5 and packages in Chapter 9.

What if you want the key, but don't want the value? In this situation, Go allows you to just leave off the second variable. This is valid Go code:

```
uniqueNames := map[string]bool{"Fred": true, "Raul": true, "Wilma": true}
for k := range uniqueNames {
    fmt.Println(k)
}
```

The most common reason for iterating over the key is when a map is being used as a set. In those situations, the value is unimportant. However, you can also leave off the value when iterating over arrays or slices. This is rare, as the usual reason for iterating over a linear data structure is to access the data. If you find yourself using this format for an array or slice, there's an excellent chance that you have chosen the wrong data structure and should consider refactoring.

 When we look at channels in Chapter 10, we'll see a situation where a for-range loop only returns a single value each time the loop iterates.

Iterating over maps

There's something interesting about how a for-range loop iterates over a map. You can run the code in Example 4-15 on The Go Playground (*https://oreil.ly/VplnA*).

Example 4-15. Map iteration order varies

```
m := map[string]int{
    "a": 1,
    "c": 3,
    "b": 2,
}

for i := 0; i < 3; i++ {
    fmt.Println("Loop", i)
    for k, v := range m {
        fmt.Println(k, v)
    }
}
```

When you build and run this program, the output varies. Here is one possibility:

```
Loop 0
c 3
b 2
a 1
Loop 1
a 1
c 3
```

```
b 2
Loop 2
b 2
a 1
c 3
```

The order of the keys and values varies; some runs may be identical. This is actually a security feature. In earlier Go versions, the iteration order for keys in a map was usually (but not always) the same if you inserted the same items into a map. This caused two problems:

- People would write code that assumed that the order was fixed, and this would break at weird times.
- If maps always hash items to the exact same values, and you know that a server is storing some user data in a map, you can actually slow down a server with an attack called *Hash DoS* by sending it specially crafted data where all of the keys hash to the same bucket.

To prevent both of these problems, the Go team made two changes to the map implementation. First, they modified the hash algorithm for maps to include a random number that's generated every time a map variable is created. Next, they made the order of a for-range iteration over a map vary a bit each time the map is looped over. These two changes make it far harder to implement a Hash DoS attack.

 There is one exception to this rule. To make it easier to debug and log maps, the formatting functions (like fmt.Println) always output maps with their keys in ascending sorted order.

Iterating over strings

As I mentioned earlier, you can also use a string with a for-range loop. Let's take a look. You can run the code in Example 4-16 on your computer or on The Go Playground (*https://oreil.ly/C3LRy*).

Example 4-16. Iterating over strings

```
samples := []string{"hello", "apple_n!"}
for _, sample := range samples {
    for i, r := range sample {
        fmt.Println(i, r, string(r))
    }
    fmt.Println()
}
```

The output when we iterate over the word "hello" has no surprises:

```
0 104 h
1 101 e
2 108 l
3 108 l
4 111 o
```

In the first column, we have the index; in the second, the numeric value of the letter; and in the third, we have the numeric value of the letter type converted to a string.

Looking at the result for "apple_π!" is more interesting:

```
0 97 a
1 112 p
2 112 p
3 108 l
4 101 e
5 95 _
6 960 π
8 33 !
```

There are two things to notice. First, notice that the first column skips the number 7. Second, the value at position 6 is 960. That's far larger than what can fit in a byte. But in Chapter 3, we said that strings were made out of bytes. What's going on?

What we are seeing is special behavior from iterating over a string with a for-range loop. It iterates over the *runes*, not the *bytes*. Whenever a for-range loop encounters a multibyte rune in a string, it converts the UTF-8 representation into a single 32-bit number and assigns it to the value. The offset is incremented by the number of bytes in the rune. If the for-range loop encounters a byte that doesn't represent a valid UTF-8 value, the Unicode replacement character (hex value 0xfffd) is returned instead.

 Use a for-range loop to access the runes in a string in order. The key is the number of bytes from the beginning of the string, but the type of the value is rune.

The for-range value is a copy

You should be aware that each time the for-range loop iterates over your compound type, it *copies* the value from the compound type to the value variable. *Modifying the value variable will not modify the value in the compound type.* Example 4-17 shows a quick program to demonstrate this. You can try it out on The Go Playground (*https://oreil.ly/ShwR0*).

Example 4-17. Modifying the value doesn't modify the source

```
evenVals := []int{2, 4, 6, 8, 10, 12}
for _, v := range evenVals {
    v *= 2
}
fmt.Println(evenVals)
```

Running this code gives the following output:

```
[2 4 6 8 10 12]
```

The implications of this behavior are subtle. When we talk about goroutines in Chapter 10, you'll see that if you launch goroutines in a for-range loop, you need to be very careful in how you pass the index and value to the goroutines, or you'll get surprisingly wrong results.

Just like the other three forms of the for statement, you can use break and continue with a for-range loop.

Labeling Your for Statements

By default, the break and continue keywords apply to the for loop that directly contains them. What if you have nested for loops and you want to exit or skip over an iterator of an outer loop? Let's look at an example. We're going to modify our earlier string iterating program to stop iterating through a string as soon as it hits a letter "l." You can run the code in Example 4-18 on The Go Playground (*https://oreil.ly/ToDkq*).

Example 4-18. Labels

```
func main() {
    samples := []string{"hello", "apple_n!"}
outer:
    for _, sample := range samples {
        for i, r := range sample {
            fmt.Println(i, r, string(r))
            if r == 'l' {
                continue outer
            }
        }
        fmt.Println()
    }
}
```

Notice that the label outer is indented by go fmt to the same level as the surrounding function. Labels are always indented to the same level as the braces for the block. This makes them easier to notice. Running our program gives the following output:

```
0 104 h
1 101 e
2 108 l
0 97 a
1 112 p
2 112 p
3 108 l
```

Nested for loops with labels are rare. They are most commonly used to implement algorithms similar to the pseudocode below:

```
outer:
    for _, outerVal := range outerValues {
        for _, innerVal := range outerVal {
            // process innerVal
            if invalidSituation(innerVal) {
                continue outer
            }
        }
        // here we have code that runs only when all of the
        // innerVal values were sucessfully processed
    }
```

Choosing the Right for Statement

Now that we've covered all of the forms of the for statement, you might be wondering when to use which format. Most of the time, you're going to use the for-range format. A for-range loop is the best way to walk through a string, since it properly gives you back runes instead of bytes. We have also seen that a for-range loop works well for iterating through slices and maps, and we'll see in Chapter 10 that channels work naturally with for-range as well.

 Favor a for-range loop when iterating over all the contents of an instance of one of the built-in compound types. It avoids a great deal of boilerplate code that's required when you use an array, slice, or map with one of the other for loop styles.

When should you use the complete for loop? The best place for it is when you aren't iterating from the first element to the last element in a compound type. While you could use some combination of if, continue, and break within a for-range loop, a standard for loop is a clearer way to indicate the start and end of your iteration. Compare these two code snippets, both of which iterate over the second through the second-to-last elements in an array. First the for-range loop:

```
evenVals := []int{2, 4, 6, 8, 10}
for i, v := range evenVals {
    if i == 0 {
        continue
```

```
    }
    if i == len(evenVals)-1 {
        break
    }
    fmt.Println(i, v)
}
```

And here's the same code, with a standard for loop:

```
evenVals := []int{2, 4, 6, 8, 10}
for i := 1; i < len(evenVals)-1; i++ {
    fmt.Println(i, evenVals[i])
}
```

The standard for loop code is both shorter and easier to understand.

 This pattern does not work for skipping over the beginning of a string. Remember, a standard for loop doesn't properly handle multibyte characters. If you want to skip over some of the runes in a string, you need to use a for-range loop so that it will properly process runes for you.

The remaining two for statement formats are used less frequently. The condition-only for loop is, like the while loop it replaces, useful when you are looping based on a calculated value.

The infinite for loop is useful in some situations. There should always be a break somewhere within the body of the for loop since it's rare that you want to loop forever. Real-world programs should bound iteration and fail gracefully when operations cannot be completed. As shown previously, an infinite for loop can be combined with an if statement to simulate the do statement that's present in other languages. An infinite for loop is also used to implement some versions of the *iterator* pattern, which we will look at when we review the standard library in "io and Friends" on page 233.

switch

Like many C-derived languages, Go has a switch statement. Most developers in those languages avoid switch statements because of their limitations on values that can be switched on and the default fall-through behavior. But Go is different. It makes switch statements useful.

 For those readers who are more familiar with Go, we're going to cover *expression switch* statements in this chapter. We'll discuss *type switch* statements when we talk about interfaces in Chapter 7.

At first glance, switch statements in Go don't look all that different from how they appear in C/C++, Java, or JavaScript, but there are a few surprises. Let's take a look at a sample switch statement. You can run the code in Example 4-19 on The Go Playground (*https://oreil.ly/VKf4N*).

Example 4-19. The switch statement

```
words := []string{"a", "cow", "smile", "gopher",
    "octopus", "anthropologist"}
for _, word := range words {
    switch size := len(word); size {
    case 1, 2, 3, 4:
        fmt.Println(word, "is a short word!")
    case 5:
        wordLen := len(word)
        fmt.Println(word, "is exactly the right length:", wordLen)
    case 6, 7, 8, 9:
    default:
        fmt.Println(word, "is a long word!")
    }
}
```

When we run this code, we get the following output:

```
a is a short word!
cow is a short word!
smile is exactly the right length: 5
anthropologist is a long word!
```

Let's go over the features of the switch statement to explain the output. As is the case with if statements, you don't put parenthesis around the value being compared in a switch. Also like an if statement, you can declare a variable that's scoped to all of the branches of the switch statement. In our case, we are scoping the variable size to all of the cases in the switch statement.

All of the case clauses (and the optional default clause) are contained inside a set of braces. But you should note that you don't put braces around the contents of the case clauses. You can have multiple lines inside a case (or default) clause and they are all considered to be part of the same block.

Inside case 5:, we declare wordLen, a new variable. Since this is a new block, you can declare new variables within it. Just like any other block, any variables declared within a case clause's block are only visible within that block.

If you are used to putting a break statement at the end of every case in your switch statements, you'll be happy to notice that they are gone. By default, cases in switch statements in Go don't fall through. This is more in line with the behavior in Ruby or (if you are an old-school programmer) Pascal.

This prompts the question: if cases don't fall through, what do you do if there are multiple values that should trigger the exact same logic? In Go, you separate multiple matches with commas, like we do when matching 1, 2, 3, and 4 or 6, 7, 8, and 9. That's why we get the same output for both a and cow.

Which leads to the next question: if you don't have fall-through, and you have an empty case (like we do in our sample program when the length of our argument is 6, 7, 8, or 9 characters), what happens? In Go, *an empty case means nothing happens*. That's why we don't see any output from our program when we use *octopus* or *gopher* as the parameter.

 For the sake of completeness, Go does include a `fallthrough` key-word, which lets one case continue on to the next one. Please think twice before implementing an algorithm that uses it. If you find yourself needing to use `fallthrough`, try to restructure your logic to remove the dependencies between cases.

In our sample program we are switching on the value of an integer, but that's not all you can do. You can switch on any type that can be compared with ==, which includes all of the built-in types except slices, maps, channels, functions, and structs that contain fields of these types.

Even though you don't need to put a `break` statement at the end of each `case` clause, you can use them in situations where you want to exit early from a `case`. However, the need for a `break` statement might indicate that you are doing something too complicated. Consider refactoring your code to remove it.

There is one more place where you might find yourself using a `break` statement in a `case` in a `switch` statement. If you have a `switch` statement inside a `for` loop, and you want to break out of the `for` loop, put a label on the `for` statement and put the name of the label on the `break`. If you don't use a label, Go assumes that you want to break out of the `case`. Let's look at a quick example. You can run the code in Example 4-20 on The Go Playground (*https://oreil.ly/o2xg2*).

Example 4-20. The case of the missing label

```go
func main() {
    for i := 0; i < 10; i++ {
        switch {
        case i%2 == 0:
            fmt.Println(i, "is even")
        case i%3 == 0:
            fmt.Println(i, "is divisible by 3 but not 2")
        case i%7 == 0:
            fmt.Println("exit the loop!")
```

```
            break
        default:
            fmt.Println(i, "is boring")
        }
    }
}
```

Running this code produces the following output:

```
0 is even
1 is boring
2 is even
3 is divisible by 3 but not 2
4 is even
5 is boring
6 is even
exit the loop!
8 is even
9 is divisible by 3 but not 2
```

That's not what we intended. The goal was to break out of the for loop when we got a 7. To do this, we need to introduce a label, just like we did when breaking out of a nested for loop. First, we label the for statement:

```
loop:
    for i := 0; i < 10; i++ {
```

Then we use the label on our break:

```
break loop
```

You can see these changes on The Go Playground (*https://oreil.ly/gA0O3*). When we run it again, we get the output that we expected:

```
0 is even
1 is boring
2 is even
3 is divisible by 3 but not 2
4 is even
5 is boring
6 is even
exit the loop!
```

Blank Switches

There's another, more powerful way to use switch statements. Just like Go allows you to leave out parts from a for statement's declaration, you can write a switch statement that doesn't specify the value that you're comparing against. This is called a *blank switch*. A regular switch only allows you to check a value for equality. A blank switch allows you to use any boolean comparison for each case. You can try out the code in Example 4-21 on The Go Playground (*https://oreil.ly/v7qI5*).

Example 4-21. The blank switch

```go
words := []string{"hi", "salutations", "hello"}
for _, word := range words {
    switch wordLen := len(word); {
    case wordLen < 5:
        fmt.Println(word, "is a short word!")
    case wordLen > 10:
        fmt.Println(word, "is a long word!")
    default:
        fmt.Println(word, "is exactly the right length.")
    }
}
```

When you run this program, you get the following output:

```
hi is a short word!
salutations is a long word!
hello is exactly the right length.
```

Just like a regular switch statement, you can optionally include a short variable declaration as part of your blank switch. But unlike a regular switch, you can write logical tests for your cases. Blank switches are pretty cool, but don't overdo them. If you find that you have written a blank switch where all of your cases are equality comparisons against the same variable:

```go
switch {
case a == 2:
    fmt.Println("a is 2")
case a == 3:
    fmt.Println("a is 3")
case a == 4:
    fmt.Println("a is 4")
default:
    fmt.Println("a is ", a)
}
```

you should replace it with an expression switch statement:

```go
switch a {
case 2:
    fmt.Println("a is 2")
case 3:
    fmt.Println("a is 3")
case 4:
    fmt.Println("a is 4")
default:
    fmt.Println("a is ", a)
}
```

Choosing Between if and switch

As a matter of functionality, there isn't a lot of difference between a series of if/else statements and a blank switch statement. Both of them allow a series of comparisons. So, when should you use switch and when should you use a set of if/else statements? A switch statement, even a blank switch, indicates that there is some relationship between the values or comparisons in each case. To demonstrate the difference in clarity, let's rewrite our random number classifier from the section on if using a switch instead, as shown in Example 4-22.

Example 4-22. Rewriting if/else with a blank switch

```
switch n := rand.Intn(10); {
case n == 0:
    fmt.Println("That's too low")
case n > 5:
    fmt.Println("That's too big:", n)
default:
    fmt.Println("That's a good number:", n)
}
```

Most people would agree that this is more readable. The value being compared is listed on a line by itself, and all of the cases line up on the lefthand side. The regularity of the location of the comparisons makes them easy to follow and modify.

Of course, there is nothing in Go that prevents you from doing all sorts of unrelated comparisons on each case in a blank switch. However, this is not idiomatic. If you find yourself in a situation where you want to do this, use a series of if/else statements (or perhaps consider refactoring your code).

 Favor blank switch statements over if/else chains when you have multiple related cases. Using a switch makes the comparisons more visible and reinforces that they are a related set of concerns.

goto—Yes, goto

There is a fourth control statement in Go, but chances are, you will never use it. Ever since Edgar Dijkstra wrote "Go To Statement Considered Harmful" (*https://oreil.ly/ YK2tl*) in 1968, the goto statement has been the black sheep of the coding family. There are good reasons for this. Traditionally, goto was dangerous because it could jump to nearly anywhere in a program; you could jump into or out of a loop, skip over variable definitions, or into the middle of a set of statements in an if statement. This made it difficult to understand what a goto-using program did.

Most modern languages don't include goto. Yet Go has a goto statement. You should still do what you can to avoid using it, but it has some uses, and the limitations that Go places on it make it a better fit with structured programming.

In Go, a goto statement specifies a labeled line of code and execution jumps to it. However, you can't jump anywhere. Go forbids jumps that skip over variable declarations and jumps that go into an inner or parallel block.

The program in Example 4-23 shows two illegal goto statements. You can attempt to run it on The Go Playground (*https://oreil.ly/lO16p*).

Example 4-23. Go's goto has rules

```
func main() {
    a := 10
    goto skip
    b := 20
skip:
    c := 30
    fmt.Println(a, b, c)
    if c > a {
        goto inner
    }
    if a < b {
    inner:
        fmt.Println("a is less than b")
    }
}
```

Trying to run this program produces the following errors:

```
goto skip jumps over declaration of b at ./main.go:8:4
goto inner jumps into block starting at ./main.go:15:11
```

So what should you use goto for? Mostly, you shouldn't. Labeled break and continue statements allow you to jump out of deeply nested loops or skip iteration. The program in Example 4-24 has a legal goto and demonstrates one of the few valid use cases.

Example 4-24. A reason to use goto

```
func main() {
    a := rand.Intn(10)
    for a < 100 {
        if a%5 == 0 {
            goto done
        }
        a = a*2 + 1
    }
```

```
    fmt.Println("do something when the loop completes normally")
done:
    fmt.Println("do complicated stuff no matter why we left the loop")
    fmt.Println(a)
}
```

This example is contrived, but it shows how goto can make a program clearer. In our simple case, there is some logic that we don't want to run in the middle of the function, but we do want to run the end of the function. There are ways to do this without goto. We could set up a boolean flag or duplicate the complicated code after the for loop instead of having a goto, but there are drawbacks to both of these approaches. Littering your code with boolean flags to control the logic flow is arguably the same functionality as the goto statement, just more verbose. Duplicating complicated code is problematic because it makes your code harder to maintain. These situations are rare, but if you cannot find a way to restructure your logic, using a goto like this actually improves your code.

If you want to see a real-world example, you can take a look at the floatBits method in the file atof.go in the strconv package in the standard library. It's too long to include in its entirety, but the method ends with this code:

```
overflow:
    // ±Inf
    mant = 0
    exp = 1<<flt.expbits - 1 + flt.bias
    overflow = true

out:
    // Assemble bits.
    bits := mant & (uint64(1)<<flt.mantbits - 1)
    bits |= uint64((exp-flt.bias)&(1<<flt.expbits-1)) << flt.mantbits
    if d.neg {
        bits |= 1 << flt.mantbits << flt.expbits
    }
    return bits, overflow
```

Before these lines, there are several condition checks. Some require the code after the overflow label to run, while other conditions require skipping that code and going directly to out. Depending on the condition, there are goto statements that jump to overflow or out. You could probably come up with a way to avoid the goto statements, but they all make the code harder to understand.

You should try very hard to avoid using goto. But in the rare situations where it makes your code more readable, it is an option.

Wrapping Up

This chapter covered a lot of important topics for writing idiomatic Go. We've learned about blocks, shadowing, and control structures, and how to use them correctly. At this point, we're able to write simple Go programs that fit within the main function. It's time to move on to larger programs, using functions to organize our code.

CHAPTER 5

Functions

So far, our programs have been limited to a few lines in the main function. It's time to get bigger. In this chapter, we're going to learn how to write functions in Go and see all of the interesting things we can do with them.

Declaring and Calling Functions

The basics of Go functions are familiar to anyone who has programmed in other languages with first-class functions, like C, Python, Ruby, or JavaScript. (Go also has methods, which we'll cover in Chapter 7.) Just like control structures, Go adds its own twist on function features. Some are improvements and others are experiments that should be avoided. We'll cover both in this chapter.

We've already seen functions being declared and used. Every program we've written has a main function that's the starting point for every Go program, and we've been calling the fmt.Println function to display output to the screen. Since main functions don't take in any parameters or return any values, let's see what it looks like when we have a function that does:

```
func div(numerator int, denominator int) int {
    if denominator == 0 {
        return 0
    }
    return numerator / denominator
}
```

Let's look at all the new things in this code sample. A function declaration has four parts: the keyword func, the name of the function, the input parameters, and the return type. The input parameters are listed in parentheses, separated by commas, with the parameter name first and the type second. Go is a typed language, so you must specify the types of the parameters. The return type is written between the input parameter's closing parenthesis and the opening brace for the function body.

Just like other languages, Go has a `return` keyword for returning values from a function. If a function returns a value, you *must* supply a `return`. If a function returns nothing, a `return` statement is not needed at the end of the function. The `return` keyword is only needed in a function that returns nothing if you are exiting from the function before the last line.

The `main` function has no input parameters or return values. When a function has no input parameters, use empty parentheses (`()`). When a function returns nothing, you write nothing between the input parameter's closing parenthesis and the opening brace for the function body:

```
func main() {
    result := div(5, 2)
    fmt.Println(result)
}
```

Calling a function should be familiar to experienced developers. On the right side of the `:=`, we call our `div` function with the values 5 and 2. On the left side, we assign the returned value to the variable `result`.

When you have multiple input parameters of the same type, you can write your input parameters like this:

```
func div(numerator, denominator int) int {
```

Simulating Named and Optional Parameters

Before we get to the unique function features that Go has, let's mention two that Go *doesn't* have: named and optional input parameters. With one exception that we will cover in the next section, you must supply all of the parameters for a function. If you want to emulate named and optional parameters, define a struct that has fields that match the desired parameters, and pass the struct to your function. Example 5-1 shows a snippet of code that demonstrates this pattern.

Example 5-1. Using a struct to simulate named parameters

```
type MyFuncOpts struct {
    FirstName string
    LastName string
    Age int
}

func MyFunc(opts MyFuncOpts) error {
```

```
        // do something here
}

func main() {
    MyFunc(MyFuncOpts {
        LastName: "Patel",
        Age: 50,
    })
    My Func(MyFuncOpts {
        FirstName: "Joe",
        LastName: "Smith",
    })
}
```

In practice, not having named and optional parameters isn't a limitation. A function shouldn't have more than a few parameters, and named and optional parameters are mostly useful when a function has many inputs. If you find yourself in that situation, your function is quite possibly too complicated.

Variadic Input Parameters and Slices

We've been using fmt.Println to print results to the screen and you've probably noticed that it allows any number of input parameters. How does it do that? Like many languages, Go supports *variadic parameters*. The variadic parameter *must* be the last (or only) parameter in the input parameter list. You indicate it with three dots (...) *before* the type. The variable that's created within the function is a slice of the specified type. You use it just like any other slice. Let's see how they work by writing a program that adds a base number to a variable number of parameters and returns the result as a slice of int. You can run this program on The Go Playground (*https://oreil.ly/nSad4*). First we'll write our variadic function:

```
func addTo(base int, vals ...int) []int {
    out := make([]int, 0, len(vals))
    for _, v := range vals {
        out = append(out, base+v)
    }
    return out
}
```

And now we'll call it a few different ways:

```
func main() {
    fmt.Println(addTo(3))
    fmt.Println(addTo(3, 2))
    fmt.Println(addTo(3, 2, 4, 6, 8))
    a := []int{4, 3}
    fmt.Println(addTo(3, a...))
    fmt.Println(addTo(3, []int{1, 2, 3, 4, 5}...))
}
```

As you can see, you can supply however many values you want for the variadic parameter, or no values at all. Since the variadic parameter is converted to a slice, you can supply a slice as the input. However, you must put three dots (...) *after* the variable or slice literal. If you do not, it is a compile-time error.

When you build and run this program, you get:

```
[]
[5]
[5 7 9 11]
[7 6]
[4 5 6 7 8]
```

Multiple Return Values

The first difference that we'll see between Go and other languages is that Go allows for multiple return values. Let's add a small feature to our previous division program. We're going to return both the dividend and the remainder from our function. Here's our updated function:

```go
func divAndRemainder(numerator int, denominator int) (int, int, error) {
    if denominator == 0 {
        return 0, 0, errors.New("cannot divide by zero")
    }
    return numerator / denominator, numerator % denominator, nil
}
```

There are a few changes to support multiple return values. When a Go function returns multiple values, the types of the return values are listed in parentheses, separated by commas. Also, if a function returns multiple values, you must return all of them, separated by commas. Don't put parentheses around the returned values; that's a compile-time error.

There's something else that we haven't seen yet: creating and returning an error. If you want to learn more about errors, skip ahead to Chapter 8. For now, you only need to know that you use Go's multiple return value support to return an error if something goes wrong in a function. If the function completes successfully, we return nil for the error's value. By convention, the error is always the last (or only) value returned from a function.

Calling our updated function looks like this:

```go
func main() {
    result, remainder, err := divAndRemainder(5, 2)
    if err != nil {
        fmt.Println(err)
        os.Exit(1)
    }
    fmt.Println(result, remainder)
}
```

We talked about assigning multiple values at once in "var Versus :=" on page 27. Here we are using that feature to assign the results of a function call to three different variables. On the right side of the :=, we call our divAndRemainder function with the values 5 and 2. On the left side, we assign the returned values to the variables result, remainder, and err. We check to see if there was an error by comparing err to nil.

Multiple Return Values Are Multiple Values

If you are familiar with Python, you might think that multiple return values are like Python functions returning a tuple that's optionally destructured if the tuple's values are assigned to multiple variables. Example 5-2 shows some sample code run in the Python interpreter.

Example 5-2. Multiple return values in Python are destructured tuples

```
>>> def div_and_remainder(n,d):
...    if d == 0:
...       raise Exception("cannot divide by zero")
...    return n / d, n % d
>>> v = div_and_remainder(5,2)
>>> v
(2.5, 1)
>>> result, remainder = div_and_remainder(5,2)
>>> result
2.5
>>> remainder
1
```

That's not how Go works. You must assign each value returned from a function. If you try to assign multiple return values to one variable, you get a compile-time error.

Ignoring Returned Values

But what if you call a function and don't want to use all of the returned values? As we covered in "Unused Variables" on page 32, Go does not allow unused variables. If a function returns multiple values, but you don't need to read one or more of the values, assign the unused values to the name _. For example, if we weren't going to read remainder, we would write the assignment as result, _, err := divAndRemainder(5, 2).

Surprisingly, Go does let you implicitly ignore *all* of the return values for a function. You can write divAndRemainder(5,2) and the returned values are dropped. We have actually been doing this since our earliest examples: fmt.Println returns two values, but it is idiomatic to ignore them. In almost all other cases, you should make it explicit that you are ignoring return values by using underscores.

Use _ whenever you don't need to read a value that's returned by a function.

Named Return Values

In addition to letting you return more than one value from a function, Go also allows you to specify *names* for your return values. Let's rewrite our divAndRemainder function one more time, this time using named return values:

```
func divAndRemainder(numerator int, denominator int) (result int, remainder int,
                                                      err error) {
    if denominator == 0 {
        err = errors.New("cannot divide by zero")
        return result, remainder, err
    }
    result, remainder = numerator/denominator, numerator%denominator
    return result, remainder, err
}
```

When you supply names to your return values, what you are doing is pre-declaring variables that you use within the function to hold the return values. They are written as a comma-separated list within parentheses. You must surround named return values with parentheses, even if there is only a single return value. Named return values are initialized to their zero values when created. This means that we can return them before any explicit use or assignment.

One important thing to note: the name that's used for a named returned value is local to the function; it doesn't enforce any name outside of the function. It is perfectly legal to assign the return values to variables of different names:

```
func main() {
    x, y, z := divAndRemainder(5, 2)
    fmt.Println(x, y, z)
}
```

If you only want to name *some* of the return values, you can do so by using _ as the name for any return values you want to remain nameless.

While named return values can sometimes help clarify your code, they do have some potential corner cases. First is the problem of shadowing. Just like any other variable, you can shadow a named return value. Be sure that you are assigning to the return value and not to a shadow of it.

The other problem with named return values is that you don't have to return them. Let's take a look at another variation on divAndRemainder. You can run it on The Go Playground (*https://oreil.ly/FzUkw*):

```
func divAndRemainder(numerator, denominator int) (result int, remainder int,
                                                  err error) {
    // assign some values
    result, remainder = 20, 30
    if denominator == 0 {
        return 0, 0, errors.New("cannot divide by zero")
    }
    return numerator / denominator, numerator % denominator, nil
}
```

Notice that we assigned values to result and remainder and then returned different values directly. Before running this code, try to guess what happens when we pass 5 and 2 to this function. The result might surprise you:

```
2 1
```

The values from the return statement were returned even though they were never assigned to the named return parameters. That's because the Go compiler inserts code that assigns whatever is returned to the return parameters. The named return parameters give a way to declare an *intent* to use variables to hold the return values, but don't *require* you to use them.

Some developers like to use named return parameters because they provide additional documentation. However, I find them of limited value. Shadowing makes them confusing, as does simply ignoring them. There is one situation where named return parameters are essential. We will talk about that when we cover defer later in the chapter.

Blank Returns—Never Use These!

If you use named return values, you need to be aware of one severe misfeature in Go: blank (sometimes called naked) returns. If you have named return values, you can just write return without specifying the values that are returned. This returns the last values assigned to the named return values. Let's rewrite our divAndRemainder function one last time, this time using blank returns:

```
func divAndRemainder(numerator, denominator int) (result int, remainder int,
                                                  err error) {
    if denominator == 0 {
        err = errors.New("cannot divide by zero")
        return
    }
    result, remainder = numerator/denominator, numerator%denominator
    return
}
```

Using blank returns makes a few additional changes to our function. When there's invalid input, we return immediately. Since no values were assigned to `result` and `remainder`, their zero values are returned. If you are returning the zero values for your named return values, be sure they make sense. Also notice that we still have to put a `return` at the end of the function. Even though we are using blank returns, this function returns values. It is a compile-time error to leave `return` out.

At first, you might find blank returns handy since they allow you to avoid some typing. However, most experienced Go developers consider blank returns a bad idea because they make it harder to understand data flow. Good software is clear and readable; it's obvious what is happening. When you use a blank return, the reader of your code needs to scan back through the program to find the last value assigned to the return parameters to see what is actually being returned.

> If your function returns values, *never* use a blank return. It can make it very confusing to figure out what value is actually returned.

Functions Are Values

Just like in many other languages, functions in Go are values. The type of a function is built out of the keyword `func` and the types of the parameters and return values. This combination is called the *signature* of the function. Any function that has the exact same number and types of parameters and return values meets the type signature.

Having functions as values allows us to do some clever things, such as build a primitive calculator using functions as values in a map. Let's see how this works. The code is available on The Go Playground (*https://oreil.ly/L59VY*). First, we'll create a set of functions that all have the same signature:

```go
func add(i int, j int) int { return i + j }

func sub(i int, j int) int { return i - j }

func mul(i int, j int) int { return i * j }

func div(i int, j int) int { return i / j }
```

Next, we create a map to associate a math operator with each function:

```go
var opMap = map[string]func(int, int) int{
    "+": add,
    "-": sub,
    "*": mul,
```

```
        "/": div,
    }
```

Finally, let's try out our calculator with a few expressions:

```
func main() {
    expressions := [][]string{
        []string{"2", "+", "3"},
        []string{"2", "-", "3"},
        []string{"2", "*", "3"},
        []string{"2", "/", "3"},
        []string{"2", "%", "3"},
        []string{"two", "+", "three"},
        []string{"5"},
    }
    for _, expression := range expressions {
        if len(expression) != 3 {
            fmt.Println("invalid expression:", expression)
            continue
        }
        p1, err := strconv.Atoi(expression[0])
        if err != nil {
            fmt.Println(err)
            continue
        }
        op := expression[1]
        opFunc, ok := opMap[op]
        if !ok {
            fmt.Println("unsupported operator:", op)
            continue
        }
        p2, err := strconv.Atoi(expression[2])
        if err != nil {
            fmt.Println(err)
            continue
        }
        result := opFunc(p1, p2)
        fmt.Println(result)
    }
}
```

We're using the strconv.Atoi function in the standard library to convert a string to an int. The second value returned by this function is an error. Just like before, we check for errors that are returned by functions and handle error conditions properly.

We use op as the key to the opMap map, and assign the value associated with the key to the variable opFunc. The type of opFunc is func(int, int) int. If there wasn't a function in the map associated with the provided key, we print an error message and skip the rest of the loop. We then call the function assigned to the opFunc variable with the p1 and p2 variables that we decoded earlier. Calling a function in a variable looks just like calling a function directly.

When you run this program, you can see our simple calculator at work:

```
5
-1
6
0
unsupported operator: %
strconv.Atoi: parsing "two": invalid syntax
invalid expression: [5]
```

 Don't write fragile programs. The core logic for this example is relatively short. Of the 22 lines inside the for loop, 6 of them implement the actual algorithm and the other 16 are error checking and data validation. You might be tempted to not validate incoming data or check errors, but doing so produces unstable, unmaintainable code. Error handling is what separates the professionals from the amateurs.

Function Type Declarations

Just like you can use the type keyword to define a struct, you can use it to define a function type, too (we'll go into more details on type declarations in Chapter 7):

```
type opFuncType func(int,int) int
```

We can then rewrite the opMap declaration to look like this:

```
var opMap = map[string]opFuncType {
    // same as before
}
```

We don't have to modify the functions at all. Any function that has two input parameters of type int and a single return value of type int automatically meets the type and can be assigned as a value in the map.

What's the advantage of declaring a function type? One use is documentation. It's useful to give something a name if you are going to refer to it multiple times. We will see another use in "Function Types Are a Bridge to Interfaces" on page 154.

Anonymous Functions

Not only can you assign functions to variables, you can also define new functions within a function and assign them to variables.

These inner functions are *anonymous functions*; they don't have a name. You don't have to assign them to a variable, either. You can write them inline and call them immediately. Here's a simple example that you can run on The Go Playground (*https://oreil.ly/EnkN6*):

```
func main() {
    for i := 0; i < 5; i++ {
        func(j int) {
            fmt.Println("printing", j, "from inside of an anonymous function")
        }(i)
    }
}
```

You declare an anonymous function with the keyword func immediately followed by the input parameters, the return values, and the opening brace. It is a compile-time error to try to put a function name between func and the input parameters.

Just like any other function, an anonymous function is called by using parenthesis. In this example, we are passing the i variable from the for loop in here. It is assigned to the j input parameter of our anonymous function.

Running the program gives the following output:

```
printing 0 from inside of an anonymous function
printing 1 from inside of an anonymous function
printing 2 from inside of an anonymous function
printing 3 from inside of an anonymous function
printing 4 from inside of an anonymous function
```

Now, this is not something that you would normally do. If you are declaring and executing an anonymous function immediately, you might as well get rid of the anonymous function and just call the code. However, there are two situations where declaring anonymous functions without assigning them to variables is useful: defer statements and launching goroutines. We'll talk about defer statements in a bit. Goroutines are covered in Chapter 10.

Closures

Functions declared inside of functions are special; they are *closures*. This is a computer science word that means that functions declared inside of functions are able to access and modify variables declared in the outer function.

All of this inner function and closure stuff might not seem all that interesting at first. What benefit do you get from making mini-functions within a larger function? Why does Go have this feature?

One thing that closures allow you to do is limit a function's scope. If a function is only going to be called from one other function, but it's called multiple times, you can use an inner function to "hide" the called function. This reduces the number of declarations at the package level, which can make it easier to find an unused name.

Closures really become interesting when they are passed to other functions or returned from a function. They allow you to take the variables within your function and use those values *outside* of your function.

Passing Functions as Parameters

Since functions are values and you can specify the type of a function using its parameter and return types, you can pass functions as parameters into functions. If you aren't used to treating functions like data, you might need a moment to think about the implications of creating a closure that references local variables and then passing that closure to another function. It's a very useful pattern and appears several times in the standard library.

One example is sorting slices. There's a function in the sort package in the standard library called sort.Slice. It takes in any slice and a function that is used to sort the slice that's passed in. Let's see how it works by sorting a slice of a struct using two different fields.

 Go doesn't have generics (yet) so sort.Slice does some internal magic to make it work with any kind of slice. We'll talk about this magic more in Chapter 14.

Let's see how we use closures to sort the same data different ways. You can run this code on The Go Playground (*https://oreil.ly/3kjg3*). First, we'll define a simple type, a slice of values of that type, and print out the slice:

```
type Person struct {
    FirstName string
    LastName  string
    Age       int
}

people := []Person{
    {"Pat", "Patterson", 37},
    {"Tracy", "Bobbert", 23},
    {"Fred", "Fredson", 18},
}
fmt.Println(people)
```

Next, we'll sort our slice by last name and print out the results:

```
// sort by last name
sort.Slice(people, func(i int, j int) bool {
    return people[i].LastName < people[j].LastName
})
fmt.Println(people)
```

The closure that's passed to sort.Slice has two parameters, i and j, but within the closure, we can refer to people so we can sort it by the LastName field. In computer science terms, people is *captured* by the closure. Next we do the same, sorting by the Age field:

```
// sort by age
sort.Slice(people, func(i int, j int) bool {
    return people[i].Age < people[j].Age
})
fmt.Println(people)
```

Running this code gives the following output:

```
[{Pat Patterson 37} {Tracy Bobbert 23} {Fred Fredson 18}]
[{Tracy Bobbert 23} {Fred Fredson 18} {Pat Patterson 37}]
[{Fred Fredson 18} {Tracy Bobbert 23} {Pat Patterson 37}]
```

The people slice is changed by the call to sort.Slice. We talk about this briefly in "Go Is Call By Value" on page 104 and in more detail in the next chapter.

 Passing functions as parameters to other functions is often useful for performing different operations on the same kind of data.

Returning Functions from Functions

Not only can you use a closure to pass some function state to another function, you can also return a closure from a function. Let's show this off by writing a function that returns a multiplier function. You can run this program on The Go Playground (*https://oreil.ly/8tpbN*). Here is our function that returns a closure:

```
func makeMult(base int) func(int) int {
    return func(factor int) int {
        return base * factor
    }
}
```

And here is how we use it:

```
func main() {
    twoBase := makeMult(2)
    threeBase := makeMult(3)
    for i := 0; i < 3; i++ {
        fmt.Println(twoBase(i), threeBase(i))
    }
}
```

Running this program gives the following output:

```
0 0
2 3
4 6
```

Now that you've seen closures in action, you might wonder how often they are used by Go developers. It turns out that they are surprisingly useful. We saw how they are used to sort slices. A closure is also used to efficiently search a sorted slice with sort.Search. As for returning closures, we will see this pattern used when we build middleware for a web server in "Middleware" on page 252. Go also uses closures to implement resource cleanup, via the defer keyword.

 If you spend any time with programmers who use functional programming languages like Haskell, you might hear the term *higher-order functions*. That's a very fancy way to say that a function has a function for an input parameter or a return value. As a Go developer, you are as cool as they are!

defer

Programs often create temporary resources, like files or network connections, that need to be cleaned up. This cleanup has to happen, no matter how many exit points a function has, or whether a function completed successfully or not. In Go, the cleanup code is attached to the function with the defer keyword.

Let's take a look at how to use defer to release resources. We'll do this by writing a simple version of cat, the Unix utility for printing the contents of a file. We can't open files on The Go Playground, but you can find the code for this example on GitHub (*https://oreil.ly/P4RuC*) in the *simple_cat* directory:

```go
func main() {
    if len(os.Args) < 2 {
        log.Fatal("no file specified")
    }
    f, err := os.Open(os.Args[1])
    if err != nil {
        log.Fatal(err)
    }
    defer f.Close()
    data := make([]byte, 2048)
    for {
        count, err := f.Read(data)
        os.Stdout.Write(data[:count])
        if err != nil {
            if err != io.EOF {
                log.Fatal(err)
            }
```

```
            break
        }
    }
}
```

This example introduces a few new features that we cover in more detail in later chapters. Feel free to read ahead to learn more.

First, we make sure that a file name was specified on the command line by checking the length of `os.Args`, a slice in the `os` package that contains the name of the program launched and the arguments passed to it. If the argument is missing, we use the `Fatal` function in the `log` package to print a message and exit the program. Next, we acquire a read-only file handle with the `Open` function in the `os` package. The second value that's returned by `Open` is an error. If there's a problem opening the file, we print the error message and exit the program. As mentioned earlier, we'll talk about errors in Chapter 8.

Once we know we have a valid file handle, we need to close it after we use it, no matter how we exit the function. To ensure the cleanup code runs, we use the `defer` keyword, followed by a function or method call. In this case, we use the `Close` method on the file variable. (We look at methods in Go in Chapter 7.) Normally, a function call runs immediately, but `defer` delays the invocation until the surrounding function exits.

We read from a file handle by passing a slice of bytes into the `Read` method on a file variable. We'll cover how to use this method in detail in "io and Friends" on page 233, but `Read` returns the number of bytes that were read into the slice and an error. If there's an error, we check to see if it's an end-of-file marker. If we are at the end of the file, we use `break` to exit the `for` loop. For all other errors, we report it and exit immediately using `log.Fatal`. We'll talk a little more about slices and function parameters in "Go Is Call By Value" on page 104 and go into details on this pattern when we discuss pointers in the next chapter.

Building and running the program from within the *simple_cat* directory produces the following result:

```
$ go build
$ ./simple_cat simple_cat.go
package main

import (
    "fmt"
    "os"
)
...
```

There are a few more things that you should know about defer. First, you can defer multiple closures in a Go function. They run in last-in-first-out order; the last defer registered runs first.

The code within defer closures runs *after* the return statement. As I mentioned, you can supply a function with input parameters to a defer. Just as defer doesn't run immediately, any variables passed into a deferred closure aren't evaluated until the closure runs.

You can supply a function that returns values to a defer, but there's no way to read those values.

```
func example() {
    defer func() int {
        return 2 // there's no way to read this value
    }()
}
```

You might be wondering if there's a way for a deferred function to examine or modify the return values of its surrounding function. There is, and it's the best reason to use named return values. It allows us to take actions based on an error. When we talk about errors in Chapter 8, we will discuss a pattern that uses a defer to add contextual information to an error returned from a function. Let's look at a way to handle database transaction cleanup using named return values and defer:

```
func DoSomeInserts(ctx context.Context, db *sql.DB, value1, value2 string)
                  (err error) {
    tx, err := db.BeginTx(ctx, nil)
    if err != nil {
        return err
    }
    defer func() {
        if err == nil {
            err = tx.Commit()
        }
        if err != nil {
            tx.Rollback()
        }
    }()
    _, err = tx.ExecContext(ctx, "INSERT INTO FOO (val) values $1", value1)
    if err != nil {
        return err
    }
    // use tx to do more database inserts here
    return nil
}
```

We're not going to cover Go's database support in this book, but the standard library includes extensive support for databases in the database/sql package. In our example function, we create a transaction to do a series of database inserts. If any of them fails, we want to roll back (not modify the database). If all of them succeed, we want to commit (store the database changes). We use a closure with defer to check if err has been assigned a value. If it hasn't, we run a tx.Commit(), which could also return an error. If it does, the value err is modified. If any database interaction returned an error, we call tx.Rollback().

 New Go developers tend to forget the parentheses when specifying a closure for defer. It is a compile-time error to leave them out and eventually the habit sets in. It helps to remember that supplying parentheses allows you to specify values that will be passed into the closure when it runs.

A common pattern in Go is for a function that allocates a resource to also return a closure that cleans up the resource. In the *simple_cat_cancel* directory in our GitHub project, there is a rewrite of our simple cat program that does this. First we write a helper function that opens a file and returns a closure:

```
func getFile(name string) (*os.File, func(), error) {
    file, err := os.Open(name)
    if err != nil {
        return nil, nil, err
    }
    return file, func() {
        file.Close()
    }, nil
}
```

Our helper function returns a file, a function, and an error. That * means that a file reference in Go is a pointer. We'll talk more about that in the next chapter.

Now in main, we use our getFile function:

```
f, closer, err := getFile(os.Args[1])
if err != nil {
    log.Fatal(err)
}
defer closer()
```

Because Go doesn't allow unused variables, returning the closer from the function means that the program will not compile if the function is not called. That reminds the user to use defer. As we covered earlier, you put parentheses after closer when you defer it.

Using `defer` can feel strange if you are used to a language that uses a block within a function to control when a resource is cleaned up, like the `try`/`catch`/`finally` blocks in Java, Javascript, and Python or the `begin`/`rescue`/`ensure` blocks in Ruby.

The downside to these resource cleanup blocks is that they create another level of indentation in your function, and that makes the code harder to read. It's not just my opinion that nested code is harder to follow. In research described in a 2017 paper in *Empirical Software Engineering* (*https://oreil.ly/VcYrR*), Vard Antinyan, Miroslaw Staron, and Anna Sandberg discovered that "Of…eleven proposed code characteristics, only two markedly influence complexity growth: the nesting depth and the lack of structure."

Research on what makes a program easier to read and understand isn't new. You can find papers that are many decades old, including a paper from 1983 (*https://oreil.ly/s0xcq*) by Richard Miara, Joyce Musseman, Juan Navarro, and Ben Shneiderman that tries to figure out the right amount of indentation to use (according to their results, two to four spaces).

Go Is Call By Value

You might hear people say that Go is a *call by value* language and wonder what that means. It means that when you supply a variable for a parameter to a function, Go *always* makes a copy of the value of the variable. Let's take a look. You can run this code on The Go Playground (*https://oreil.ly/yo_rY*). First, we define a simple struct:

```
type person struct {
    age  int
    name string
}
```

Next, we write a function that takes in an `int`, a `string`, and a `person`, and modifies their values:

```
func modifyFails(i int, s string, p person) {
    i = i * 2
    s = "Goodbye"
    p.name = "Bob"
}
```

We then call this function from `main` and see if the modifications stick:

```
func main() {
    p := person{}
    i := 2
    s := "Hello"
    modifyFails(i, s, p)
```

```
    fmt.Println(i, s, p)
}
```

As the name of the function indicates, running this code shows that a function won't change the values of the parameters passed into it:

```
2 Hello {0 }
```

I included the person struct to show that this isn't just true for primitive types. If you have programming experience in Java, JavaScript, Python, or Ruby, you might find the struct behavior very strange. After all, those languages let you modify the fields in an object when you pass an object as a parameter to a function. The reason for the difference is something we will cover when we talk about pointers.

The behavior is a little different for maps and slices. Let's see what happens when we try to modify them within a function. You can run this code on The Go Playground (*https://oreil.ly/kKL4R*). We're going to write a function to modify a map parameter and a function to modify a slice parameter:

```
func modMap(m map[int]string) {
    m[2] = "hello"
    m[3] = "goodbye"
    delete(m, 1)
}

func modSlice(s []int) {
    for k, v := range s {
        s[k] = v * 2
    }
    s = append(s, 10)
}
```

We then call these functions from main:

```
func main() {
    m := map[int]string{
        1: "first",
        2: "second",
    }
    modMap(m)
    fmt.Println(m)

    s := []int{1, 2, 3}
    modSlice(s)
    fmt.Println(s)
}
```

When you run this code, you'll see something interesting:

```
map[2:hello 3:goodbye]
[2 4 6]
```

For the map, it's easy to explain what happens: any changes made to a map parameter are reflected in the variable passed into the function. For a slice, it's more complicated. You can modify any element in the slice, but you can't lengthen the slice. This is true for maps and slices that are passed directly into functions as well as map and slice fields in structs.

This program leads to the question: why do maps and slices behave differently than other types? It's because maps and slices are both implemented with pointers. We'll go into more detail in the next chapter.

 Every type in Go is a value type. It's just that sometimes the value is a pointer.

Call by value is one reason why Go's limited support for constants is only a minor handicap. Since variables are passed by value, you can be sure that calling a function doesn't modify the variable whose value was passed in (unless the variable is a slice or map). In general, this is a good thing. It makes it easier to understand the flow of data through your program when functions don't modify their input parameters and instead return newly computed values.

While this approach is easy to understand, there are cases where you need to pass something mutable to a function. What do you do then? That's when you need a pointer.

Wrapping Up

In this chapter, we've looked at functions in Go, how they are similar to functions in other languages, and their unique features. In the next chapter, we're going to look at pointers, find out that they aren't nearly as scary as many new Go developers expect them to be, and learn how to take advantage of them to write efficient programs.

CHAPTER 6

Pointers

Now that we've seen variables and functions, we're going to take a quick look at pointer syntax. Then we'll clarify the behavior of pointers in Go by comparing them to the behavior of classes in other languages. We'll also learn how and when to use pointers, how memory is allocated in Go, and how using pointers and values properly makes Go programs faster and more efficient.

A Quick Pointer Primer

A pointer is simply a variable that holds the location in memory where a value is stored. If you've taken computer science courses, you might have seen a graphic to represent how variables are stored in memory. The representation of the following two variables would look something like Figure 6-1:

```
var x int32 = 10
var y bool = true
```

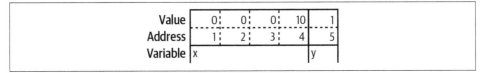

Figure 6-1. *Storing two variables in memory*

Every variable is stored in one or more contiguous memory locations, called *addresses*. Different types of variables can take up different amounts of memory. In this example, we have two variables, x, which is a 32-bit int, and y, which is a boolean. Storing a 32-bit int requires four bytes, so the value for x is stored in four bytes, starting at address 1 and ending at address 4. A boolean only requires a single byte (you only need a bit to represent true or false, but the smallest amount of memory that can be independently addressed is a byte), so the value for y is stored in one byte at address 5, with true represented by the value 1.

A pointer is simply a variable whose contents are the address where another variable is stored. Figure 6-2 demonstrates how pointers are stored in memory:

```
var x int32 = 10
var y bool = true
pointerX := &x
pointerY := &y
var pointerZ *string
```

Value	0	0	0	10	1	0	0	0	1	0	0	0	5	0	0	0	0
Address	1	2	3	4	5	6	7	8	9	10	11	12	13	14	15	16	17
Variable	x				y	pointerX				pointerY				pointerZ			

Figure 6-2. Storing pointers in memory

While different types of variables can take up different numbers of memory locations, every pointer, no matter what type it is pointing to, is always the same size: a number that holds the location in memory where the data is stored. Our pointer to x, pointerX, is stored at location 6 and has the value 1, the address of x. Similarly, our pointer to y, pointerY, is stored at location 10 and has the value 5, the address of y. The last pointer, pointerZ, is stored at location 14 and has the value 0, because it doesn't point to anything.

The zero value for a pointer is nil. We've seen nil a few times before, as the zero value for slices, maps, and functions. All of these types are implemented with pointers. (Two more types, channels and interfaces, are also implemented with pointers. We'll look at them in detail in "A Quick Lesson on Interfaces" on page 141 and "Channels" on page 206.) As we covered in Chapter 3, nil is an untyped identifier that represents the lack of a value for certain types. Unlike NULL in C, nil is not another name for 0; you can't convert it back and forth with a number.

 As alluded to in Chapter 4, nil is defined in the universe block. Because nil is a value defined in the universe block, it can be shadowed. Never name a variable or function nil, unless you are trying to trick your coworker and are unconcerned about your annual review.

Go's pointer syntax is partially borrowed from C and C++. Since Go has a garbage collector, most of the pain of memory management is removed. Furthermore, some of the tricks that you can do with pointers in C and C++, including *pointer arithmetic*, are not allowed in Go.

 The Go standard library does have an unsafe package that lets you do some low-level operations on data structures. While pointer manipulation is used in C for common operations, it is exceedingly rare for Go developers to use unsafe. We'll take a quick look at it in Chapter 14.

The & is the *address* operator. It precedes a value type and returns the address of the memory location where the value is stored:

```
x := "hello"
pointerToX := &x
```

The * is the *indirection* operator. It precedes a variable of pointer type and returns the pointed-to value. This is called *dereferencing*:

```
x := 10
pointerToX := &x
fmt.Println(pointerToX)  // prints a memory address
fmt.Println(*pointerToX) // prints 10
z := 5 + *pointerToX
fmt.Println(z)           // prints 15
```

Before dereferencing a pointer, you must make sure that the pointer is non-nil. Your program will panic if you attempt to dereference a nil pointer:

```
var x *int
fmt.Println(x == nil) // prints true
fmt.Println(*x)       // panics
```

A *pointer type* is a type that represents a pointer. It is written with a * before a type name. A pointer type can be based on any type:

```
x := 10
var pointerToX *int
pointerToX = &x
```

The built-in function new creates a pointer variable. It returns a pointer to a zero value instance of the provided type:

```
var x = new(int)
fmt.Println(x == nil) // prints false
fmt.Println(*x)       // prints 0
```

The new function is rarely used. For structs, use an & before a struct literal to create a pointer instance. You can't use an & before a primitive literal (numbers, booleans, and strings) or a constant because they don't have memory addresses; they exist only at compile time. When you need a pointer to a primitive type, declare a variable and point to it:

```
x := &Foo{}
var y string
z := &y
```

Not being able to take the address of a constant is sometimes inconvenient. If you have a struct with a field of a pointer to a primitive type, you can't assign a literal directly to the field:

```
type person struct {
    FirstName  string
    MiddleName *string
    LastName   string
}

p := person{
  FirstName:  "Pat",
  MiddleName: "Perry", // This line won't compile
  LastName:   "Peterson",
}
```

Compiling this code returns the error:

```
cannot use "Perry" (type string) as type *string in field value
```

If you try to put an & before "Perry", you'll get the error message:

```
cannot take the address of "Perry"
```

There are two ways around this problem. The first is to do what we showed previously, introduce a variable to hold the constant value. The second way is to write a helper function that takes in a boolean, numeric, or string type and returns a pointer to that type:

```
func stringp(s string) *string {
    return &s
}
```

With that function, you can now write:

```
p := person{
  FirstName:  "Pat",
  MiddleName: stringp("Perry"), // This works
  LastName:   "Peterson",
}
```

Why does this work? When we pass a constant to a function, the constant is copied to a parameter, which is a variable. Since it's a variable, it has an address in memory. The function then returns the variable's memory address.

Use a helper function to turn a constant value into a pointer.

Don't Fear the Pointers

The first rule of pointers is to not be afraid of them. If you are used to Java, JavaScript, Python, or Ruby, you might find pointers intimidating. However, pointers are actually the familiar behavior for classes. It's the nonpointer structs in Go that are unusual.

In Java and JavaScript, there is a difference in the behavior between primitive types and classes (Python and Ruby don't have primitive values, but use immutable instances to simulate them). When a primitive value is assigned to another variable or passed to a function or method, any changes made to the other variable aren't reflected in the original, as shown in Example 6-1.

Example 6-1. Assigning primitive variables doesn't share memory in Java

```
int x = 10;
int y = x;
y = 20;
System.out.println(x); // prints 10
```

However, let's take a look at what happens when an instance of a class is assigned to another variable or passed to a function or method (the code in Example 6-2 is written in Python, but similar code for Java, JavaScript, and Ruby can be found on GitHub (*https://oreil.ly/9IpUK*)).

Example 6-2. Passing a class instance into a function

```
class Foo:
    def __init__(self, x):
        self.x = x


def outer():
    f = Foo(10)
    inner1(f)
    print(f.x)
    inner2(f)
    print(f.x)
```

```
    g = None
    inner2(g)
    print(g is None)


def inner1(f):
    f.x = 20


def inner2(f):
    f = Foo(30)


outer()
```

Running this code prints out:

```
20
20
True
```

That's because the following things are true in Java, Python, JavaScript, and Ruby:

- If you pass an instance of a class to a function and you change the value of a field, the change is reflected in the variable that was passed in.
- If you reassign the parameter, the change is *not* reflected in the variable that was passed in.
- If you pass nil/null/None for a parameter value, setting the parameter itself to a new value doesn't modify the variable in the calling function.

Some people explain this behavior by saying that class instances are passed by reference in these languages. This is untrue. If they were being passed by reference, cases two and three would change the variable in the calling function. These languages are always pass-by-value, just like Go.

What we are seeing is that every instance of a class in these languages is implemented as a pointer. When a class instance is passed to a function or method, the value being copied is the pointer to the instance. Since outer and inner1 are referring to the same memory, changes made to fields in f in inner1 are reflected in the variable in outer. When inner2 reassigns f to a new class instance, this creates a separate instance and does not affect the variable in outer.

When you use a pointer variable or parameter in Go, you see the exact same behaviors. The difference between Go and these languages is that Go gives you the *choice* to use pointers or values for both primitives and structs. Most of the time, you should use a value. They make it easier to understand how and when your data is modified. A secondary benefit is that using values reduces the amount of work that the garbage collector has to do. We'll talk about that in "Reducing the Garbage Collector's Workload" on page 123.

Pointers Indicate Mutable Parameters

As we've already seen, Go constants provide names for literal expressions that can be calculated at compile time. There is no mechanism in the language to declare that other kinds of values are immutable. Modern software engineering embraces immutability. MIT's course on Software Construction (*https://oreil.ly/FbUTJ*) sums up the reasons why: "[I]mmutable types are safer from bugs, easier to understand, and more ready for change. Mutability makes it harder to understand what your program is doing, and much harder to enforce contracts."

The lack of immutable declarations in Go might seem problematic, but the ability to choose between value and pointer parameter types addresses the issue. As the Software Construction course materials go on to explain: "[U]sing mutable objects is just fine if you are using them entirely locally within a method, and with only one reference to the object." Rather than declare that some variables and parameters are immutable, Go developers use pointers to indicate that a parameter is mutable.

Since Go is a call by value language, the values passed to functions are copies. For nonpointer types like primitives, structs, and arrays, this means that the called function cannot modify the original. Since the called function has a copy of the original data, the immutability of the original data is guaranteed.

We'll talk about passing maps and slices to functions in "The Difference Between Maps and Slices" on page 119.

However, if a pointer is passed to a function, the function gets a copy of the pointer. This still points to the original data, which means that the original data can be modified by the called function.

There are a couple of related implications of this.

The first implication is that when you pass a nil pointer to a function, you cannot make the value non-nil. You can only reassign the value if there was a value already assigned to the pointer. While confusing at first, it makes sense. Since the memory location was passed to the function via call-by-value, we can't change the memory address, any more than we could change the value of an int parameter. We can demonstrate this with the following program:

```
func failedUpdate(g *int) {
    x := 10
    g = &x
}

func main() {
    var f *int // f is nil
    failedUpdate(f)
    fmt.Println(f) // prints nil
}
```

The flow through this code is shown in Figure 6-3.

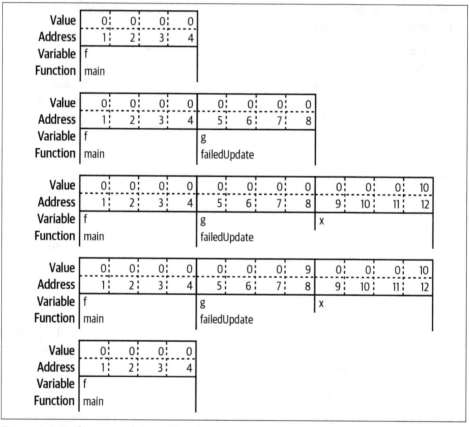

Figure 6-3. Failing to update a nil pointer

We start with a nil variable f in main. When we call failedUpdate, we copy the value of f, which is nil, into the parameter named g. This means that g is also set to nil. We then declare a new variable x within failedUpdate with the value 10. Next, we change g in failedUpdate to point to x. This does not change the f in main, and when we exit failedUpdate and return to main, f is still nil.

The second implication of copying a pointer is that if you want the value assigned to a pointer parameter to still be there when you exit the function, you must dereference the pointer and set the value. If you change the pointer, you have changed the copy, not the original. Dereferencing puts the new value in the memory location pointed to by both the original and the copy. Here's a short program that shows how this works:

```
func failedUpdate(px *int) {
    x2 := 20
    px = &x2
}

func update(px *int) {
    *px = 20
}

func main() {
    x := 10
    failedUpdate(&x)
    fmt.Println(x) // prints 10
    update(&x)
    fmt.Println(x) // prints 20
}
```

The flow through this code is shown in Figure 6-4.

In this example, we start with x in main set to 10. When we call failedUpdate, we copy the address of x into the parameter px. Next, we declare x2 in failedUpdate, set to 20. We then point px in failedUpdate to the address of x2. When we return to main, the value of x is unchanged. When we call update, we copy the address of x into px again. However, this time we change the value of what px in update points to, the variable x in main. When we return to main, x has been changed.

Value	0	0	0	10
Address	1	2	3	4
Variable	x			
Function	main			

Value	0	0	0	10	0	0	0	1
Address	1	2	3	4	5	6	7	8
Variable	x				px			
Function	main				failedUpdate			

Value	0	0	0	10	0	0	0	1	0	0	0	20
Address	1	2	3	4	5	6	7	8	9	10	11	12
Variable	x				px				x2			
Function	main				failedUpdate							

Value	0	0	0	10	0	0	0	9	0	0	0	20
Address	1	2	3	4	5	6	7	8	9	10	11	12
Variable	x				px				x2			
Function	main				failedUpdate							

Value	0	0	0	10
Address	1	2	3	4
Variable	x			
Function	main			

Value	0	0	0	10	0	0	0	1
Address	1	2	3	4	5	6	7	8
Variable	x				px			
Function	main				Update			

Value	0	0	0	20	0	0	0	1
Address	1	2	3	4	5	6	7	8
Variable	x				px			
Function	main				Update			

Value	0	0	0	20
Address	1	2	3	4
Variable	x			
Function	main			

Figure 6-4. The wrong way and the right way to update a pointer

Pointers Are a Last Resort

That said, you should be careful when using pointers in Go. As discussed earlier, they make it harder to understand data flow and can create extra work for the garbage collector. Rather than populating a struct by passing a pointer to it into a function, have the function instantiate and return the struct (see Example 6-3 and Example 6-4).

Example 6-3. Don't do this

```go
func MakeFoo(f *Foo) error {
  f.Field1 = "val"
  f.Field2 = 20
  return nil
}
```

Example 6-4. Do this

```go
func MakeFoo() (Foo, error) {
  f := Foo{
    Field1: "val",
    Field2: 20,
  }
  return f, nil
}
```

The only time you should use pointer parameters to modify a variable is when the function expects an interface. You see this pattern when working with JSON (we'll talk more about the JSON support in Go's standard library in "encoding/json" on page 241):

```go
f := struct {
  Name string `json:"name"`
  Age int `json:"age"`
}{}
err := json.Unmarshal([]byte(`{"name": "Bob", "age": 30}`), &f)
```

The Unmarshal function populates a variable from a slice of bytes containing JSON. It is declared to take a slice of bytes and an interface{} parameter. The value passed in for the interface{} parameter must be a pointer. If it is not, an error is returned. This pattern is used because Go doesn't have generics. That means there isn't a convenient way to pass a type into a function to specify what to unmarshal into nor is there a way to specify a different return type for different types.

Because JSON integration is so common, this API is sometimes treated as a common case by new Go developers, instead of the exception that it should be.

There is a way to represent a type in Go in a variable, by using the Type type in the `reflect` package. The `reflect` package is reserved for situations where there is no other way to accomplish a task. We'll look at reflection in Chapter 14.

When returning values from a function, you should favor value types. Only use a pointer type as a return type if there is state within the data type that needs to be modified. When we look at I/O in "io and Friends" on page 233, we'll see that with buffers for reading or writing data. In addition, there are data types that are used with concurrency that must always be passed as pointers. We'll see those in Chapter 10.

Pointer Passing Performance

If a struct is large enough, there are performance improvements from using a pointer to the struct as either an input parameter or a return value. The time to pass a pointer into a function is constant for all data sizes, roughly one nanosecond. This makes sense, as the size of a pointer is the same for all data types. Passing a value into a function takes longer as the data gets larger. It takes about a millisecond once the value gets to be around 10 megabytes of data.

The behavior for returning a pointer versus returning a value is more interesting. For data structures that are smaller than a megabyte, it is actually *slower* to return a pointer type than a value type. For example, a 100-byte data structure takes around 10 nanoseconds to be returned, but a pointer to that data structure takes about 30 nanoseconds. Once your data structures are larger than a megabyte, the performance advantage flips. It takes nearly 2 milliseconds to return 10 megabytes of data, but a little more than half a millisecond to return a pointer to it.

You should be aware that these are very short times. For the vast majority of cases, the difference between using a pointer and a value won't affect your program's performance. But if you are passing megabytes of data between functions, consider using a pointer even if the data is meant to be immutable.

All of these numbers are from an i7-8700 computer with 32GB of RAM. You can run your own performance tests by using the code on GitHub (*https://oreil.ly/uVEin*).

The Zero Value Versus No Value

The other common usage of pointers in Go is to indicate the difference between a variable or field that's been assigned the zero value and a variable or field that hasn't been assigned a value at all. If this distinction matters in your program, use a `nil` pointer to represent an unassigned variable or struct field.

Because pointers also indicate mutability, be careful when using this pattern. Rather than return a pointer set to nil from a function, use the comma ok idiom that we saw for maps and return a value type and a boolean.

Remember, if a nil pointer is passed into a function via a parameter or a field on a parameter, you cannot set the value within the function as there's nowhere to store the value. If a non-nil value is passed in for the pointer, do not modify it unless you document the behavior.

Again, JSON conversions are the exception that proves the rule. When converting data back and forth from JSON (yes, we'll talk more about the JSON support in Go's standard library in "encoding/json" on page 241), you often need a way to differentiate between the zero value and not having a value assigned at all. Use a pointer value for fields in the struct that are nullable.

When not working with JSON (or other external protocols), resist the temptation to use a pointer field to indicate no value. While a pointer does provide a handy way to indicate no value, if you are not going to modify the value, you should use a value type instead, paired with a boolean.

The Difference Between Maps and Slices

As we saw in the previous chapter, any modifications made to a map that's passed to a function are reflected in the original variable that was passed in. Now that we know about pointers, we can understand why: within the Go runtime, a map is implemented as a pointer to a struct. Passing a map to a function means that you are copying a pointer.

Because of this, you should avoid using maps for input parameters or return values, especially on public APIs. On an API-design level, maps are a bad choice because they say nothing about what values are contained within; there's nothing that explicitly defines what keys are in the map, so the only way to know what they are is to trace through the code. From the standpoint of immutability, maps are bad because the only way to know what ended up in the map is to trace through all of the functions that interact with it. This prevents your API from being self-documenting. If you are used to dynamic languages, don't use a map as a replacement for another language's lack of structure. Go is a strongly typed language; rather than passing a map around, use a struct. (We'll learn another reason to prefer structs when we talk about memory layout in "Reducing the Garbage Collector's Workload" on page 123.)

Meanwhile, passing a slice to a function has more complicated behavior: any modification to the contents of the slice is reflected in the original variable, but using append to change the length isn't reflected in the original variable, even if the slice has a capacity greater than its length. That's because a slice is implemented as a struct with three fields: an int field for length, an int field for capacity, and a pointer to a block of memory. Figure 6-5 demonstrates the relationship.

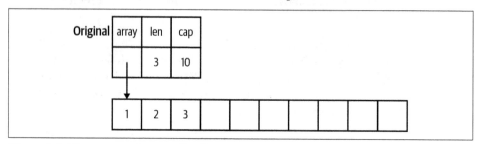

Figure 6-5. The memory layout of a slice

When a slice is copied to a different variable or passed to a function, a copy is made of the length, capacity, and the pointer. Figure 6-6 shows how both slice variables point to the same memory.

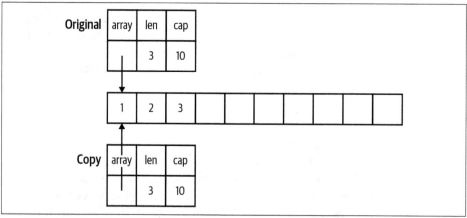

Figure 6-6. The memory layout of a slice and its copy

Changing the values in the slice changes the memory that the pointer points to, so the changes are seen in both the copy and the original. We see in Figure 6-7 how this looks in memory.

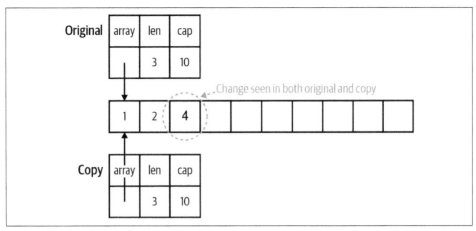

Figure 6-7. Modifying the contents of a slice

Changes to the length and capacity are not reflected back in the original, because they are only in the copy. Changing the capacity means that the pointer is now pointing to a new, bigger block of memory. In Figure 6-8 we show how each slice variable now points to a different memory block.

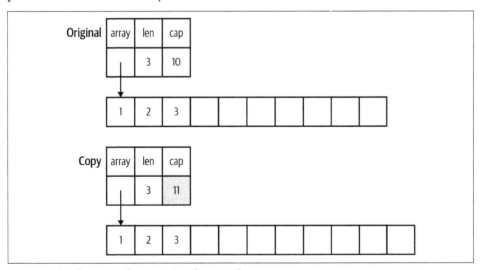

Figure 6-8. Changing the capacity changes the storage

If the slice copy is appended to and there is enough capacity to not allocate a new slice, the length changes in the copy and the new values are stored in the block of memory that's shared by the copy and the original. However, the length in the original slice remains unchanged. This means the Go runtime prevents the original slice from seeing those values since they are beyond the length of the original slice.

Figure 6-9 highlights the values that are visible in one slice variable but not in the other.

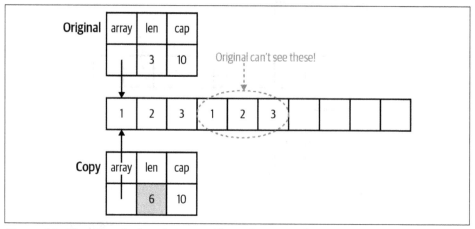

Figure 6-9. Changing the length is invisible in the original

The result is that a slice that's passed to a function can have its contents modified, but the slice can't be resized. As the only usable linear data structure, slices are frequently passed around in Go programs. By default, you should assume that a slice is not modified by a function. Your function's documentation should specify if it modifies the slice's contents.

> The reason you can pass a slice of any size to a function is that the data that's passed to the function is the same for any size slice: two int values and a pointer. The reason that you can't write a function that takes an array of any size is because the entire array is passed to the function, not just a pointer to the data.

There's another use for slices as input parameters: they are ideal for reusable buffers.

Slices as Buffers

When reading data from an external resource (like a file or a network connection), many languages use code like this:

```
r = open_resource()
while r.has_data() {
    data_chunk = r.next_chunk()
    process(data_chunk)
}
close(r)
```

The problem with this pattern is that every time we iterate through that `while` loop, we allocate another `data_chunk` even though each one is only used once. This creates lots of unnecessary memory allocations. Garbage-collected languages handle those allocations for you automatically, but the work still needs to be done to clean them up when you are done processing.

Even though Go is a garbage-collected language, writing idiomatic Go means avoiding unneeded allocations. Rather than returning a new allocation each time we read from a data source, we create a slice of bytes once and use it as a buffer to read data from the data source:

```
file, err := os.Open(fileName)
if err != nil {
    return err
}
defer file.Close()
data := make([]byte, 100)
for {
    count, err := file.Read(data)
    if err != nil {
        return err
    }
    if count == 0 {
        return nil
    }
    process(data[:count])
}
```

Remember that we can't change the length or capacity of a slice when we pass it to a function, but we can change the contents up to the current length. In this code, we create a buffer of 100 bytes and each time through the loop, we copy the next block of bytes (up to 100) into the slice. We then pass the populated portion of the buffer to `process`. We'll look at more details about I/O in "io and Friends" on page 233.

Reducing the Garbage Collector's Workload

Using buffers is just one example of how we reduce the work done by the garbage collector. When programmers talk about "garbage" what they mean is "data that has no more pointers pointing to it." Once there are no more pointers pointing to some data, the memory that this data takes up can be reused. If the memory isn't recovered, the program's memory usage would continue to grow until the computer ran out of RAM. The job of a garbage collector is to automatically detect unused memory and recover it so it can be reused. It is fantastic that Go has a garbage collector, because decades of experience have shown that it is very difficult for people to properly manage memory manually. But just because we have a garbage collector doesn't mean we should create lots of garbage.

If you've spent time learning how programming languages are implemented, you've probably learned about the *heap* and the *stack*. If you're unfamiliar, here's how a stack works. A stack is a consecutive block of memory, and every function call in thread of execution shares the same stack. Allocating memory on the stack is fast and simple. A *stack pointer* tracks the last location where memory was allocated; allocating additional memory is done by moving the stack pointer. When a function is invoked, a new *stack frame* is created for the function's data. Local variables are stored on the stack, along with parameters passed into a function. Each new variable moves the stack pointer by the size of the value. When a function exits, its return values are copied back to the calling function via the stack and the stack pointer is moved back to the beginning of the stack frame for the exited function, deallocating all of the stack memory that was used by that function's local variables and parameters.

 Go is unusual in that it can actually increase the size of a stack while the program is running. This is possible because each goroutine has its own stack and goroutines are managed by the Go runtime, not by the underlying operating system (we discuss goroutines when we talk about concurrency in Chapter 10). This has advantages (Go stacks start small and use less memory) and disadvantages (when the stack needs to grow, all of the data on the stack needs to be copied, which is slow). It's also possible to write worst-case scenario code that causes the stack to grow and shrink over and over.

To store something on the stack, you have to know exactly how big it is at compile time. When you look at the value types in Go (primitive values, arrays, and structs), they all have one thing in common: we know exactly how much memory they take at compile time. This is why the size is considered part of the type for an array. Because their sizes are known, they can be allocated on the stack instead of the heap. The size of a pointer type is also known, and it is also stored on the stack.

The rules are more complicated when it comes to the data that the pointer points to. In order for Go to allocate the data the pointer points to on the stack, several conditions must be true. It must be a local variable whose data size is known at compile time. The pointer cannot be returned from the function. If the pointer is passed into a function, the compiler must be able to ensure that these conditions still hold. If the size isn't known, you can't make space for it by simply moving the stack pointer. If the pointer variable is returned, the memory that the pointer points to will no longer be valid when the function exits. When the compiler determines that the data can't be stored on the stack, we say that the data the pointer points to *escapes* the stack and the compiler stores the data on the heap.

The heap is the memory that's managed by the garbage collector (or by hand in languages like C and C++). We're not going to discuss garbage collector algorithm implementation details, but they are much more complicated than simply moving a stack pointer. Any data that's stored on the heap is valid as long as it can be tracked back to a pointer type variable on a stack. Once there are no more pointers pointing to that data (or to data that points to that data), the data becomes *garbage* and it's the job of the garbage collector to clear it out.

A common source of bugs in C programs is returning a pointer to a local variable. In C, this results in a pointer pointing to invalid memory. The Go compiler is smarter. When it sees that a pointer to a local variable is returned, the local variable's value is stored on the heap.

The *escape analysis* done by the Go compiler isn't perfect. There are some cases where data that could be stored on the stack escapes to the heap. However, the compiler has to be conservative; it can't take the chance of leaving a value on the stack when it might need to be on the heap because leaving a reference to invalid data causes memory corruption. Newer Go releases improve escape analysis.

You might be wondering: what's so bad about storing things on the heap? There are two problems related to performance. First is that the garbage collector takes time to do its work. It isn't trivial to keep track of all of the available chunks of free memory on the heap or tracking which used blocks of memory still have valid pointers. This is time that's taken away from doing the processing that your program is written to do. Many garbage collection algorithms have been written, and they can be placed into two rough categories: those that are designed for higher throughput (find the most garbage possible in a single scan) or lower latency (finish the garbage scan as quickly as possible). Jeff Dean (*https://oreil.ly/x2Rxr*), the genius behind many of Google's engineering successes, co-wrote a paper in 2013 called The Tail at Scale (*https://oreil.ly/cvLpa*). It argues that systems should be optimized for latency, to keep response times low. The garbage collector used by the Go runtime favors low latency. Each garbage collection cycle is designed to take less than 500 microseconds. However, if your Go program creates lots of garbage, then the garbage collector won't be able to find all of the garbage during a cycle, slowing down the collector and increasing memory usage.

If you are interested in the implementation details, you may want to listen to the talk Rick Hudson gave at the International Symposium on Memory Management in 2018, describing the history and implementation (*https://oreil.ly/UUhGK*) of the Go garbage collector.

The second problem deals with the nature of computer hardware. RAM might mean "random access memory," but the fastest way to read from memory is to read it sequentially. A slice of structs in Go has all of the data laid out sequentially in memory. This makes it fast to load and fast to process. A slice of pointers to structs (or structs whose fields are pointers) has its data scattered across RAM, making it far slower to read and process. Forrest Smith wrote an in-depth blog post (*https://oreil.ly/v_urr*) that explores how much this can affect performance. His numbers indicate that it's roughly two orders of magnitude slower to access data via pointers that are stored randomly in RAM.

This approach of writing software that's aware of the hardware it's running on is called *mechanical sympathy*. The term comes from the world of car racing, where the idea is that a driver who understands what the car is doing can best squeeze the last bits of performance out of it. In 2011, Martin Thompson began applying the term to software development. Following best practices in Go gives it to you automatically.

Compare Go's approach to Java's. In Java, local variables and parameters are stored in the stack, just like Go. However, as we discussed earlier, objects in Java are implemented as pointers. That means for every object variable instance, only the pointer to it is allocated on the stack; the data within the object is allocated on the heap. Only primitive values (numbers, booleans, and chars) are stored entirely on the stack. This means that the garbage collector in Java has to do a great deal of work. It also means that things like Lists in Java are actually a pointer to an array of pointers. Even though it *looks* like a linear data structure, reading it actually involves bouncing through memory, which is highly inefficient. There are similar behaviors in Python, Ruby, and JavaScript. To work around all of this inefficiency, the Java Virtual Machine includes some very clever garbage collectors that do lots of work, some optimized for throughput, some for latency, and all with configuration settings to tune them for the best performance. The virtual machines for Python, Ruby, and JavaScript are less optimized and their performance suffers accordingly.

Now you can see why Go encourages you to use pointers sparingly. We reduce the workload of the garbage collector by making sure that as much as possible is stored on the stack. Slices of structs or primitive types have their data lined up sequentially in memory for rapid access. And when the garbage collector does do work, it is optimized to return quickly rather than gather the most garbage. The key to making this approach work is to simply create less garbage in the first place. While focusing on optimizing memory allocations can feel like premature optimization, the idiomatic approach in Go is also the most efficient.

If you want to learn more about heap versus stack allocation and escape analysis in Go, there are excellent blog posts that cover the topic, including ones by Bill Kennedy of Arden Labs (*https://oreil.ly/juu44*) and Achille Roussel and Rick Branson of Segment (*https://oreil.ly/c_gvC*).

Wrapping Up

This chapter peeked under the covers a bit to help us understand pointers, what they are, how to use them, and, most importantly, when to use them. In the next chapter, we'll take a look at Go's implementation of methods, interfaces, and types, how they differ from other languages, and the power they possess.

CHAPTER 7

Types, Methods, and Interfaces

As we saw in earlier chapters, Go is a statically typed language with both built-in types and user-defined types. Like most modern languages, Go allows you to attach methods to types. It also has type abstraction, allowing you to write code that invokes methods without explicitly specifying the implementation.

However, Go's approach to methods, interfaces, and types is very different from most other languages in common use today. Go is designed to encourage the best practices that are advocated by software engineers, avoiding inheritance while encouraging composition. In this chapter, we'll take a look at types, methods, and interfaces, and see how to use them to build testable and maintainable programs.

Types in Go

Back in "Structs" on page 56 we saw how to define a struct type:

```
type Person struct {
    FirstName string
    LastName string
    Age int
}
```

This should be read as declaring a user-defined type with the name Person to have the *underlying type* of the struct literal that follows. In addition to struct literals, you can use any primitive type or compound type literal to define a concrete type. Here are a few examples:

```
type Score int
type Converter func(string)Score
type TeamScores map[string]Score
```

Go allows you to declare a type at any block level, from the package block down. However, you can only access the type from within its scope. The only exceptions are exported package block level types. We'll talk more about those in Chapter 9.

 To make it easier to talk about types, we're going to define a couple of terms. An *abstract type* is one that specifies *what* a type should do, but not *how* it is done. A *concrete type* specifies what and how. This means that it has a specified way to store its data and provides an implementation of any methods declared on the type. While all types in Go are either abstract or concrete, some languages allow hybrid types, such as abstract classes or interfaces with default methods in Java.

Methods

Like most modern languages, Go supports methods on user-defined types.

The methods for a type are defined at the package block level:

```
type Person struct {
    FirstName string
    LastName string
    Age int
}

func (p Person) String() string {
    return fmt.Sprintf("%s %s, age %d", p.FirstName, p.LastName, p.Age)
}
```

Method declarations look just like function declarations, with one addition: the *receiver* specification. The receiver appears between the keyword func and the name of the method. Just like all other variable declarations, the receiver name appears before the type. By convention, the receiver name is a short abbreviation of the type's name, usually its first letter. It is nonidiomatic to use this or self.

Just like functions, method names cannot be overloaded. You can use the same method names for different types, but you can't use the same method name for two different methods on the same type. While this philosophy feels limiting when coming from languages that have method overloading, not reusing names is part of Go's philosophy of making clear what your code is doing.

We'll talk more about packages in Chapter 9, but be aware that methods must be declared in the same package as their associated type; Go doesn't allow you to add methods to types you don't control. While you can define a method in a different file within the same package as the type declaration, it is best to keep your type definition and its associated methods together so that it's easy to follow the implementation.

Method invocations should look familiar to those who have used methods in other languages:

```
p := Person {
    FirstName: "Fred",
    LastName:"Fredson",
    Age: 52,
}
output := p.String()
```

Pointer Receivers and Value Receivers

As we covered in Chapter 6, Go uses parameters of pointer type to indicate that a parameter might be modified by the function. The same rules apply for method receivers, too. They can be *pointer receivers* (the type is a pointer) or *value receivers* (the type is a value type). The following rules help you determine when to use each kind of receiver:

- If your method modifies the receiver, you *must* use a pointer receiver.
- If your method needs to handle nil instances (see "Code Your Methods for nil Instances" on page 133), then it *must* use a pointer receiver.
- If your method doesn't modify the receiver, you *can* use a value receiver.

Whether or not you use a value receiver for a method that doesn't modify the receiver depends on the other methods declared on the type. When a type has *any* pointer receiver methods, a common practice is to be consistent and use pointer receivers for *all* methods, even the ones that don't modify the receiver.

Here's some simple code to demonstrate pointer and value receivers. We'll start with a type that has two methods on it, one using a value receiver, the other with a pointer receiver:

```
type Counter struct {
    total       int
    lastUpdated time.Time
}

func (c *Counter) Increment() {
    c.total++
    c.lastUpdated = time.Now()
}

func (c Counter) String() string {
    return fmt.Sprintf("total: %d, last updated: %v", c.total, c.lastUpdated)
}
```

We can then try out these methods with the following code. You can run it yourself on The Go Playground (*https://oreil.ly/aqY0i*):

```
var c Counter
fmt.Println(c.String())
c.Increment()
fmt.Println(c.String())
```

You should see the following output:

```
total: 0, last updated: 0001-01-01 00:00:00 +0000 UTC
total: 1, last updated: 2009-11-10 23:00:00 +0000 UTC m=+0.000000001
```

One thing you might notice is that we were able to call the pointer receiver method even though c is a value type. When you use a pointer receiver with a local variable that's a value type, Go automatically converts it to a pointer type. In this case, c.Increment() is converted to (&c).Increment().

However, be aware that the rules for passing values to functions still apply. If you pass a value type to a function and call a pointer receiver method on the passed value, you are invoking the method on a *copy*. You can try out the following code on The Go Playground (*https://oreil.ly/bGdDi*):

```
func doUpdateWrong(c Counter) {
    c.Increment()
    fmt.Println("in doUpdateWrong:", c.String())
}

func doUpdateRight(c *Counter) {
    c.Increment()
    fmt.Println("in doUpdateRight:", c.String())
}

func main() {
    var c Counter
    doUpdateWrong(c)
    fmt.Println("in main:", c.String())
    doUpdateRight(&c)
    fmt.Println("in main:", c.String())
}
```

When you run this code, you'll get the output:

```
in doUpdateWrong: total: 1, last updated: 2009-11-10 23:00:00 +0000 UTC
    m=+0.000000001
in main: total: 0, last updated: 0001-01-01 00:00:00 +0000 UTC
in doUpdateRight: total: 1, last updated: 2009-11-10 23:00:00 +0000 UTC
    m=+0.000000001
in main: total: 1, last updated: 2009-11-10 23:00:00 +0000 UTC m=+0.000000001
```

The parameter in doUpdateRight is of type *Counter, which is a pointer instance. As you can see, we can call both Increment and String on it. Go considers both pointer and value receiver methods to be in the *method set* for a pointer instance. For a value instance, only the value receiver methods are in the method set. This seems like a

---

pedantic detail right now, but we'll come back to it when talking about interfaces in just a bit.

One final note: do not write getter and setter methods for Go structs, unless you need them to meet an interface (we'll start covering interfaces in "A Quick Lesson on Interfaces" on page 141). Go encourages you to directly access a field. Reserve methods for business logic. The exceptions are when you need to update multiple fields as a single operation or when the update isn't a straightforward assignment of a new value. The Increment method defined earlier demonstrates both of these properties.

Code Your Methods for nil Instances

We just mentioned pointer instances, which might make you wonder what happens when you call a method on a nil instance. In most languages, this produces some sort of error. (Objective-C allows you to call a method on a nil instance, but it always does nothing.)

Go does something a little different. It actually tries to invoke the method. If it's a method with a value receiver, you'll get a panic (we discuss panics in "panic and recover" on page 174), as there is no value being pointed to by the pointer. If it's a method with a pointer receiver, it can work if the method is written to handle the possibility of a nil instance.

In some cases, expecting a nil receiver actually makes the code simpler. Here's an implementation of a binary tree that takes advantage of nil values for the receiver:

```
type IntTree struct {
    val         int
    left, right *IntTree
}

func (it *IntTree) Insert(val int) *IntTree {
    if it == nil {
        return &IntTree{val: val}
    }
    if val < it.val {
        it.left = it.left.Insert(val)
    } else if val > it.val {
        it.right = it.right.Insert(val)
    }
    return it
}

func (it *IntTree) Contains(val int) bool {
    switch {
    case it == nil:
        return false
    case val < it.val:
        return it.left.Contains(val)
```

```
        case val > it.val:
            return it.right.Contains(val)
        default:
            return true
        }
}
```

 The Contains method doesn't modify the *IntTree, but it is
declared with a pointer receiver. This demonstrates the rule mentioned previously about supporting a nil receiver. A method with a
value receiver can't check for nil and as mentioned earlier, panics
if invoked with a nil receiver.

The following code uses the tree. You can try it out on The Go Playground (*https://oreil.ly/-F2i-*):

```
func main() {
    var it *IntTree
    it = it.Insert(5)
    it = it.Insert(3)
    it = it.Insert(10)
    it = it.Insert(2)
    fmt.Println(it.Contains(2))  // true
    fmt.Println(it.Contains(12)) // false
}
```

It's very clever that Go allows you to call a method on a nil receiver, and there are
situations where it is useful, like our tree node example. However, most of the time it's
not very useful. Pointer receivers work just like pointer function parameters; it's a
copy of the pointer that's passed into the method. Just like nil parameters passed to
functions, if you change the copy of the pointer, you haven't changed the original.
This means you can't write a pointer receiver method that handles nil and makes the
original pointer non-nil. If your method has a pointer receiver and won't work for a
nil receiver, check for nil and return an error (we discuss errors in Chapter 8).

Methods Are Functions Too

Methods in Go are so much like functions that you can use a method as a replacement for a function any time there's a variable or parameter of a function type.

Let's start with this simple type:

```
type Adder struct {
    start int
}

func (a Adder) AddTo(val int) int {
    return a.start + val
}
```

We create an instance of the type in the usual way and invoke its method:

```
myAdder := Adder{start: 10}
fmt.Println(myAdder.AddTo(5)) // prints 15
```

We can also assign the method to a variable or pass it to a parameter of type func(int)int. This is called a *method value*:

```
f1 := myAdder.AddTo
fmt.Println(f1(10))          // prints 20
```

A method value is a bit like a closure, since it can access the values in the fields of the instance from which it was created.

You can also create a function from the type itself. This is called a *method expression*:

```
f2 := Adder.AddTo
fmt.Println(f2(myAdder, 15))  // prints 25
```

In the case of a method expression, the first parameter is the receiver for the method; our function signature is func(Adder, int) int.

Method values and method expressions aren't just clever corner cases. We'll see one way to use them when we look at dependency injection in "Implicit Interfaces Make Dependency Injection Easier" on page 155.

Functions Versus Methods

Since you can use a method as a function, you might wonder when you should declare a function and when you should use a method.

The differentiator is whether or not your function depends on other data. As we've covered several times, package-level state should be effectively immutable. Any time your logic depends on values that are configured at startup or changed while your program is running, those values should be stored in a struct and that logic should be implemented as a method. If your logic only depends on the input parameters, then it should be a function.

Types, packages, modules, testing, and dependency injection are interrelated concepts. We'll look at dependency injection later in this chapter. You can find out more about packages and modules in Chapter 9 and testing in Chapter 13.

Type Declarations Aren't Inheritance

In addition to declaring types based on built-in Go types and struct literals, you can also declare a user-defined type based on another user-defined type:

```
type HighScore Score
type Employee Person
```

There are many concepts that can be considered "object-oriented," but one stands out: *inheritance*. This is where the state and methods of a *parent* type are declared to be available on a *child* type and values of the child type can be substituted for the parent type. (For the computer scientists in the audience, I realize that subtyping is not inheritance. However, most programming languages use inheritance to implement subtyping so the definitions are often conflated in popular usage.)

Declaring a type based on another type looks a bit like inheritance, but it isn't. The two types have the same underlying type, but that's all. There is no hierarchy between these types. In languages with inheritance, a child instance can be used anywhere the parent instance is used. The child instance also has all the methods and data structures of the parent instance. That's not the case in Go. You can't assign an instance of type HighScore to a variable of type Score or vice versa without a type conversion, nor can you assign either of them to a variable of type int without a type conversion. Furthermore, any methods defined on Score aren't defined on HighScore:

```
// assigning untyped constants is valid
var i int = 300
var s Score = 100
var hs HighScore = 200
hs = s                    // compilation error!
s = i                     // compilation error!
s = Score(i)              // ok
hs = HighScore(s)         // ok
```

For user-defined types whose underlying types are built-in types, a user-declared type can be used with the operators for those types. As we see in the preceding code, they can also be assigned literals and constants compatible with the underlying type.

 A type conversion between types that share an underlying type keeps the same underlying storage but associates different methods.

Types Are Executable Documentation

While it's well understood that you should declare a struct type to hold a set of related data, it's less clear when you should declare a user-defined type based on other built-in types or one user-defined type that's based on another user-defined type. The short answer is that types are documentation. They make code clearer by providing a name for a concept and describing the kind of data that is expected. It's clearer for someone reading your code when a method has a parameter of type Percentage than of type int, and it's harder for it to be invoked with an invalid value.

The same logic applies when declaring one user-defined type based on another user-defined type. When you have the same underlying data, but different sets of operations to perform, make two types. Declaring one as being based on the other avoids some repetition and makes it clear that the two types are related.

iota Is for Enumerations—Sometimes

Many programming languages have the concept of enumerations, where you can specify that a type can only have a limited set of values. Go doesn't have an enumeration type. Instead, it has iota, which lets you assign an increasing value to a set of constants.

 The concept of iota comes from the programming language APL (which stood for "A Programming Language"). APL is famous for being so reliant on its own custom notation that it required computers with a special keyboard. For example, (~R∈R∘.×R)/R←1↓ιR is an APL program to find all the prime numbers up to the value of the variable R.

It may seem ironic that a language as focused on readability as Go would borrow a concept from a language that is concise to a fault, but this is why you should learn many different programming languages: you can find inspiration everywhere.

When using iota, the best practice is to first define a type based on int that will represent all of the valid values:

```
type MailCategory int
```

Next, use a const block to define a set of values for your type:

```
const (
    Uncategorized MailCategory = iota
    Personal
    Spam
    Social
    Advertisements
)
```

The first constant in the const block has the type specified and its value is set to iota. Every subsequent line has neither the type nor a value assigned to it. When the Go compiler sees this, it repeats the type and the assignment to all of the subsequent constants in the block, and increments the value of iota on each line. This means that it assigns 0 to the first constant (Uncategorized), 1 to the second constant (Personal), and so on. When a new const block is created, iota is set back to 0.

This is the best advice I've seen on `iota`:

> Don't use iota for defining constants where its values are explicitly defined (elsewhere).
> For example, when implementing parts of a specification and the specification says
> which values are assigned to which constants, you should explicitly write the constant
> values. Use iota for "internal" purposes only. That is, where the constants are referred
> to by name rather than by value. That way you can optimally enjoy iota by inserting
> new constants at any moment in time / location in the list without the risk of breaking
> everything.
>
> —Danny van Heumen (*https://oreil.ly/3MKwn*)

The important thing to understand is that there is nothing in Go to stop you (or anyone else) from creating additional values of your type. Furthermore, if you insert a
new identifier in the middle of your list of literals, all of the subsequent ones will be
renumbered. This will break your application in a subtle way if those constants represented values in another system or in a database. Given these two limitations, iota-
based enumerations only make sense when you care about being able to differentiate
between a set of values, and don't particularly care what the value is behind the
scenes. If the actual value matters, specify it explicitly.

Because you can assign a literal expression to a constant, you'll see
sample code that suggests you should use `iota` for cases like this:

```
type BitField int

const (
    Field1 BitField = 1 << iota // assigned 1
    Field2                      // assigned 2
    Field3                      // assigned 4
    Field4                      // assigned 8
)
```

While this is clever, be careful when using this pattern. If you do so,
document what you are doing. As mentioned previously, using
iota with constants is fragile when you care about the value. You
don't want a future maintainer to insert a new constant in the middle of the list and break your code.

Be aware that `iota` starts numbering from 0. If you are using your set of constants to
represent different configuration states, the zero value might be useful. We saw this
earlier in our `MailCategory` type. When mail first arrives, it is uncategorized, so the
zero value makes sense. If there isn't a sensical default value for your constants, a
common pattern is to assign the first `iota` value in the constant block to _ or to a
constant that indicates the value is invalid. This makes it easy to detect when a variable has not been properly initialized.

Use Embedding for Composition

The software engineering advice "Favor object composition over class inheritance" dates back to at least the 1994 book *Design Patterns* by Gamma, Helm, Johnson, and Vlissides (Addison-Wesley), better known as the Gang of Four book. While Go doesn't have inheritance, it encourages code reuse via built-in support for composition and promotion:

```
type Employee struct {
    Name        string
    ID          string
}

func (e Employee) Description() string {
    return fmt.Sprintf("%s (%s)", e.Name, e.ID)
}

type Manager struct {
    Employee
    Reports []Employee
}

func (m Manager) FindNewEmployees() []Employee {
    // do business logic
}
```

Note that `Manager` contains a field of type `Employee`, but no name is assigned to that field. This makes `Employee` an *embedded field*. Any fields or methods declared on an embedded field are *promoted* to the containing struct and can be invoked directly on it. That makes the following code valid:

```
m := Manager{
    Employee: Employee{
        Name:       "Bob Bobson",
        ID:         "12345",
    },
    Reports: []Employee{},
}
fmt.Println(m.ID)            // prints 12345
fmt.Println(m.Description()) // prints Bob Bobson (12345)
```

 You can embed any type within a struct, not just another struct. This promotes the methods on the embedded type to the containing struct.

If the containing struct has fields or methods with the same name as an embedded field, you need to use the embedded field's type to refer to the obscured fields or methods. If you have types defined like this:

```
type Inner struct {
    X int
}

type Outer struct {
    Inner
    X int
}
```

You can only access the X on Inner by specifying Inner explicitly:

```
o := Outer{
    Inner: Inner{
        X: 10,
    },
    X: 20,
}
fmt.Println(o.X)       // prints 20
fmt.Println(o.Inner.X) // prints 10
```

Embedding Is Not Inheritance

Built-in embedding support is rare in programming languages (I'm not aware of another popular language that supports it). Many developers who are familiar with inheritance (which is available in many languages) try to understand embedding by treating it as inheritance. That way lies tears. You cannot assign a variable of type Manager to a variable of type Employee. If you want to access the Employee field in Manager, you must do so explicitly. You can run the following code on The Go Playground (*https://oreil.ly/vBl7o*):

```
var eFail Employee = m        // compilation error!
var eOK Employee = m.Employee // ok!
```

You'll get the error:

```
cannot use m (type Manager) as type Employee in assignment
```

Furthermore, there is no *dynamic dispatch* for concrete types in Go. The methods on the embedded field have no idea they are embedded. If you have a method on an embedded field that calls another method on the embedded field, and the containing struct has a method of the same name, the method on the embedded field will not invoke the method on the containing struct. This behavior is demonstrated in the following code, which you can run on The Go Playground (*https://oreil.ly/yN6bV*):

```
type Inner struct {
    A int
}

func (i Inner) IntPrinter(val int) string {
    return fmt.Sprintf("Inner: %d", val)
}

func (i Inner) Double() string {
    return i.IntPrinter(i.A * 2)
}

type Outer struct {
    Inner
    S string
}

func (o Outer) IntPrinter(val int) string {
    return fmt.Sprintf("Outer: %d", val)
}

func main() {
    o := Outer{
        Inner: Inner{
            A: 10,
        },
        S: "Hello",
    }
    fmt.Println(o.Double())
}
```

Running this code produces the output:

```
Inner: 20
```

While embedding one concrete type inside another won't allow you to treat the outer type as the inner type, the methods on an embedded field do count toward the *method set* of the containing struct. This means they can make the containing struct implement an interface.

A Quick Lesson on Interfaces

While Go's concurrency model (which we cover in Chapter 10) gets all of the publicity, the real star of Go's design is its implicit interfaces, the only abstract type in Go. Let's see what makes them so great.

We'll start by taking a quick look at how to declare interfaces. At their core, interfaces are simple. Like other user-defined types, you use the type keyword.

Here's the definition of the `Stringer` interface in the `fmt` package:

```
type Stringer interface {
    String() string
}
```

In an interface declaration, an interface literal appears after the name of the interface type. It lists the methods that must be implemented by a concrete type to meet the interface. The methods defined by an interface are called the method set of the interface.

Like other types, interfaces can be declared in any block.

Interfaces are usually named with "er" endings. We've already seen `fmt.Stringer`, but there are many more, including `io.Reader`, `io.Closer`, `io.ReadCloser`, `json.Mar shaler`, and `http.Handler`.

Interfaces Are Type-Safe Duck Typing

So far, nothing that's been said is much different from interfaces in other languages. What makes Go's interfaces special is that they are implemented *implicitly*. A concrete type does not declare that it implements an interface. If the method set for a concrete type contains all of the methods in the method set for an interface, the concrete type implements the interface. This means that the concrete type can be assigned to a variable or field declared to be of the type of the interface.

This implicit behavior makes interfaces the most interesting thing about types in Go, because they enable both type-safety and decoupling, bridging the functionality in both static and dynamic languages.

To understand why, let's talk about why languages have interfaces. Earlier we mentioned that *Design Patterns* taught developers to favor composition over inheritance. Another piece of advice from the book is "Program to an interface, not an implementation." Doing so allows you to depend on behavior, not on implementation, allowing you to swap implementations as needed. This allows your code to evolve over time, as requirements inevitably change.

Dynamically typed languages like Python, Ruby, and JavaScript don't have interfaces. Instead, those developers use "duck typing," which is based on the expression "If it walks like a duck and quacks like a duck, it's a duck." The concept is that you can pass an instance of a type as a parameter to a function as long as the function can find a method to invoke that it expects:

```
class Logic:
def process(self, data):
    # business logic

def program(logic):
```

```
    # get data from somewhere
    logic.process(data)

logicToUse = Logic()
program(logicToUse)
```

Duck typing might sound weird at first, but it's been used to build large and successful systems. If you program in a statically typed language, this sounds like utter chaos. Without an explicit type being specified, it's hard to know exactly what functionality should be expected. As new developers move on to a project or the existing developers forget what the code is doing, they have to trace through the code to figure out what the actual dependencies are.

Java developers use a different pattern. They define an interface, create an implementation of the interface, but only refer to the interface in the client code:

```
public interface Logic {
    String process(String data);
}

public class LogicImpl implements Logic {
    public String process(String data) {
        // business logic
    }
}

public class Client {
    private final Logic logic;
    // this type is the interface, not the implementation

    public Client(Logic logic) {
        this.logic = logic;
    }

    public void program() {
        // get data from somewhere
        this.logic.process(data);
    }
}

public static void main(String[] args) {
    Logic logic = new LogicImpl();
    Client client = new Client(logic);
    client.program();
}
```

Dynamic language developers look at the explicit interfaces in Java and don't see how you can possibly refactor your code over time when you have explicit dependencies. Switching to a new implementation from a different provider means rewriting your code to depend on a new interface.

Go's developers decided that both groups are right. If your application is going to grow and change over time, you need flexibility to change implementation. However, in order for people to understand what your code is doing (as new people work on the same code over time), you also need to specify what the code depends on. That's where implicit interfaces come in. Go code is a blend of the previous two styles:

```go
type LogicProvider struct {}

func (lp LogicProvider) Process(data string) string {
    // business logic
}

type Logic interface {
    Process(data string) string
}

type Client struct{
    L Logic
}

func(c Client) Program() {
    // get data from somewhere
    c.L.Process(data)
}

main() {
    c := Client{
        L: LogicProvider{},
    }
    c.Program()
}
```

In the Go code, there is an interface, but only the caller (Client) knows about it; there is nothing declared on LogicProvider to indicate that it meets the interface. This is sufficient to both allow a new logic provider in the future and provide executable documentation to ensure that any type passed into the client will match the client's need.

 Interfaces specify what callers need. The client code defines the interface to specify what functionality it requires.

This doesn't mean that interfaces can't be shared. We've already seen several interfaces in the standard library that are used for input and output. Having a standard interface is powerful; if you write your code to work with io.Reader and io.Writer, it will function correctly whether it is writing to a file on local disk or a value in memory.

Furthermore, using standard interfaces encourages the *decorator pattern*. It is common in Go to write factory functions that take in an instance of an interface and return another type that implements the same interface. For example, say you have a function with the following definition:

```
func process(r io.Reader) error
```

You can process data from a file with the following code:

```
r, err := os.Open(fileName)
if err != nil {
    return err
}
defer r.Close()
return process(r)
```

The os.File instance returned by os.Open meets the io.Reader interface and can be used in any code that reads in data. If the file is gzip-compressed, you can wrap the io.Reader in another io.Reader:

```
r, err := os.Open(fileName)
if err != nil {
    return err
}
defer r.Close()
gz, err = gzip.NewReader(r)
if err != nil {
    return err
}
defer gz.Close()
return process(gz)
```

Now the exact same code that was reading from an uncompressed file is reading from a compressed file instead.

 If there's an interface in the standard library that describes what your code needs, use it!

It's perfectly fine for a type that meets an interface to specify additional methods that aren't part of the interface. One set of client code may not care about those methods, but others do. For example, the io.File type also meets the io.Writer interface. If your code only cares about reading from a file, use the io.Reader interface to refer to the file instance and ignore the other methods.

Embedding and Interfaces

Just like you can embed a type in a struct, you can also embed an interface in an interface. For example, the io.ReadCloser interface is built out of an io.Reader and an io.Closer:

```
type Reader interface {
        Read(p []byte) (n int, err error)
}

type Closer interface {
        Close() error
}

type ReadCloser interface {
        Reader
        Closer
}
```

 Just like you can embed a concrete type in a struct, you can also embed an interface in a struct. We'll see a use for this in "Stubs in Go" on page 288.

Accept Interfaces, Return Structs

You'll often hear experienced Go developers say that your code should "Accept interfaces, return structs." What this means is that the business logic invoked by your functions should be invoked via interfaces, but the output of your functions should be a concrete type. We've already covered why functions should accept interfaces: they make your code more flexible and explicitly declare exactly what functionality is being used.

If you create an API that returns interfaces, you are losing one of the main advantages of implicit interfaces: decoupling. You want to limit the third-party interfaces that your client code depends on because your code is now permanently dependent on the module that contains those interfaces, as well as any dependencies of that module, and so on. (We talk about modules and dependencies in Chapter 9.) This limits future flexibility. To avoid the coupling, you'd have to write another interface and do a type conversion from one to the other. While depending on concrete instances can lead to dependencies, using a dependency injection layer in your application limits the effect. We'll talk more about dependency injection in "Implicit Interfaces Make Dependency Injection Easier" on page 155.

Another reason to avoid returning interfaces is versioning. If a concrete type is returned, new methods and fields can be added without breaking existing code. The same is not true for an interface. Adding a new method to an interface means that you need to update all existing implementations of the interface, or your code breaks. If you make a backward-breaking change to an API, you should increment your major version number.

Rather than writing a single factory function that returns different instances behind an interface based on input parameters, try to write separate factory functions for each concrete type. In some situations (such as a parser that can return one or more different kinds of tokens), it's unavoidable and you have no choice but to return an interface.

Errors are an exception to this rule. As we'll see in Chapter 8, Go functions and methods declare a return parameter of the error interface type. In the case of error, it's quite likely that different implementation of the interface could be returned, so you need to use an interface to handle all possible options, as interfaces are the only abstract type in Go.

There is one potential drawback to this pattern. As we discussed in "Reducing the Garbage Collector's Workload" on page 123, reducing heap allocations improves performance by reducing the amount of work for the garbage collector. Returning a struct avoids a heap allocation, which is good. However, when invoking a function with parameters of interface types, a heap allocation occurs for each of the interface parameters. Figuring out the trade-off between better abstraction and better performance is something that should be done over the life of your program. Write your code so that it is readable and maintainable. If you find that your program is too slow *and* you have profiled it *and* you have determined that the performance problems are due to a heap allocation caused by an interface parameter, then you should rewrite the function to use a concrete type parameter. If multiple implementations of an interface are passed into the function, this will mean creating multiple functions with repeated logic.

Interfaces and nil

When discussing pointers in Chapter 6, we also talked about nil, the zero value for pointer types. We also use nil to represent the zero value for an interface instance, but it's not as simple as it is for concrete types.

In order for an interface to be considered nil *both* the type and the value must be nil. The following code prints out true on the first two lines and false on the last:

```
var s *string
fmt.Println(s == nil) // prints true
var i interface{}
fmt.Println(i == nil) // prints true
i = s
fmt.Println(i == nil) // prints false
```

You can run it for yourself on The Go Playground (*https://oreil.ly/NBPbC*).

In the Go runtime, interfaces are implemented as a pair of pointers, one to the underlying type and one to the underlying value. As long as the type is non-nil, the interface is non-nil. (Since you cannot have a variable without a type, if the value pointer is non-nil, the type pointer is always non-nil.)

What nil indicates for an interface is whether or not you can invoke methods on it. As we covered earlier, you can invoke methods on nil concrete instances, so it makes sense that you can invoke methods on an interface variable that was assigned a nil concrete instance. If an interface is nil, invoking any methods on it triggers a panic (which we'll discuss in "panic and recover" on page 174). If an interface is non-nil, you can invoke methods on it. (But note that if the value is nil and the methods of the assigned type don't properly handle nil, you could still trigger a panic.)

Since an interface instance with a non-nil type is not equal to nil, it is not straightforward to tell whether or not the value associated with the interface is nil when the type is non-nil. You must use reflection (which we'll discuss in "Use Reflection to Check If an Interface's Value Is nil" on page 308) to find out.

The Empty Interface Says Nothing

Sometimes in a statically typed language, you need a way to say that a variable could store a value of any type. Go uses interface{} to represent this:

```
var i interface{}
i = 20
i = "hello"
i = struct {
    FirstName string
    LastName string
} {"Fred", "Fredson"}
```

You should note that interface{} isn't special case syntax. An empty interface type simply states that the variable can store any value whose type implements zero or more methods. This just happens to match every type in Go. Because an empty interface doesn't tell you anything about the value it represents, there isn't a lot you can do with it. One common use of the empty interface is as a placeholder for data of uncertain schema that's read from an external source, like a JSON file:

```
// one set of braces for the interface{} type,
// the other to instantiate an instance of the map
data := map[string]interface{}{}
contents, err := ioutil.ReadFile("testdata/sample.json")
if err != nil {
    return err
}
defer contents.Close()
```

```
json.Unmarshal(contents, &data)
// the contents are now in the data map
```

Another use of `interface{}` is as a way to store a value in a user-created data structure. This is due to Go's current lack of user-defined generics. If you need a data structure beyond a slice, array, or map, and you don't want it to only work with a single type, you need to use a field of type `interface{}` to hold its value. You can try the following code on The Go Playground (*https://oreil.ly/SBisO*):

```go
type LinkedList struct {
    Value interface{}
    Next    *LinkedList
}

func (ll *LinkedList) Insert(pos int, val interface{}) *LinkedList {
    if ll == nil || pos == 0 {
        return &LinkedList{
            Value: val,
            Next:    ll,
        }
    }
    ll.Next = ll.Next.Insert(pos-1, val)
    return ll
}
```

> This is *not* an efficient implementation of insert for a linked list, but it's short enough to fit in a book. Please don't use it in real code.

If you see a function that takes in an empty interface, it's likely that it is using reflection (which we'll talk about in Chapter 14) to either populate or read the value. In our preceding example, the second parameter of the `json.Unmarshal` function is declared to be of type `interface{}`.

These situations should be relatively rare. Avoid using `interface{}`. As we've seen, Go is designed as a strongly typed language and attempts to work around this are unidiomatic.

If you find yourself in a situation where you had to store a value into an empty interface, you might be wondering how to read the value back again. To do that, we need to look at type assertions and type switches.

Type Assertions and Type Switches

Go provides two ways to see if a variable of an interface type has a specific concrete type or if the concrete type implements another interface. Let's start by looking at *type assertions*. A type assertion names the concrete type that implemented the interface, or names another interface that is also implemented by the concrete type underlying the interface. You can try it out on The Go Playground (*https://oreil.ly/_nUSw*):

```
type MyInt int

func main() {
    var i interface{}
    var mine MyInt = 20
    i = mine
    i2 := i.(MyInt)
    fmt.Println(i2 + 1)
}
```

In the preceding code, the variable i2 is of type MyInt.

You might wonder what happens if a type assertion is wrong. In that case, your code panics. You can try it out on The Go Playground (*https://oreil.ly/qoXu_*):

```
i2 := i.(string)
fmt.Println(i2)
```

Running this code produces the following panic:

```
panic: interface conversion: interface {} is main.MyInt, not string
```

As we've already seen, Go is very careful about concrete types. Even if two types share an underlying type, a type assertion must match the type of the underlying value. The following code panics. You can try it out on The Go Playground (*https://oreil.ly/YUaka*):

```
i2 := i.(int)
fmt.Println(i2 + 1)
```

Obviously, crashing is not desired behavior. We avoid this by using the comma ok idiom, just as we saw in "The comma ok Idiom" on page 54 when detecting whether or not a zero value was in a map:

```
i2, ok := i.(int)
if !ok {
    return fmt.Errorf("unexpected type for %v",i)
}
fmt.Println(i2 + 1)
```

The boolean ok is set to true if the type conversion was successful. If it was not, ok is set to false and the other variable (in this case i2) is set to its zero value. We then handle the unexpected condition within an `if` statement, but in idiomatic Go, we indent the error handling code. We'll talk more about error handling in Chapter 8.

 A type assertion is very different from a type conversion. Type conversions can be applied to both concrete types and interfaces and are checked at compilation time. Type assertions can only be applied to interface types and are checked at runtime. Because they are checked at runtime, they can fail. Conversions change, assertions reveal.

Even if you are absolutely certain that your type assertion is valid, use the comma ok idiom version. You don't know how other people (or you in six months) will reuse your code. Sooner or later, your unvalidated type assertions will fail at runtime.

When an interface could be one of multiple possible types, use a *type switch* instead:

```go
func doThings(i interface{}) {
    switch j := i.(type) {
    case nil:
        // i is nil, type of j is interface{}
    case int:
        // j is of type int
    case MyInt:
        // j is of type MyInt
    case io.Reader:
        // j is of type io.Reader
    case string:
        // j is a string
    case bool, rune:
        // i is either a bool or rune, so j is of type interface{}
    default:
        // no idea what i is, so j is of type interface{}
    }
}
```

A type `switch` looks a lot like the `switch` statement that we saw way back in "switch" on page 78. Instead of specifying a boolean operation, you specify a variable of an interface type and follow it with `.(type)`. Usually, you assign the variable being checked to another variable that's only valid within the `switch`.

 Since the purpose of a type `switch` is to derive a new variable from an existing one, it is idiomatic to assign the variable being switched on to a variable of the same name (`i := i.(type)`), making this one of the few places where shadowing is a good idea. To make the comments more readable, our example doesn't use shadowing.

The type of the new variable depends on which case matches. You can use nil for one case to see if the interface has no associated type. If you list more than one type on a case, the new variable is of type interface{}. Just like a switch statement, you can have a default case that matches when no specified type does. Otherwise, the new variable has the type of the case that matches.

 If you *don't* know the underlying type, you need to use reflection. We'll talk more about reflection in Chapter 14.

Use Type Assertions and Type Switches Sparingly

While it might seem handy to be able to extract the concrete implementation from an interface variable, you should use these techniques infrequently. For the most part, treat a parameter or return value as the type that was supplied and not what else it could be. Otherwise, your function's API isn't accurately declaring what types it needs to perform its task. If you needed a different type, then it should be specified.

That said, there are use cases where type assertions and type switches are useful. One common use of a type assertion is to see if the concrete type behind the interface also implements another interface. This allows you to specify optional interfaces. For example, the standard library uses this technique to allow more efficient copies when the io.Copy function is called. This function has two parameters of types io.Writer and io.Reader and calls the io.copyBuffer function to do its work. If the io.Writer parameter also implements io.WriterTo, or the io.Reader parameter also implements io.ReaderFrom, most of the work in the function can be skipped:

```
// copyBuffer is the actual implementation of Copy and CopyBuffer.
// if buf is nil, one is allocated.
func copyBuffer(dst Writer, src Reader, buf []byte) (written int64, err error) {
    // If the reader has a WriteTo method, use it to do the copy.
    // Avoids an allocation and a copy.
    if wt, ok := src.(WriterTo); ok {
        return wt.WriteTo(dst)
    }
    // Similarly, if the writer has a ReadFrom method, use it to do the copy.
    if rt, ok := dst.(ReaderFrom); ok {
        return rt.ReadFrom(src)
    }
    // function continues...
}
```

Another place optional interfaces are used is when evolving an API. In Chapter 12 we'll discuss the context. Context is a parameter that's passed to functions that provides, among other things, a standard way to manage cancellation. It was added to Go in version 1.7, which means older code doesn't support it. This includes older database drivers.

In Go 1.8, new context-aware analogues of existing interfaces were defined in the database/sql/driver package. For example, the StmtExecContext interface defines a method called ExecContext, which is a context-aware replacement for the Exec method in Stmt. When an implementation of Stmt is passed into standard library database code, it checks to see if it also implements StmtExecContext. If it does, ExecContext is invoked. If not, the Go standard library provides a fallback implementation of the cancellation support provided by newer code:

```
func ctxDriverStmtExec(ctx context.Context, si driver.Stmt,
                       nvdargs []driver.NamedValue) (driver.Result, error) {
    if siCtx, is := si.(driver.StmtExecContext); is {
        return siCtx.ExecContext(ctx, nvdargs)
    }
    // fallback code is here
}
```

There is one drawback to the optional interface technique. We saw earlier that it is common for implementations of interfaces to use the decorator pattern to wrap other implementations of the same interface to layer behavior. The problem is that if there is an optional interface implemented by one of the wrapped implementations, you cannot detect it with a type assertion or type switch. For example, the standard library includes a bufio package that provides a buffered reader. You can buffer any other io.Reader implementation by passing it to the bufio.NewReader function and using the returned *bufio.Reader. If the passed-in io.Reader also implemented io.ReaderFrom, wrapping it in a buffered reader prevents the optimization.

We also see this when handling errors. As mentioned earlier, they implement the error interface. Errors can include additional information by wrapping other errors. A type switch or type assertion cannot detect or match wrapped errors. If you want different behaviors to handle different concrete implementations of a returned error, use the errors.Is and errors.As functions to test for and access the wrapped error.

Type switch statements provide the ability to differentiate between multiple implementations of an interface that require different processing. They are most useful when there are only certain possible valid types that can be supplied for an interface. Be sure to include a default case in the type switch to handle implementations that aren't known at development time. This protects you if you forget to update your type switch statements when adding new interface implementations:

```
func walkTree(t *treeNode) (int, error) {
    switch val := t.val.(type) {
    case nil:
        return 0, errors.New("invalid expression")
    case number:
```

```
        // we know that t.val is of type number, so return the
        // int value
        return int(val), nil
    case operator:
        // we know that t.val is of type operator, so
        // find the values of the left and right children, then
        // call the process() method on operator to return the
        // result of processing their values.
        left, err := walkTree(t.lchild)
        if err != nil {
            return 0, err
        }
        right, err := walkTree(t.rchild)
        if err != nil {
            return 0, err
        }
        return val.process(left, right), nil
    default:
        // if a new treeVal type is defined, but walkTree wasn't updated
        // to process it, this detects it
        return 0, errors.New("unknown node type")
    }
}
```

You can see the complete implementation on The Go Playground (*https://oreil.ly/jDhqM*).

 You can further protect yourself from unexpected interface implementations by making the interface unexported and at least one
method unexported. If the interface is exported, then it can be
embedded in a struct in another package, making the struct implement the interface. We'll talk more about packages and exporting
identifiers in Chapter 9.

Function Types Are a Bridge to Interfaces

There's one last thing that we haven't talked about with type declarations. It's pretty
easy to wrap your head around adding a method to an int or a string, but Go allows
methods on *any* user-defined type, including user-defined function types. This
sounds like an academic corner case, but they are actually very useful. They allow
functions to implement interfaces. The most common usage is for HTTP handlers.
An HTTP handler processes an HTTP server request. It's defined by an interface:

```
type Handler interface {
    ServeHTTP(http.ResponseWriter, *http.Request)
}
```

By using a type conversion to `http.HandlerFunc`, any function that has the signature
`func(http.ResponseWriter,*http.Request)` can be used as an `http.Handler`:

```
type HandlerFunc func(http.ResponseWriter, *http.Request)

func (f HandlerFunc) ServeHTTP(w http.ResponseWriter, r *http.Request) {
    f(w, r)
}
```

This lets you implement HTTP handlers using functions, methods, or closures using the exact same code path as the one used for other types that meet the http.Handler interface.

Functions in Go are first-class concepts, and as such, they are often passed as parameters into functions. Meanwhile, Go encourages small interfaces, and an interface of only one method could easily replace a parameter of function type. The question becomes: when should your function or method specify an input parameter of a function type and when should you use an interface?

If your single function is likely to depend on many other functions or other state that's not specified in its input parameters, use an interface parameter and define a function type to bridge a function to the interface. That's what's done in the http package; it's likely that a Handler is just the entry point for a chain of calls that needs to be configured. However, if it's a simple function (like the one used in sort.Slice), then a parameter of function type is a good choice.

Implicit Interfaces Make Dependency Injection Easier

Anyone who has been programming for any length of time quickly learns that applications need to change over time. One of the techniques that has been developed to ease decoupling is called *dependency injection*. Dependency injection is the concept that your code should explicitly specify the functionality it needs to perform its task. It's quite a bit older than you might think; in 1996, Robert Martin wrote an article called "The Dependency Inversion Principle" (*https://oreil.ly/6HVob*).

One of the surprising benefits of Go's implicit interfaces is that they make dependency injection an excellent way to decouple your code. While developers in other languages often use large, complicated frameworks to inject their dependencies, the truth is that it is easy to implement dependency injection in Go without any additional libraries. Let's work through a simple example to see how we use implicit interfaces to compose applications via dependency injection.

To understand this concept better and see how to implement dependency injection in Go, let's build a very simple web application. (We'll talk more about Go's built-in HTTP server support in "The Server" on page 249; consider this a preview.) We'll start by writing a small utility function, a logger:

```
func LogOutput(message string) {
    fmt.Println(message)
}
```

Another thing our app needs is a data store. Let's create a simple one:

```go
type SimpleDataStore struct {
    userData map[string]string
}

func (sds SimpleDataStore) UserNameForID(userID string) (string, bool) {
    name, ok := sds.userData[userID]
    return name, ok
}
```

Let's also define a factory function to create an instance of a SimpleDataStore:

```go
func NewSimpleDataStore() SimpleDataStore {
    return SimpleDataStore{
        userData: map[string]string{
            "1": "Fred",
            "2": "Mary",
            "3": "Pat",
        },
    }
}
```

Next, we'll write some business logic that looks up a user and says hello or goodbye. Our business logic needs some data to work with, so it requires a data store. We also want our business logic to log when it is invoked, so it depends on a logger. However, we don't want to force it to depend on LogOutput or SimpleDataStore, because we might want to use a different logger or data store later. What our business logic needs are interfaces to describe what it depends on:

```go
type DataStore interface {
    UserNameForID(userID string) (string, bool)
}

type Logger interface {
    Log(message string)
}
```

To make our LogOutput function meet this interface, we define a function type with a method on it:

```go
type LoggerAdapter func(message string)

func (lg LoggerAdapter) Log(message string) {
    lg(message)
}
```

By a stunning coincidence, our LoggerAdapter and SimpleDataStore happen to meet the interfaces needed by our business logic, but neither type has any idea that it does.

Now that we have the dependencies defined, let's look at the implementation of our business logic:

```
type SimpleLogic struct {
    l  Logger
    ds DataStore
}

func (sl SimpleLogic) SayHello(userID string) (string, error) {
    sl.l.Log("in SayHello for " + userID)
    name, ok := sl.ds.UserNameForID(userID)
    if !ok {
        return "", errors.New("unknown user")
    }
    return "Hello, " + name, nil
}

func (sl SimpleLogic) SayGoodbye(userID string) (string, error) {
    sl.l.Log("in SayGoodbye for " + userID)
    name, ok := sl.ds.UserNameForID(userID)
    if !ok {
        return "", errors.New("unknown user")
    }
    return "Goodbye, " + name, nil
}
```

We have a struct with two fields, one a Logger, the other a DataStore. There's nothing in SimpleLogic that mentions the concrete types, so there's no dependency on them. There's no problem if we later swap in new implementations from an entirely different provider, because the provider has nothing to do with our interface. This is very different from explicit interfaces in languages like Java. Even though Java uses an interface to decouple implementation from interface, the explicit interfaces bind the client and the provider together. This makes replacing a dependency in Java (and other languages with explicit interfaces) far more difficult than it is in Go.

When we want a SimpleLogic instance, we call a factory function, passing in interfaces and returning a struct:

```
func NewSimpleLogic(l Logger, ds DataStore) SimpleLogic {
    return SimpleLogic{
        l:  l,
        ds: ds,
    }
}
```

The fields in SimpleLogic are unexported. This means they can only be accessed by code within the same package as SimpleLogic. We can't enforce immutability in Go, but limiting which code can access these fields makes their accidental modification less likely. We'll talk more about exported and unexported identifiers in Chapter 9.

Now we get to our API. We're only going to have a single endpoint, /hello, which says hello to the person whose user ID is supplied. (Please do not use query parameters in your real applications for authentication information; this is just a quick sample.) Our controller needs business logic that says hello, so we define an interface for that:

```
type Logic interface {
    SayHello(userID string) (string, error)
}
```

This method is available on our SimpleLogic struct, but once again, the concrete type is not aware of the interface. Furthermore, the other method on SimpleLogic, SayGoodbye, is not in the interface because our controller doesn't care about it. The interface is owned by the client code, so its method set is customized to the needs of the client code:

```
type Controller struct {
    l     Logger
    logic Logic
}

func (c Controller) SayHello(w http.ResponseWriter, r *http.Request) {
    c.l.Log("In SayHello")
    userID := r.URL.Query().Get("user_id")
    message, err := c.logic.SayHello(userID)
    if err != nil {
        w.WriteHeader(http.StatusBadRequest)
        w.Write([]byte(err.Error()))
        return
    }
    w.Write([]byte(message))
}
```

Just as we have factory functions for our other types, let's write one for the Controller:

```
func NewController(l Logger, logic Logic) Controller {
    return Controller{
        l:     l,
        logic: logic,
    }
}
```

Again, we accept interfaces and return structs.

Finally, we wire up all of our components in our `main` function and start our server:

```
func main() {
    l := LoggerAdapter(LogOutput)
    ds := NewSimpleDataStore()
    logic := NewSimpleLogic(l, ds)
    c := NewController(l, logic)
    http.HandleFunc("/hello", c.SayHello)
    http.ListenAndServe(":8080", nil)
}
```

The `main` function is the only part of the code that knows what all the concrete types actually are. If we want to swap in different implementations, this is the only place that needs to change. Externalizing the dependencies via dependency injection means that we limit the changes that are needed to evolve our code over time.

Dependency injection is also a great pattern for making testing easier. It shouldn't be surprising, since writing unit tests is effectively reusing your code in a different environment, one where the inputs and outputs are constrained to validate functionality. For example, we can validate the logging output in a test by injecting a type that captures the log output and meets the `Logger` interface. We'll talk about this more in Chapter 13.

> The line `http.HandleFunc("/hello", c.SayHello)` demonstrates two things we talked about earlier.
>
> First, we are treating the `SayHello` method as a function.
>
> Second, the `http.HandleFunc` function takes in a function and converts it to an `http.HandlerFunc` function type, which declares a method to meet the `http.Handler` interface, which is the type used to represent a request handler in Go. We took a method from one type and converted it into another type with its own method. That's pretty neat.

Wire

Those who feel like writing dependency injection code by hand is too much work, can use Wire (*https://oreil.ly/Akwt_*), a dependency injection helper written by Google. It uses code generation to automatically create the concrete type declarations that we wrote ourselves in `main`.

Go Isn't Particularly Object-Oriented (and That's Great)

Now that we've taken a look at the idiomatic use of types in Go, you can see that it's hard to categorize Go as a particular style of language. It clearly isn't a strictly procedural language. At the same time, Go's lack of method overriding, inheritance, or, well, objects means that it is not a particularly object-oriented language, either. Go has function types and closures, but it isn't a functional language, either. If you attempt to shoehorn Go into one of these categories, the result is nonidiomatic code.

If you had to label Go's style, the best word to use is *practical*. It borrows concepts from many places with the overriding goal of creating a language that is simple, readable, and maintainable by large teams for many years.

Wrapping Up

In this chapter, we covered types, methods, interfaces, and their best practices. In our next chapter, we are going to learn how to properly use one of Go's most controversial features: errors.

CHAPTER 8

Errors

Error handling is one of the biggest challenges for developers moving to Go from other languages. For those used to exceptions, Go's approach feels anachronistic. But there are solid software engineering principles underlying Go's approach. In this chapter, we'll learn how to work with errors in Go. We'll also take a look at panic and recover, Go's system for handling errors that should stop execution.

How to Handle Errors: The Basics

As we covered briefly in Chapter 5, Go handles errors by returning a value of type error as the last return value for a function. This is entirely by convention, but it is such a strong convention that it should never be breached. When a function executes as expected, nil is returned for the error parameter. If something goes wrong, an error value is returned instead. The calling function then checks the error return value by comparing it to nil, handling the error, or returning an error of its own. The code looks like this:

```
func calcRemainderAndMod(numerator, denominator int) (int, int, error) {
    if denominator == 0 {
        return 0, 0, errors.New("denominator is 0")
    }
    return numerator / denominator, numerator % denominator, nil
}
```

A new error is created from a string by calling the New function in the errors package. Error messages should not be capitalized nor should they end with punctuation or a newline. In most cases, you should set the other return values to their zero values when a non-nil error is returned. We'll see an exception to this rule when we look at sentinel errors.

Unlike languages with exceptions, Go doesn't have special constructs to detect if an error was returned. Whenever a function returns, use an `if` statement to check the error variable to see if it is non-nil:

```
func main() {
    numerator := 20
    denominator := 3
    remainder, mod, err := calcRemainderAndMod(numerator, denominator)
    if err != nil {
        fmt.Println(err)
        os.Exit(1)
    }
    fmt.Println(remainder, mod)
}
```

`error` is a built-in interface that defines a single method:

```
type error interface {
    Error() string
}
```

Anything that implements this interface is considered an error. The reason why we return `nil` from a function to indicate that no error occurred is that `nil` is the zero value for any interface type.

There are two very good reasons why Go uses a returned error instead of thrown exceptions. First, exceptions add at least one new code path through the code. These paths are sometimes unclear, especially in languages whose functions don't include a declaration that an exception is possible. This produces code that crashes in surprising ways when exceptions aren't properly handled, or, even worse, code that doesn't crash but whose data is not properly initialized, modified, or stored.

The second reason is more subtle, but demonstrates how Go's features work together. The Go compiler requires that all variables must be read. Making errors returned values forces developers to either check and handle error conditions or make it explicit that they are ignoring errors by using an underscore (_) for the returned error value.

 As noted in Chapter 5, while you cannot ignore *some* values returned from a function, you can ignore *all* of the return values from a function. If you ignore all the return values, you would be able to ignore the error, too. In most cases, it is very bad form to ignore the values returned from a function. Please avoid this, except for cases like `fmt.Println`.

Exception handling may produce shorter code, but having fewer lines doesn't necessarily make code easier to understand or maintain. As we've seen, idiomatic Go favors clear code, even if it takes more lines.

Another thing to note is how code flows in Go. The error handling is indented inside an `if` statement. The business logic is not. This gives a quick visual clue to which code is along the "golden path" and which code is the exceptional condition.

Use Strings for Simple Errors

Go's standard library provides two ways to create an error from a string. The first is the `errors.New` function. It takes in a `string` and returns an `error`. This string is returned when you call the `Error` method on the returned error instance. If you pass an error to `fmt.Println`, it calls the `Error` method automatically:

```
func doubleEven(i int) (int, error) {
    if i % 2 != 0 {
        return 0, errors.New("only even numbers are processed")
    }
    return i * 2, nil
}
```

The second way is to use the `fmt.Errorf` function. This function allows you to use all of the formatting verbs for `fmt.Printf` to create an error. Like `errors.New`, this string is returned when you call the `Error` method on the returned error instance:

```
func doubleEven(i int) (int, error) {
    if i % 2 != 0 {
        return 0, fmt.Errorf("%d isn't an even number", i)
    }
    return i * 2, nil
}
```

Sentinel Errors

Some errors are meant to signal that processing cannot continue due to a problem with the current state. In his blog post "Don't just check errors, handle them gracefully" (*https://oreil.ly/TiJnS*), Dave Cheney, a developer who has been active in the Go community for many years, coined the term *sentinel errors* to describe these errors:

> The name descends from the practice in computer programming of using a specific value to signify that no further processing is possible. So to [sic] with Go, we use specific values to signify an error.
>
> —Dave Cheney (*https://oreil.ly/3fMAI*)

Sentinel errors are one of the few variables that are declared at the package level. By convention, their names start with `Err` (with the notable exception of `io.EOF`). They should be treated as read-only; there's no way for the Go compiler to enforce this, but it is a programming error to change their value.

Sentinel errors are usually used to indicate that you cannot start or continue processing. For example, the standard library includes a package for processing ZIP files, archive/zip. This package defines several sentinel errors, including ErrFormat, which is returned when data that doesn't represent a ZIP file is passed in. Try out this code on The Go Playground (*https://oreil.ly/DaW-s*):

```
func main() {
    data := []byte("This is not a zip file")
    notAZipFile := bytes.NewReader(data)
    _, err := zip.NewReader(notAZipFile, int64(len(data)))
    if err == zip.ErrFormat {
        fmt.Println("Told you so")
    }
}
```

Another example of a sentinel error in the standard library is rsa.ErrMessageToo Long in the crypto/rsa package. It indicates that a message cannot be encrypted because it is too long for the provided public key. When we discuss the context in Chapter 12, you'll see another commonly used sentinel error, context.Canceled.

Be sure you need a sentinel error before you define one. Once you define one, it is part of your public API and you have committed to it being available in all future backward-compatible releases. It's far better to reuse one of the existing ones in the standard library or to define an error type that includes information about the condition that caused the error to be returned (we'll see how to do that in the next section). But if you have an error condition that indicates a specific state has been reached in your application where no further processing is possible and no contextual information needs to be used to explain the error state, a sentinel error is the correct choice.

How do you test for a sentinel error? As you can see in the preceding code sample, use == to test if the error was returned when calling a function whose documentation explicitly says it returns a sentinel error. In an upcoming section, we will discuss how to check for sentinel errors in other situations.

Using Constants for Sentinel Errors

In Constant errors (*https://oreil.ly/1AnVg*), Dave Cheney proposed that constants would make useful sentinel errors. You'd have a type like this in a package (we'll talk about creating packages in Chapter 9):

```
package consterr

type Sentinel string

func(s Sentinel) Error() string {
    return string(s)
}
```

and then use it like this:

```
package mypkg

const (
    ErrFoo = consterr.Sentinel("foo error")
    ErrBar = consterr.Sentinel("bar error")
)
```

This looks like a function call, but it's actually casting a string literal to a type that implements the error interface. It would be impossible to change the values of Err Foo and ErrBar. At first glance, this looks like a good solution.

However, this practice isn't considered idiomatic. If you used the same type to create constant errors across packages, two errors would be equal if their error strings are equal. They'd also be equal to a string literal with the same value. Meanwhile, an error created with errors.New is only equal to itself or to variables explicitly assigned its value. You almost certainly do not want to make errors in different packages equal to each other; otherwise, why declare two different errors? (You could avoid this by creating a nonpublic error type in every package, but that's a lot of boilerplate.)

The sentinel error pattern is another example of the Go design philosophy. Sentinel errors should be rare, so they can be handled by convention instead of language rules. Yes, they are public package-level variables. This makes them mutable, but it's highly unlikely someone would accidentally reassign a public variable in a package. In short, it's a corner case that is handled by other features and patterns. The Go philosophy is that it's better to keep the language simple and trust the developers and tooling than it is to add additional features.

So far, all the errors that we've seen are strings. But Go errors can contain more information. Let's see how.

Errors Are Values

Since error is an interface, you can define your own errors that include additional information for logging or error handling. For example, you might want to include a status code as part of the error to indicate the kind of error that should be reported back to the user. This lets you avoid string comparisons (whose text might change) to determine error causes. Let's see how this works. First, define your own enumeration to represent the status codes:

```
type Status int

const (
    InvalidLogin Status = iota + 1
    NotFound
)
```

Next, define a `StatusErr` to hold this value:

```
type StatusErr struct {
    Status    Status
    Message string
}

func (se StatusErr) Error() string {
    return se.Message
}
```

Now we can use `StatusErr` to provide more details about what went wrong:

```
func LoginAndGetData(uid, pwd, file string) ([]byte, error) {
    err := login(uid, pwd)
    if err != nil {
        return nil, StatusErr{
            Status:  InvalidLogin,
            Message: fmt.Sprintf("invalid credentials for user %s", uid),
        }
    }
    data, err := getData(file)
    if err != nil {
        return nil, StatusErr{
            Status:  NotFound,
            Message: fmt.Sprintf("file %s not found", file),
        }
    }
    return data, nil
}
```

Even when you define your own custom error types, always use `error` as the return type for the error result. This allows you to return different types of errors from your function and allows callers of your function to choose not to depend on the specific error type.

If you are using your own error type, be sure you don't return an uninitialized instance. This means that you shouldn't declare a variable to be the type of your custom error and then return that variable. Let's see what happens if you do. Try out the following code on The Go Playground (*https://oreil.ly/5QJVN*):

```
func GenerateError(flag bool) error {
    var genErr StatusErr
    if flag {
        genErr = StatusErr{
            Status: NotFound,
        }
    }
    return genErr
}

func main() {
```

```
    err := GenerateError(true)
    fmt.Println(err != nil)
    err = GenerateError(false)
    fmt.Println(err != nil)
}
```

Running this program produces the following output:

```
true
true
```

This isn't a pointer type versus value type issue; if we declared genErr to be of type *StatusErr, we'd see the same output. The reason why err is non-nil is that error is an interface. As we discussed in "Interfaces and nil" on page 147, for an interface to be considered nil, both the underlying type and the underlying value must be nil. Whether or not genErr is a pointer, the underlying type part of the interface is not nil.

There are two ways to fix this. The most common approach is to explicitly return nil for the error value when a function completes successfully:

```
func GenerateError(flag bool) error {
    if flag {
        return StatusErr{
            Status: NotFound,
        }
    }
    return nil
}
```

This has the advantage of not requiring you to read through code to make sure that the error variable on the return statement is correctly defined.

Another approach is to make sure that any local variable that holds an error is of type error:

```
func GenerateError(flag bool) error {
    var genErr error
    if flag {
        genErr = StatusErr{
            Status: NotFound,
        }
    }
    return genErr
}
```

 When using custom errors, never define a variable to be of the type of your custom error. Either explicitly return nil when no error occurs or define the variable to be of type error.

As we covered in "Use Type Assertions and Type Switches Sparingly" on page 152, don't use a type assertion or a type switch to access the fields and methods of a custom error. Instead, use `errors.As`, which we'll look at in "Is and As" on page 170.

Wrapping Errors

When an error is passed back through your code, you often want to add additional context to it. This context can be the name of the function that received the error or the operation it was trying to perform. When you preserve an error while adding additional information, it is called *wrapping* the error. When you have a series of wrapped errors, it is called an *error chain*.

There's a function in the Go standard library that wraps errors, and we've already seen it. The `fmt.Errorf` function has a special verb, `%w`. Use this to create an error whose formatted string includes the formatted string of another error and which contains the original error as well. The convention is to write : `%w` at the end of the error format string and make the error to be wrapped the last parameter passed to `fmt.Errorf`.

The standard library also provides a function for unwrapping errors, the `Unwrap` function in the `errors` package. You pass it an error and it returns the wrapped error, if there is one. If there isn't, it returns `nil`. Here's a quick program that demonstrates wrapping with `fmt.Errorf` and unwrapping with `errors.Unwrap`. You can run it on The Go Playground (*https://oreil.ly/HxdHz*):

```go
func fileChecker(name string) error {
    f, err := os.Open(name)
    if err != nil {
        return fmt.Errorf("in fileChecker: %w", err)
    }
    f.Close()
    return nil
}

func main() {
    err := fileChecker("not_here.txt")
    if err != nil {
        fmt.Println(err)
        if wrappedErr := errors.Unwrap(err); wrappedErr != nil {
            fmt.Println(wrappedErr)
        }
    }
}
```

When you run this program, you see the following output:

```
in fileChecker: open not_here.txt: no such file or directory
open not_here.txt: no such file or directory
```

You don't usually call errors.Unwrap directly. Instead, you use errors.Is and errors.As to find a specific wrapped error. We'll talk about these two functions in the next section.

If you want to wrap an error with your custom error type, your error type needs to implement the method Unwrap. This method takes in no parameters and returns an error. Here's an update to the error that we defined earlier to demonstrate how this works:

```
type StatusErr struct {
    Status Status
    Message string
    Err error
}

func (se StatusErr) Error() string {
    return se.Message
}

func (se StatusError) Unwrap() error {
    return se.Err
}
```

Now we can use StatusErr to wrap underlying errors:

```
func LoginAndGetData(uid, pwd, file string) ([]byte, error) {
    err := login(uid,pwd)
    if err != nil {
        return nil, StatusErr {
            Status: InvalidLogin,
            Message: fmt.Sprintf("invalid credentials for user %s",uid),
            Err: err,
        }
    }
    data, err := getData(file)
    if err != nil {
        return nil, StatusErr {
            Status: NotFound,
            Message: fmt.Sprintf("file %s not found",file),
            Err: err,
        }
    }
    return data, nil
}
```

Not all errors need to be wrapped. A library can return an error that means processing cannot continue, but the error message contains implementation details that aren't needed in other parts of your program. In this situation it is perfectly acceptable to create a brand-new error and return that instead. Understand the situation and determine what needs to be returned.

 If you want to create a new error that contains the message from another error, but don't want to wrap it, use fmt.Errorf to create an error, but use the %v verb instead of %w:

```
err := internalFunction()
if err != nil {
    return fmt.Errorf("internal failure: %v", err)
}
```

Is and As

Wrapping errors is a useful way to get additional information about an error, but it introduces problems. If a sentinel error is wrapped, you cannot use == to check for it, nor can you use a type assertion or type switch to match a wrapped custom error. Go solves this problem with two functions in the errors package, Is and As.

To check if the returned error or any errors that it wraps match a specific sentinel error instance, use errors.Is. It takes in two parameters, the error that is being checked and the instance you are comparing against. The errors.Is function returns true if there is an error in the error chain that matches the provided sentinel error. Let's write a short program to see errors.Is in action. You can run it yourself on The Go Playground (*https://oreil.ly/5_6rI*):

```
func fileChecker(name string) error {
    f, err := os.Open(name)
    if err != nil {
        return fmt.Errorf("in fileChecker: %w", err)
    }
    f.Close()
    return nil
}

func main() {
    err := fileChecker("not_here.txt")
    if err != nil {
        if errors.Is(err, os.ErrNotExist) {
            fmt.Println("That file doesn't exist")
        }
    }
}
```

Running this program produces the output:

```
That file doesn't exist
```

By default, `errors.Is` uses == to compare each wrapped error with the specified error. If this does not work for an error type that you define (for example, if your error is a noncomparable type), implement the Is method on your error:

```
type MyErr struct {
    Codes []int
}

func (me MyErr) Error() string {
    return fmt.Sprintf("codes: %v", me.Codes)
}

func (me MyErr) Is(target error) bool {
    if me2, ok := target.(MyErr); ok {
        return reflect.DeepEqual(me, me2)
    }
    return false
}
```

(We mentioned `reflect.DeepEqual` back in Chapter 3. It can compare anything, including slices.)

Another use for defining your own Is method is to allow comparisons against errors that aren't identical instances. You might want to pattern match your errors, specifying a filter instance that matches errors that have some of the same fields. Let's define a new error type, `ResourceErr`:

```
type ResourceErr struct {
    Resource    string
    Code        int
}

func (re ResourceErr) Error() string {
    return fmt.Sprintf("%s: %d", re.Resource, re.Code)
}
```

If we want two `ResourceErr` instances to match when either field is set, we can do so by writing a custom Is method:

```
func (re ResourceErr) Is(target error) bool {
    if other, ok := target.(ResourceErr); ok {
        ignoreResource := other.Resource == ""
        ignoreCode := other.Code == 0
        matchResource := other.Resource == re.Resource
        matchCode := other.Code == re.Code
        return matchResource && matchCode ||
            matchResource && ignoreCode ||
            ignoreResource && matchCode
    }
    return false
}
```

Now we can find, for example, all errors that refer to the database, no matter the code:

```
if errors.Is(err, ResourceErr{Resource: "Database"}) {
    fmt.Println("The database is broken:", err)
    // process the codes
}
```

You can see this code on The Go Playground (*https://oreil.ly/Mz_Op*).

The `errors.As` function allows you to check if a returned error (or any error it wraps) matches a specific type. It takes in two parameters. The first is the error being examined and the second is a pointer to a variable of the type that you are looking for. If the function returns `true`, an error in the error chain was found that matched, and that matching error is assigned to the second parameter. If the function returns `false`, no match was found in the error chain. Let's try it out with `MyErr`:

```
err := AFunctionThatReturnsAnError()
var myErr MyErr
if errors.As(err, &myErr) {
    fmt.Println(myErr.Code)
}
```

Note that you use `var` to declare a variable of a specific type set to the zero value. You then pass a pointer to this variable into `errors.As`.

You don't have to pass a pointer to a variable of an error type as the second parameter to `errors.As`. You can pass a pointer to an interface to find an error that meets the interface:

```
err := AFunctionThatReturnsAnError()
var coder interface {
    Code() int
}
if errors.As(err, &coder) {
    fmt.Println(coder.Code())
}
```

We're using an anonymous interface here, but any interface type is acceptable.

> If the second parameter to `errors.As` is anything other than a pointer to an error or a pointer to an interface, the method panics.

Just like you can override the default `errors.Is` comparison with an `Is` method, you can override the default `errors.As` comparison with an `As` method on your error. Implementing an `As` method is nontrivial and requires reflection (we will talk about reflection in Go we in Chapter 14). You should only do it in unusual circumstances, such as when you want to match an error of one type and return another.

 Use errors.Is when you are looking for a specific *instance* or specific *values*. Use errors.As when you are looking for a specific *type*.

Wrapping Errors with defer

Sometimes you find yourself wrapping multiple errors with the same message:

```go
func DoSomeThings(val1 int, val2 string) (string, error) {
    val3, err := doThing1(val1)
    if err != nil {
        return "", fmt.Errorf("in DoSomeThings: %w", err)
    }
    val4, err := doThing2(val2)
    if err != nil {
        return "", fmt.Errorf("in DoSomeThings: %w", err)
    }
    result, err := doThing3(val3, val4)
    if err != nil {
        return "", fmt.Errorf("in DoSomeThings: %w", err)
    }
    return result, nil
}
```

We can simplify this code by using defer:

```go
func DoSomeThings(val1 int, val2 string) (_ string, err error) {
    defer func() {
        if err != nil {
            err = fmt.Errorf("in DoSomeThings: %w", err)
        }
    }()
    val3, err := doThing1(val1)
    if err != nil {
        return "", err
    }
    val4, err := doThing2(val2)
    if err != nil {
        return "", err
    }
    return doThing3(val3, val4)
}
```

We have to name our return values so that we can refer to err in the deferred function. If you name a single return value, you must name all of them, so we use an underscore here for the string return value since we don't explicitly assign to it.

In the `defer` closure, we check if an error was returned. If so, we reassign the error to a new error that wraps the original error with a message that indicates which function detected the error.

This pattern works well when you are wrapping every error with the same message. If you want to customize the wrapping error to provide more context about what caused the error, then put both the specific and the general message in every `fmt.Errorf`.

panic and recover

In previous chapters, we've mentioned panics in passing without going into any details on what they are. Go generates a panic whenever there is a situation where the Go runtime is unable to figure out what should happen next. This could be due to a programming error (like an attempt to read past the end of a slice) or environmental problem (like running out of memory). As soon as a panic happens, the current function exits immediately and any defers attached to the current function start running. When those defers complete, the defers attached to the calling function run, and so on, until `main` is reached. The program then exits with a message and a stack trace.

If there are situations in your programs that are unrecoverable, you can create your own panics. The built-in function `panic` takes one parameter, which can be of any type. Usually, it is a string. Let's make a trivial program that panics and run it on The Go Playground (*https://oreil.ly/yCBib*):

```go
func doPanic(msg string) {
    panic(msg)
}

func main() {
    doPanic(os.Args[0])
}
```

Running this code produces the following output:

```
panic: /tmpfs/play

goroutine 1 [running]:
main.doPanic(...)
    /tmp/sandbox567884271/prog.go:6
main.main()
    /tmp/sandbox567884271/prog.go:10 +0x5f
```

As you can see, a `panic` prints out its message followed by a stack trace.

Go provides a way to capture a panic to provide a more graceful shutdown or to prevent shutdown at all. The built-in `recover` function is called from within a `defer` to check if a panic happened. If there was a panic, the value assigned to the panic is returned. Once a recover happens, execution continues normally. Let's take a look with another sample program. Run it on The Go Playground (*https://oreil.ly/f5Ybe*):

```go
func div60(i int) {
    defer func() {
        if v := recover(); v != nil {
            fmt.Println(v)
        }
    }()
    fmt.Println(60 / i)
}

func main() {
    for _, val := range []int{1, 2, 0, 6} {
        div60(val)
    }
}
```

There's a specific pattern for using recover. We register a function with defer to handle a potential panic. We call recover within an if statement and check to see if a non-nil value was found. You must call recover from within a defer because once a panic happens, only deferred functions are run.

Running this code produces the following output:

```
60
30
runtime error: integer divide by zero
10
```

While panic and recover look a lot like exception handling in other languages, they are not intended to be used that way. Reserve panics for fatal situations and use recover as a way to gracefully handle these situations. If your program panics, be very careful about trying to continue executing after the panic. It's very rare that you want to keep your program running after a panic occurs. If the panic was triggered because the computer is out of a resource like memory or disk space, the safest thing to do is use recover to log the situation to monitoring software and shut down with os.Exit(1). If there's a programming error that caused the panic, you can try to continue, but you'll likely hit the same problem again. In the preceding sample program, it would be idiomatic to check for division by zero and return an error if one was passed in.

The reason we don't rely on panic and recover is that recover doesn't make clear *what* could fail. It just ensures that *if* something fails, we can print out a message and continue. Idiomatic Go favors code that explicitly outlines the possible failure conditions over shorter code that handles anything while saying nothing.

There is one situation where recover is recommended. If you are creating a library for third parties, do not let panics escape the boundaries of your public API. If a panic is possible, a public function should use a `recover` to convert the `panic` into an error, return it, and let the calling code decide what to do with them.

 While the HTTP server built into Go recovers from panics in handlers, David Symonds said in a GitHub comment (*https://oreil.ly/BGOmg*) that this is now considered a mistake by the Go team.

Getting a Stack Trace from an Error

One of the reasons why new Go developers are tempted by `panic` and `recover` is that they want to get a stack trace when something goes wrong. By default, Go doesn't provide that. As we've shown, you can use error wrapping to build a call stack by hand, but there are third-party libraries with error types that generate those stacks automatically (see Chapter 9 to learn how to incorporate third-party code in your program). The best known third-party library (*https://github.com/pkg/errors*) provides functions for wrapping errors with stack traces.

By default, the stack trace is not printed out. If you want to see the stack trace, use `fmt.Printf` and the verbose output verb (`%+v`). Check the documentation (*https://oreil.ly/mBQRA*) to learn more.

 When you have a stack trace in your error, the output includes the full path to the file on the computer where the program was compiled. If you don't want to expose the path, use the `-trimpath` flag when building your code. This replaces the full path with the package.

Wrapping Up

In this chapter, we learned about errors in Go, what they are, how to define your own, and how to examine them. We also took a look at `panic` and `recover`. In the next chapter, we discuss packages and modules, how to use third-party code in your programs, and how to publish your own code for others to use.

CHAPTER 9

Modules, Packages, and Imports

Most modern programming languages have a system for organizing code into namespaces and libraries, and Go is no exception. As we've seen while exploring other features, Go introduces some new approaches to this old idea. In this chapter, we'll learn about organizing code with packages and modules, how to import them, how to work with third-party libraries, and how to create libraries of your own.

Repositories, Modules, and Packages

Library management in Go is based around three concepts: *repositories*, *modules*, and *packages*. A repository is familiar to all developers. It is a place in a version control system where the source code for a project is stored. A module is the root of a Go library or application, stored in a repository. Modules consist of one or more packages, which give the module organization and structure.

 While you can store more than one module in a repository, it isn't encouraged. Everything within a module is versioned together. Maintaining two modules in one repository means tracking separate versions for two different projects in a single repository.

Before we can use code from packages outside of the standard library, we need to make sure that we have declared that our project is a module. Every module has a globally unique identifier. This is not unique to Go. Java uses globally unique package declarations like com.companyname.projectname.library.

In Go, we usually use the path to the module repository where the module is found. For example, Proteus, a module I wrote to simplify relational database access in Go, can be found at GitHub (*https://github.com/jonbodner/proteus*). It has a module path of *github.com/jonbodner/proteus*.

go.mod

A collection of Go source code becomes a module when there's a valid *go.mod* file in its root directory. Rather than create this file manually, we use the subcommands of the go mod command to manage modules. The command go mod init *MODULE_PATH* creates the *go.mod* file that makes the current directory the root of a module. The *MODULE_PATH* is the globally unique name that identifies your module. The module path is case-sensitive. To reduce confusion, do not use uppercase letters within it.

Let's take a quick look at the contents of a *go.mod* file:

```
module github.com/learning-go-book/money

go 1.15

require (
    github.com/learning-go-book/formatter v0.0.0-20200921021027-5abc380940ae
    github.com/shopspring/decimal v1.2.0
)
```

Every *go.mod* file starts with a module declaration that consists of the word module and the module's unique path. Next, the *go.mod* file specifies the minimum compatible version of Go. Finally, the require section lists the modules that your module depends on and the minimum version required for each one. We'll talk more about what those versions mean in "Importing Third-Party Code" on page 190. Omit the require section when your module doesn't depend on any other modules.

There are two optional sections as well. The replace section lets you override the location where a dependent module is located, and the exclude section prevents a specific version of a module from being used.

Building Packages

Now that we've learned how to make our directory of code into a module, it's time to start using packages to organize our code. We'll start by looking at how import works, move on to creating and organizing packages, and then look at some of the features of Go's packages, both good and bad.

Imports and Exports

We've been using the import statement in Go without discussing what it does and how it differs from other languages. Go's import statement allows you to access exported constants, variables, functions, and types in another package. A package's exported identifiers (an *identifier* is the name of a variable, constant, type, function, method, or a field in a struct) cannot be accessed from another current package without an `import` statement.

This leads to the question: how do you export an identifier in Go? Rather than use a special keyword, Go uses *capitalization* to determine if a package-level identifier is visible outside of the package where it is declared. An identifier whose name starts with an uppercase letter is *exported*. Conversely, an identifier whose name starts with a lowercase letter or underscore can only be accessed from within the package where it is declared.

Anything you export is part of your package's API. Before you export an identifier, be sure that you intend to expose it to clients. Document all exported identifiers and keep them backward-compatible unless you are intentionally making a major version change (see "Versioning Your Module" on page 199 for more information).

Creating and Accessing a Package

Making packages in Go is easy. Let's look at a small program to demonstrate this. You can find it on GitHub (*https://oreil.ly/WE7RN*). Inside `package_example`, you'll see two additional directories, *math* and *formatter*. In *math*, there's a file called *math.go* with the following contents:

```
package math

func Double(a int) int {
    return a * 2
}
```

The first line of the file is called the *package clause*. It consists of the keyword `package` and the name for the package. The package clause is always the first nonblank, non-comment line in a Go source file.

In *formatter*, there's a file called *formatter.go* with the following contents:

```
package print

import "fmt"

func Format(num int) string {
    return fmt.Sprintf("The number is %d", num)
}
```

Note that we said the package name is `print` in the package clause, but it's in the *formatter* directory. We'll talk more about this in a bit.

Finally, the following contents are in the file *main.go* in the root directory:

```
package main

import (
    "fmt"

    "github.com/learning-go-book/package_example/formatter"
    "github.com/learning-go-book/package_example/math"
)

func main() {
    num := math.Double(2)
    output := print.Format(num)
    fmt.Println(output)
}
```

The first line of this file is familiar. All of our programs before this chapter have put package main as the first line in our code. We'll talk more about what this means in just a bit.

Next we have our import section. We're importing three packages. The first is fmt, which is in the standard library. We've done this in previous chapters. The next two imports refer to the packages within our program. You must specify an *import path* when importing from anywhere besides the standard library. The import path is built by appending the path to the package within the module to the module path.

It is a compile-time error to import a package but not use any of the identifiers exported by the package. This ensures that the binary produced by the Go compiler only includes code that's actually used in the program.

 While you can use a relative path to import a dependent package within the same module, don't do this. Absolute import paths clarify what you are importing and make it easier to refactor your code. You must fix the imports when a file with a relative path in its imports is moved to another package, and if you move that file to another module entirely, you must make the import reference absolute.

When you run this program, you'll see the following output:

```
$ go run main.go
The number is 4
```

In our main function, we called the Double function in the math package by prefixing the function name with the package name. We've seen this in previous chapters when calling functions in the standard library. We also called the Format function in the print package. You might wonder where this `print` package came from, since we imported `github.com/learning-go-book/package_example/formatter`.

Every Go file in a directory must have an identical package clause. (There is one tiny exception to this rule that we'll see in "Testing Your Public API" on page 278.) We imported the `print` package with the import path *github.com/learning-go-book/package_example/formatter*. That's because *the name of a package is determined by its package clause, not its import path*.

As a general rule, you should make the name of the package match the name of the directory that contains the package. It is hard to discover a package's name if it does not match the containing directory. However, there are a few situations where you use a different name for the package than for the directory.

The first is something we have been doing all along without realizing it. We declare a package to be a starting point for a Go application by using the special package name `main`. Since you cannot import the `main` package, this doesn't produce confusing import statements.

The other reasons for having a package name not match your directory name are less common. If your directory name contains a character that's not valid in a Go identifier, then you must choose a package name that's different from your directory name. It's better to avoid this by never creating a directory with a name that's not a valid identifier.

The final reason for creating a directory whose name doesn't match the package name is to support versioning using directories. We'll talk about this more in "Versioning Your Module" on page 199.

Package names are in the file block. If you use the same package in two different files in the same package, you must import the package in both files.

Naming Packages

Having the package name as part of the name used to refer to items in the package has some implications. The first is that package names should be descriptive. Rather than have a package called `util`, create a package name that describes the functionality provided by the package. For example, say you have two helper functions: one to extract all names from a string and another to format names properly. Don't create two functions in a `util` package called `ExtractNames` and `FormatNames`. If you do, every time you use these functions, they will be referred to as `util.ExtractNames` and `util.FormatNames`, and that `util` package tells you nothing about what the functions do.

It's better to create one function called Names in a package called extract and a second function called Names in a package called format. It's OK for these two functions to have the same name, because they will always be disambiguated by their package names. The first will be referred to as extract.Names when imported, and the second will be referred to as format.Names.

You should also avoid repeating the name of the package in the names of functions and types within the package. Don't name your function ExtractNames when it is in the extract package. The exception to this rule is when the name of the identifier is the same as the name of the package. For example, the package sort in the standard library has a function called Sort, and the context package defines the Context interface.

How to Organize Your Module

There's no one official way to structure the Go packages in your module, but several patterns have emerged over the years. They are guided by the principle that you should focus on making your code easy to understand and maintain. When your module is small, keep all of your code in a single package. As long as there are no other modules that depend on your module, there is no harm in delaying organization.

As your project grows, you'll want to impose some order to make your code more readable. If your module consists of one or more applications, create a directory called *cmd* at the root of your module. Within *cmd*, create one directory for each binary built from your module. For example, you might have a module that contains both a web application and a command-line tool that analyzes data in the web application's database. Use main as the package name within each of these directories.

If your module's root directory contains many files for managing the testing and deployment of your project (such as shell scripts, continuous integration configuration files, or Dockerfiles), place all of your Go code (besides the main packages under *cmd*) into packages under a directory called *pkg*.

Within the *pkg* directory, organize your code to limit the dependencies between packages. One common pattern is to organize your code by slices of functionality. For example, if you wrote a shopping site in Go, you might place all of the code to support customer management in one package and all of the code to manage inventory in another. This style limits the dependencies between packages, which makes it easier to later refactor a single web application into multiple microservices.

For a good overview of Go project structure advice, watch Kat Zien's talk from GopherCon 2018, How Do You Structure Your Go Apps (*https://oreil.ly/0zHY4*).

Overriding a Package's Name

Sometimes you might find yourself importing two packages whose names collide. For example, the standard library includes two packages for generating random numbers; one is cryptographically secure (crypto/rand) and the other is not (math/rand). The regular generator is fine when you aren't generating random numbers for encryption, but you need to seed it with an unpredictable value. A common pattern is to seed a regular random number generator with a value from a cryptographic generator. In Go, both packages have the same name (rand). When that happens, you provide an alternate name for one package within the current file. You can try out this code on The Go Playground (*https://oreil.ly/YVwkm*). First, look at the import section:

```
import (
    crand "crypto/rand"
    "encoding/binary"
    "fmt"
    "math/rand"
)
```

We import crypto/rand with the name crand. This overrides the name rand that's declared within the package. We then import math/rand normally. When you look at the seedRand function, you see that we access identifiers in math/rand with the rand prefix, and use the crand prefix with the crypto/rand package:

```
func seedRand() *rand.Rand {
    var b [8]byte
    _, err := crand.Read(b[:])
    if err != nil {
        panic("cannot seed with cryptographic random number generator")
    }
    r := rand.New(rand.NewSource(int64(binary.LittleEndian.Uint64(b[:]))))
    return r
}
```

 There are two other symbols you can use as a package name. The package name . places all the exported identifiers in the imported package into the current package's namespace; you don't need a prefix to refer to them. This is discouraged because it makes your source code less clear as you no longer know whether something is defined in the current package or an imported one by simply looking at its name.

You can also use _ as the package name. We'll explore what this does when we talk about init in "The init Function: Avoid if Possible" on page 186.

As we discussed in "Shadowing Variables" on page 62, package names can be shadowed. Declaring variables, types, or functions with the same name as a package makes the package inaccessible within the block with that declaration. If this is unavoidable (for example, a newly imported package has a name that conflicts with an existing identifier), override the package's name to resolve the conflict.

Package Comments and godoc

Go has its own format for writing comments that are automatically converted into documentation. It's called *godoc* format and it's very simple. There are no special symbols in a godoc comment. They just follow a convention. Here are the rules:

- Place the comment directly before the item being documented with no blank lines between the comment and the declaration of the item.
- Start the comment with two forward slashes (//) followed by the name of the item.
- Use a blank comment to break your comment into multiple paragraphs.
- Insert preformatted comments by indenting the lines.

Comments before the package declaration create package-level comments. If you have lengthy comments for the package (such as the extensive formatting documentation in the fmt package), the convention is to put the comments in a file in your package called *doc.go*.

Let's go through a well-commented file. We'll start with the package-level comment in Example 9-1.

Example 9-1. A package-level comment

```
// Package money provides various utilities to make it easy to manage money.
package money
```

Next, we place a comment on an exported struct (see Example 9-2). Notice that it starts with the name of the struct.

Example 9-2. A struct comment

```
// Money represents the combination of an amount of money
// and the currency the money is in.
type Money struct {
    Value decimal.Decimal
    Currency string
}
```

Finally, we have a comment on a function (see Example 9-3).

Example 9-3. A well-commented function

```
// Convert converts the value of one currency to another.
//
// It has two parameters: a Money instance with the value to convert,
// and a string that represents the currency to convert to. Convert returns
// the converted currency and any errors encountered from unknown or unconvertible
// currencies.
// If an error is returned, the Money instance is set to the zero value.
//
// Supported currencies are:
//        USD - US Dollar
//        CAD - Canadian Dollar
//        EUR - Euro
//        INR - Indian Rupee
//
// More information on exchange rates can be found
// at https://www.investopedia.com/terms/e/exchangerate.asp
func Convert(from Money, to string) (Money, error) {
    // ...
}
```

Go includes a command-line tool called go doc that views godocs. The command go doc *PACKAGE_NAME* displays the package godocs for the specified package and a list of the identifiers in the package. Use go doc *PACKAGE_NAME.IDENTIFIER_NAME* to display the documentation for a specific identifier in the package.

> Make sure you comment your code properly. At the very least, any exported identifier should have a comment. Go linting tools such as golint and golangci-lint can report missing comments on exported identifiers.

The internal Package

Sometimes you want to share a function, type, or constant between packages in your module, but you don't want to make it part of your API. Go supports this via the special internal package name.

When you create a package called internal, the exported identifiers in that package and its subpackages are only accessible to the direct parent package of internal and the sibling packages of internal. Let's look at an example to see how this works. You can find the code on GitHub (*https://oreil.ly/ksyAO*). The directory tree is shown in Figure 9-1.

We've declared a simple function in the *internal.go* file in the internal package:

```
func Doubler(a int) int {
    return a * 2
}
```

We can access this function from *foo.go* in the foo package and from *sibling.go* in the sibling package.

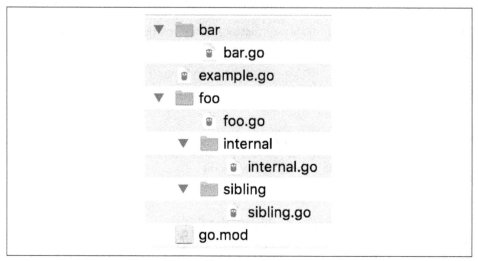

Figure 9-1. The file tree for `internal_package_example`

Be aware that attempting to use the internal function from *bar.go* in the bar package or from *example.go* in the root package results in a compilation error:

```
$ go build ./...
package github.com/learning-go-book/internal_example
example.go:3:8: use of internal package
github.com/learning-go-book/internal_example/foo/internal not allowed

package github.com/learning-go-book/internal_example/bar
bar/bar.go:3:8: use of internal package
github.com/learning-go-book/internal_example/foo/internal not allowed
```

The init Function: Avoid if Possible

When you read Go code, it is usually clear which methods and functions are invoked and when they are called. One of the reasons why Go doesn't have method overriding or function overloading is to make it easier to understand what code is running. However, there is a way to set up state in a package without explicitly calling anything: the init function. When you declare a function named init that takes no parameters and returns no values, it runs the first time the package is referenced by another package. Since init functions do not have any inputs or outputs, they can only work by side effect, interacting with package-level functions and variables.

The `init` function has another unique feature. Go allows you to declare multiple `init` functions in a single package, or even in a single file in a package. There's a documented order for running multiple `init` functions in a single package, but rather than remembering it, it's better to simply avoid them.

Some packages, like database drivers, use `init` functions to register the database driver. However, you don't use any of the identifiers in the package. As mentioned earlier, Go doesn't allow you to have unused imports. To work around this, Go allows *blank imports*, where the name assigned to an import is the underscore (_). Just as an underscore allows you to skip an unused return value from a function, a blank import triggers the `init` function in a package but doesn't give you access to any of the exported identifiers in the package:

```
import (
    "database/sql"

    _ "github.com/lib/pq"
)
```

This pattern is considered obsolete because it's unclear that a registration operation is being performed. Go's compatibility guarantee for its standard library means that we are stuck using it to register database drivers and image formats, but if you have a registry pattern in your own code, register your plug-ins explicitly.

The primary use of `init` functions today is to initialize package-level variables that can't be configured in a single assignment. It's a bad idea to have mutable state at the top level of a package, since it makes it harder to understand how data flows through your application. That means that any package-level variables configured via `init` should be *effectively immutable*. While Go doesn't provide a way to enforce that their value does not change, you should make sure that your code does not change them. If you have package-level variables that need to be modified while your program is running, see if you can refactor your code to put that state into a struct that's initialized and returned by a function in the package.

There are a couple of additional caveats on the use of `init`. You should only declare a single `init` function per package, even though Go allows you to define multiple. If your `init` function loads files or accesses the network, document this behavior, so that security-conscious users of your code aren't surprised by unexpected I/O.

Circular Dependencies

Two of the goals of Go are a fast compiler and easy to understand source code. To support this, Go does not allow you to have a *circular dependency* between packages. This means that if package A imports package B, directly or indirectly, package B cannot import package A, directly or indirectly. Let's look at a quick example to explain the concept. You can download the code from GitHub (*https://oreil.ly/CXsyd*). Our project has two sub-directories, *pet* and *person*. In *pet.go* in the `pet` package, we import `github.com/learning-go-book/circular_dependency_example/person`:

```
var owners = map[string]person.Person{
    "Bob":    {"Bob", 30, "Fluffy"},
    "Julia": {"Julia", 40, "Rex"},
}
```

While in *person.go* in the `person` package, we import `github.com/learning-go-book/circular_dependency_example/pet`:

```
var pets = map[string]pet.Pet{
    "Fluffy": {"Fluffy", "Cat", "Bob"},
    "Rex":    {"Rex", "Dog", "Julia"},
}
```

If you try to build this project, you'll get an error:

```
$ go build
package github.com/learning-go-book/circular_dependency_example
    imports github.com/learning-go-book/circular_dependency_example/person
    imports github.com/learning-go-book/circular_dependency_example/pet
    imports github.com/learning-go-book/circular_dependency_example/person:
        import cycle not allowed
```

If you find yourself with a circular dependency, you have a few options. In some cases, this is caused by splitting packages up too finely. If two packages depend on each other, there's a good chance they should be merged into a single package. We can merge our `person` and `pet` packages into a single package and that solves our problem.

If you have a good reason to keep your packages separated, it may be possible to move just the items that cause the circular dependency to one of the two packages or to a new package.

Gracefully Renaming and Reorganizing Your API

After using a module for a while, you might realize that its API is not ideal. You might want to rename some of the exported identifiers or move them to another package within your module. To avoid a backward-breaking change, don't remove the original identifiers; provide an alternate name instead.

With a function or method, this is easy. You declare a function or method that calls the original. For a constant, simply declare a new constant with the same type and value, but a different name.

When you want to rename or move an exported type, you have to use an *alias*. Quite simply, an alias is a new name for a type. We saw in Chapter 7 how to use the `type` keyword to declare a new type based on an existing one. We also use the `type` keyword to declare an alias. Let's say we have a type called Foo:

```
type Foo struct {
    x int
    S string
}

func (f Foo) Hello() string {
    return "hello"
}

func (f Foo) goodbye() string {
    return "goodbye"
}
```

If we want to allow users to access Foo by the name Bar, all we need to do is:

```
type Bar = Foo
```

To create an alias, we use the type keyword, the name of the alias, an equals sign, and the name of the original type. The alias has the same fields and methods as the original type.

The alias can even be assigned to a variable of the original type without a type conversion:

```
func MakeBar() Bar {
    bar := Bar{
        x: 20,
        S: "Hello",
    }
    var f Foo = bar
    fmt.Println(f.Hello())
    return bar
}
```

One important point to remember: an alias is just another name for a type. If you want to add new methods or change the fields in an aliased struct, you must add them to the original type.

You can alias a type that's defined in the same package as the original type or in a different package. You can even alias a type from another module. There is one drawback to an alias in another package: you cannot use an alias to refer to the unexported methods and fields of the original type. This limitation makes sense, as aliases exist to allow a gradual change to a package's API, and the API only consists of the exported parts of the package. To work around this limitation, call code in the type's original package to manipulate unexported fields and methods.

There are two kinds of exported identifiers that can't have alternate names. The first is a package-level variable. The second is a field in a struct. Once you choose a name for an exported struct field, there's no way to create an alternate name.

Working with Modules

We've seen how to work with packages within a single module, and now it's time to see how to integrate with other modules and the packages within them. After that, we'll learn about publishing and versioning our own modules and Go's centralized services: pkg.go.dev, the module proxy, and the sum database.

Importing Third-Party Code

So far, we've imported packages from the standard library like fmt, errors, os, and math. Go uses the same import system to integrate packages from third parties. Unlike many other compiled languages, Go compiles all code for your application into a single binary, whether it was code you wrote or code from third parties. Just as we saw when we imported a package from within our own project, when you import a third-party package, you specify the location in the source code repository where the package is located.

Let's look at an example. We mentioned back in Chapter 2 that you should never use floating point numbers when you need an exact representation of a decimal number. If you do need an exact representation, one good library is the decimal module from ShopSpring (*https://github.com/shopspring/decimal*). We are also going to look at a simple formatting library (*https://github.com/learning-go-book/money*) that I've written for this book. We'll use both of these modules in a small program that accurately calculates the price of an item with the tax included and prints the output in a neat format. The following code is in *main.go*:

```go
package main

import (
    "fmt"
    "log"
    "os"

    "github.com/learning-go-book/formatter"
    "github.com/shopspring/decimal"
)

func main() {
    if len(os.Args) < 3 {
        fmt.Println("Need two parameters: amount and percent")
        os.Exit(1)
    }
    amount, err := decimal.NewFromString(os.Args[1])
    if err != nil {
        log.Fatal(err)
    }
    percent, err := decimal.NewFromString(os.Args[2])
    if err != nil {
```

```
        log.Fatal(err)
    }
    percent = percent.Div(decimal.NewFromInt(100))
    total := amount.Add(amount.Mul(percent)).Round(2)
    fmt.Println(formatter.Space(80, os.Args[1], os.Args[2],
                          total.StringFixed(2)))
}
```

The two imports github.com/learning-go-book/formatter and github.com/shop
spring/decimal specify third-party imports. Note that they include the location of
the package in the repository. Once imported, we access the exported items in these
packages just like any other imported package.

Before we build our application, look at the *go.mod* file. Its contents should be:

```
module github.com/learning-go-book/money

go 1.15
```

Do a build and we'll see what happens:

```
$ go build
go: finding module for package github.com/shopspring/decimal
go: finding module for package github.com/learning-go-book/formatter
go: found github.com/learning-go-book/formatter in
    github.com/learning-go-book/formatter v0.0.0-20200921021027-5abc380940ae
go: found github.com/shopspring/decimal in github.com/shopspring/decimal v1.2.0
```

Because the location of the package is in the source code, go build is able to get the
package's module and download it. If you look in the *go.mod* file now, you'll see:

```
module github.com/learning-go-book/money

go 1.15

require (
    github.com/learning-go-book/formatter v0.0.0-20200921021027-5abc380940ae
    github.com/shopspring/decimal v1.2.0
)
```

The require section of the *go.mod* file lists the modules that you've imported into
your module. After the module name is a version number. In the case of the
formatter module, it doesn't have a version tag, so Go makes up a *pseudo-version*.

Meanwhile, a *go.sum* file has been created with the contents:

```
github.com/google/go-cmp v0.5.2/go.mod h1:v8dTdLbMG2kIc/vJvl+f65V22db...
github.com/learning-go-book/formatter v0.0.0-20200921021027-5abc38094...
github.com/learning-go-book/formatter v0.0.0-20200921021027-5abc38094...
github.com/shopspring/decimal v1.2.0 h1:abSATXmQEYyShuxI4/vyW3tV1MrKA...
github.com/shopspring/decimal v1.2.0/go.mod h1:DKyhrW/HYNuLGql+MJL6WC...
golang.org/x/xerrors v0.0.0-20191204190536-9bdfabe68543/go.mod h1:I/5...
```

Whenever you run any go command that requires dependencies (such as go run, go build, go test, or even go list), any imports that aren't already in *go.mod* are downloaded to a cache. The *go.mod* file is automatically updated to include the module path that contains the package and the version of the module. The *go.sum* file is updated with two entries: one with the module, its version, and a hash of the module, the other with the hash of the *go.mod* file for the module. We'll see what these hashes are used for in "Module Proxy Servers" on page 200.

Let's validate that our code works by passing it some arguments:

```
$ ./money 99.99 7.25
99.99          7.25                                              107.24
```

 Our sample program was checked in without *go.sum* and with an incomplete *go.mod*. This was done so you could see what happens when these files are populated. When committing your own projects to source control, always include up-to-date *go.mod* and *go.sum* files. Doing so specifies exactly what versions of your dependencies are being used.

Working with Versions

Let's see how Go's module system uses versions. I've written a simple module (*https://github.com/learning-go-book/simpletax*) that we're going to use in another tax collection program (*https://oreil.ly/gjxYL*). In *main.go*, we have the following third-party imports:

```
"github.com/learning-go-book/simpletax"
"github.com/shopspring/decimal"
```

Like before, our sample program wasn't checked in with *go.mod* and *go.sum* updated, so we could see what happens. When we build our program, we see the following:

```
$ go build
go: finding module for package github.com/learning-go-book/simpletax
go: finding module for package github.com/shopspring/decimal
go: downloading github.com/learning-go-book/simpletax v1.1.0
go: found github.com/learning-go-book/simpletax in
    github.com/learning-go-book/simpletax v1.1.0
go: found github.com/shopspring/decimal in github.com/shopspring/decimal v1.2.0
```

The *go.mod* file has been updated to:

```
module region_tax

go 1.15

require (
    github.com/learning-go-book/simpletax v1.1.0
```

```
    github.com/shopspring/decimal v1.2.0
)
```

We also have a *go.sum* with hashes for our dependencies. Let's run our code and see if it's working:

```
$ ./region_tax 99.99 12345
unknown zip: 12345
```

That looks like a wrong answer. There might be a bug in this latest version of the library. By default, Go picks the latest version of a dependency when you add it to your project. However, one of the things that makes versioning useful is that you can specify an earlier version of a module. First we can see what versions of the module are available with the `go list` command:

```
$ go list -m -versions github.com/learning-go-book/simpletax
github.com/learning-go-book/simpletax v1.0.0 v1.1.0
```

By default, the `go list` command lists the packages that are used in your project. The -m flag changes the output to list the modules instead, and the -versions flag changes `go list` to report on the available versions for the specified module. In this case, we see that there are two versions, v1.0.0 and v1.1.0. Let's downgrade to version v1.0.0 and see if that fixes our problem. We do that with the `go get` command:

```
$ go get github.com/learning-go-book/simpletax@v1.0.0
```

The `go get` command lets us work with modules, updating the versions of our dependencies.

Now if we look at *go.mod*, we'll see the version has been changed:

```
module region_tax

go 1.15

require (
    github.com/learning-go-book/simpletax v1.0.0
    github.com/shopspring/decimal v1.2.0
)
```

We also see in *go.sum* that it contains both versions of `simpletax`:

```
github.com/learning-go-book/simpletax v1.0.0 h1:iH+7ADkdyrSqrMR2GzuWS...
github.com/learning-go-book/simpletax v1.0.0/go.mod h1:/YqHwHy95m0M4Q...
github.com/learning-go-book/simpletax v1.1.0 h1:Z/6s1ydS/vjblI6PFuDEn...
github.com/learning-go-book/simpletax v1.1.0/go.mod h1:/YqHwHy95m0M4Q...
```

This is fine; if you change a module's version, or even remove a module from your project, there still might be an entry for it in *go.sum*. This doesn't cause any problems.

When we build and run our code again, the bug is fixed:

```
$ go build
$ ./region_tax 99.99 12345
107.99
```

 You might see dependencies labeled // indirect in your *go.mod* file. These are dependencies that aren't declared in your project directly. There are a few reasons why they are added to your *go.mod* file. One reason is that your project depends on an older module that doesn't have a *go.mod* file or the *go.mod* file has an error and is missing some of its dependencies. When building with modules, all dependencies must be listed in a *go.mod* file. Since the dependency declarations have to go somewhere, your *go.mod* is modified.

An indirect declaration might also be present if a direct dependency properly specifies the indirect dependency, but it specifies an older version than what's installed in your project. This happens when you explicitly update an indirect dependency with go get or downgrade a dependency's version.

Semantic Versioning

Software has had version numbers from time immemorial, but there has been little consistency in what version numbers mean. The version numbers attached to Go modules follow the rules of *semantic versioning*, also known as *SemVer*. By requiring semantic versioning for modules, Go makes its module management code simpler while ensuring that users of a module understand what a new release promises.

If you aren't familiar with SemVer, check out the full specification (*https://semver.org*). The very short explanation is that semantic versioning divides a version number into three parts: the *major* version, the *minor* version, and the *patch* version, which are written as major.minor.patch and preceded by a v. The patch version number is incremented when fixing a bug, the minor version number is incremented (and the patch version is set back to 0) when a new, backward-compatible feature is added, and the major version number is incremented (and minor and patch are set back to 0) when making a change that breaks backward compatibility.

Minimal Version Selection

At some point, your project will depend on two or more modules that all depend on the same module. As often happens, these modules declare that they depend on different minor or patch versions of that module. How does Go resolve this?

The module system uses the principle of *minimal version selection*. This means that you will always get the lowest version of a dependency that is declared to work in all of the *go.mod* files across all of your dependencies. Let's say that your module directly depends on modules A, B, and C. All three of these modules depend on module D. The *go.mod* file for module A declares that it depends on v1.1.0, module B declares that it depends on v1.2.0, and module C declares that it depends on v1.2.3. Go will import module D only once, and it will choose version v1.2.3, as that, in the words of the Go Modules Reference (*https://oreil.ly/6YRBy*), is the minimum version that satisfies all requirements.

However, as sometimes happens, you might find that while module A works with version v1.1.0 of module D, it does not work with version v1.2.3. What do you do then? Go's answer is that you need to contact the module authors to fix their incompatibilities. The import compatibility rule says that all minor and patch versions of a module must be backward compatible. If they aren't, it's a bug. In our example, either module D needs to be fixed because it broke backward compatibility, or module A needs to be fixed because it made a faulty assumption about the behavior of module D.

This isn't the most satisfying answer, but it's the most honest. Some build systems, like npm, will include multiple versions of the same package. This can introduce its own set of bugs, especially when there is package-level state. It also increases the size of your application. In the end, some things are better solved by community than code.

Updating to Compatible Versions

What about the case where you explicitly want to upgrade a dependency? Let's assume that after we wrote our initial program, there are three more versions of `simpletax`. The first fixes problems in the initial v1.1.0 release. Since it's a bug patch release with no new functionality, it would be released as v1.1.1. The second keeps the current functionality, but also adds a new function. It would get the version number v1.2.0. Finally, the third fixes a bug that was found in version v1.2.0. It has the version number v1.2.1.

To upgrade to the bug patch release for the current minor version, use the command `go get -u=patch github.com/learning-go-book/simpletax`. Since we had downgraded to v1.0.0, we would remain on that version, since there is no patch version with the same minor version.

If we upgraded to version v1.1.0 using `go get github.com/learning-go-book/simpletax@v1.1.0` and then ran `go get -u=patch github.com/learning-go-book/simpletax`, we would be upgraded to version v1.1.1.

Finally, use the command `go get -u github.com/learning-go-book/simpletax` to get the most recent version of `simpletax`. That upgrades us to version v1.2.1.

Updating to Incompatible Versions

Let's go back to our program. We're expanding to Canada, and luckily, there's a version of the simpletax module that handles both the US and Canada. However, this version has a slightly different API than the previous one, so its version is v2.0.0.

To handle incompatibility, Go modules follow the *semantic import versioning* rule. There are two parts to this rule:

- The major version of the module must be incremented.
- For all major versions besides 0 and 1, the path to the module must end in vN, where N is the major version.

The path changes because an import path uniquely identifies a package and, by definition, incompatible versions of a package are not the same package. Using different paths means that you can import two incompatible versions of a package into different parts of your program, allowing you to upgrade gracefully.

Let's see how this changes our program. First, we are going to change our import of simpletax to:

```
"github.com/learning-go-book/simpletax/v2"
```

This changes our import to refer to the v2 module.

Next, we're going to change the code in main to the following:

```
func main() {
    amount, err := decimal.NewFromString(os.Args[1])
    if err != nil {
        log.Fatal(err)
    }
    zip := os.Args[2]
    country := os.Args[3]
    percent, err := simpletax.ForCountryPostalCode(country, zip)
    if err != nil {
        log.Fatal(err)
    }
    total := amount.Add(amount.Mul(percent)).Round(2)
    fmt.Println(total)
}
```

We are now reading a third parameter from the command line, which is the country code, and we call a different function in the simpletax package. When we call go build, our dependency is automatically updated:

```
$ go build
go: finding module for package github.com/learning-go-book/simpletax/v2
go: downloading github.com/learning-go-book/simpletax/v2 v2.0.0
```

```
go: found github.com/learning-go-book/simpletax/v2 in
    github.com/learning-go-book/simpletax/v2 v2.0.0
```

We can run the program and see our new output:

```
$ ./region_tax 99.99 M4B1B4 CA
112.99
$ ./region_tax 99.99 12345 US
107.99
```

We can look at the *go.mod* file and we'll see that the new version of `simpletax` is included:

```
module region_tax

go 1.15

require (
    github.com/learning-go-book/simpletax v1.0.0 // indirect
    github.com/learning-go-book/simpletax/v2 v2.0.0
    github.com/shopspring/decimal v1.2.0
)
```

And *go.sum* has been updated as well:

```
github.com/learning-go-book/simpletax v1.0.0 h1:iH+7ADkdyrSqrMR2GzuWS...
github.com/learning-go-book/simpletax v1.0.0/go.mod h1:YqHwHy95m0M4Q...
github.com/learning-go-book/simpletax v1.1.0 h1:Z/6s1ydS/vjblI6PFuDEn...
github.com/learning-go-book/simpletax v1.1.0/go.mod h1:YqHwHy95m0M4Q...
github.com/learning-go-book/simpletax/v2 v2.0.0 h1:cZURCo1tEqdw/cJygg...
github.com/learning-go-book/simpletax/v2 v2.0.0/go.mod h1:DVMa7zPtIFG...
github.com/shopspring/decimal v1.2.0 h1:abSATXmQEYyShuxI4/vyW3tV1MrKA...
github.com/shopspring/decimal v1.2.0/go.mod h1:DKyhrW/HYNuLGql+MJL6WC...
```

The old versions of `simpletax` are still referenced, even though they are no longer used. While this doesn't cause any problems, Go includes a command to remove unused versions:

```
go mod tidy
```

After running this command, you'll see that the only version referenced in *go.mod* and *go.sum* is v2.0.0.

Vendoring

To ensure that a module always builds with identical dependencies, some organizations like to keep copies of their dependencies inside their module. This is known as *vendoring*. It's enabled by running the command `go mod vendor`. This creates a directory called *vendor* at the top level of your module that contains all of your module's dependencies.

If new dependencies are added to *go.mod* or versions of existing dependencies are upgraded with go get, you need to run go mod vendor again to update the *vendor* directory. If you forget to do this, go build, go run, and go test will refuse to run and display an error message.

Whether or not you want to vendor your dependencies is up to your organization. Older Go dependency management systems required it, but with the advent of Go modules and proxy servers (see "Module Proxy Servers" on page 200 for details), the practice is falling out of favor. The advantage of vendoring is that you know exactly what third-party code is going to be used by your project. The downside is that it dramatically increases the size of your project in version control.

pkg.go.dev

While there isn't a single centralized repository of Go modules, there is a single service that gathers together documentation on Go modules. The Go team has created a site called *pkg.go.dev* (*https://pkg.go.dev*) that automatically indexes open source Go projects. For each module, the package index publishes the godocs, the license used, the *README*, the module's dependencies, and what open source projects depends on the module. You can see the info that *pkg.go.dev* has on our simpletax module in Figure 9-2.

Figure 9-2. Use pkg.go.dev to find and learn about third-party modules

Additional Information

We've covered the most important parts of working with Go modules here, but you can learn more at the Go wiki page on Modules (*https://oreil.ly/LfIUi*).

Publishing Your Module

Making your module available to other people is as simple as putting it in a version control system. This is true whether you are releasing your project as open source on a public version control system like GitHub or a private one that's hosted within your organization. Since Go programs build from source code and use a repository path to identify themselves, there's no need to explicitly upload your module to a central library repository, like you do for Maven Central or npm. Make sure you check in both your *go.mod* file and your *go.sum* file.

When releasing an open source module, you should include a file named *LICENSE* in the root of your repository that specifies the open source license under which you are releasing your code. It's FOSS (*https://oreil.ly/KVlrd*) has a good resource for learning more about the various kinds of open source licenses.

Roughly speaking, you can divide open source licenses into two categories: permissive (which allows users of your code to keep their code private) and nonpermissive (which requires users of your code to make their code open source). While the license you choose is up to you, the Go community favors permissive licenses, such as BSD, MIT, and Apache. Since Go compiles third-party code directly into every application, the use of a nonpermissive license like the GPL would require people who use your code to release their code as open source as well. For many organizations, this is not acceptable.

One final note: do not write your own license. Few people will trust that it has been properly reviewed by a lawyer, and they can't tell what claims you are making on their project.

Versioning Your Module

Whether your module is public or private, you must properly version your module so that it works correctly with Go's module system. As long as you are adding functionality or patching bugs, the process is simple. Store your changes in your source code repository, then apply a tag that follows the semantic versioning rules we discussed in "Semantic Versioning" on page 194.

If you reach a point where you need to break backward compatibility, the process is more complicated. As we saw when we imported version 2 of the simpletax module, a backward-breaking change requires a different import path. There are a few steps to take.

First you need to choose a way to store your new version. Go supports two ways for creating the different import paths:

- Create a subdirectory within your module named *vN*, where *N* is the major version of your module. For example, if you are creating version 2 of your module, call this directory *v2*. Copy your code into this subdirectory, including the *README* and *LICENSE* files.
- Create a branch in your version control system. You can either put the old code on the branch or the new code. Name the branch *vN* if you are putting the new code on the branch, or *vN-1* if you are putting the old code there. For example, if you are creating version 2 of your module and want to put version 1 code on the branch, name the branch *v1*.

After you decide how to store your new code, you need to change the import path in the code in your subdirectory or branch. The module path in your *go.mod* file must end with */vN*, and all of the imports within your module must use */vN* as well. Going through all of your code can be tedious, but Marwan Sulaiman has created a tool that automates (*https://oreil.ly/BeOAr*) the work. Once the paths are fixed, go ahead and implement your changes.

 Technically, you could just change *go.mod* and your import statements, tag your main branch with the latest version, and not bother with a subdirectory or versioned branch. However, this is not a good practice, as it will break Go code built with older versions of the language or third-party dependency managers.

When you are ready to publish your new code, place a tag on your repository that looks like vN.0.0. If you are using the subdirectory system or keeping the latest code on your main branch, tag the main branch. If you are placing your new code on a different branch, tag that branch instead.

You can find more details on updating your code to an incompatible version in the post Go Modules: v2 and Beyond (*https://oreil.ly/E-3Qo*) on the Go Blog.

Module Proxy Servers

Rather than rely on a single, central repository for libraries, Go uses a hybrid model. Every Go module is stored in a source code repository, like GitHub or GitLab. But by default, go get doesn't fetch code directly from source code repositories. Instead, it sends requests to a *proxy server* (*https://proxy.golang.org*) run by Google. This server keeps copies of every version of virtually all public Go modules. If a module or a version of a module isn't present on the proxy server, it downloads the module from the module's repository, stores a copy, and returns the module.

In addition to the proxy server, Google also maintains a *sum database*. It stores information on every version of every module. This includes the entries that appear in a *go.sum* file for the module at that version and a signed, encoded tree description that contains the record. Just as the proxy server protects you from a module or a version of a module being removed from the internet, the sum database protects you against modifications to a version of a module. This could be malicious (someone has hijacked a module and slipped in malicious code), or it could be inadvertent (a module maintainer fixes a bug or adds a new feature and reuses an existing version tag). In either case, you don't want to use a module version that has changed because you won't be building the same binary and don't know what the effects are on your application.

Every time you download a module via `go build`, `go test`, or `go get`, the Go tools calculate a hash for the module and contact the sum database to compare the calculated hash to the hash stored for that module's version. If they don't match, the module isn't installed.

Specifying a Proxy Server

Some people object to sending requests for third-party libraries to Google. There are a few options:

- If you don't mind a public proxy server, but don't want to use Google's, you can switch to GoCenter (which is run by JFrog) by setting the `GOPROXY` environment variable to *https://gocenter.io,direct*.

- You can disable proxying entirely by setting the `GOPROXY` environment variable to `direct`. You'll download modules directly from their repositories, but if you depend on a version that's removed from the repository, you won't be able to access it.

- You can run your own proxy server. Both Artifactory and Sonatype have Go proxy server support built into their enterprise repository products. The Athens Project (*https://docs.gomods.io*) provides an open source proxy server. Install one of these products on your network and then point `GOPROXY` to the URL.

Private Repositories

Most organizations keep their code in private repositories. If you want to use a private module in another Go project, you can't request it from Google's proxy server. Go will fall back to checking the private repository directly, but you might not want to leak the names of private servers and repositories to external services.

If you are using your own proxy server, or if you have disabled proxying, this isn't an issue. Running a private proxy server has some additional benefits. First, it speeds up downloading of third-party modules, as they are cached in your company's network. If accessing your private repositories requires authentication, using a private proxy server means that you don't have to worry about exposing authentication information in your CI/CD pipeline. The private proxy server is configured to authenticate to your private repositories (see the authentication configuration documentation (*https://oreil.ly/Nl4hv*) for Athens), while the calls to the private proxy server are unauthenticated.

If you are using a public proxy server, you can set the GOPRIVATE environment variable to a comma-separated list of your private repositories. For example, if you set GOPRIVATE to:

```
GOPRIVATE=*.example.com,company.com/repo
```

Any module stored in a repository that's located at any subdomain of *example.com* or at a URL that starts with *company.com/repo* will be downloaded directly.

Wrapping Up

In this chapter, we've learned how to organize code and interact with the ecosystem of Go source code. We've seen how modules work, how to organize your code into packages, how to use third-party modules, and how to release modules of your own. In the next chapter, we're going to explore one of the signature features in Go: concurrency.

CHAPTER 10

Concurrency in Go

Concurrency is the computer science term for breaking up a single process into independent components and specifying how these components safely share data. Most languages provide concurrency via a library that uses operating system–level threads that share data by attempting to acquire locks. Go is different. Its main concurrency model, arguably Go's most famous feature, is based on CSP (Communicating Sequential Processes). It's a style for concurrency that was described in 1978 in a paper by Tony Hoare (*https://oreil.ly/x1IVG*), the man who invented the Quicksort algorithm. The patterns implemented with CSP are just as powerful as the standard ones, but are far easier to understand.

In this chapter, we are going to go through a quick review of the features that are the backbone of concurrency in Go: goroutines, channels, and the `select` keyword. Then we are going to look at some common Go concurrency patterns, and we will then learn about the situations where lower-level techniques are a better approach.

When to Use Concurrency

Let's start with a word of caution. Be sure that your program benefits from concurrency. When new Go developers start experimenting with concurrency, they tend to go through a series of stages:

1. This is *amazing*; I'm going to put everything in goroutines!
2. My program isn't any faster. I'm adding buffers to my channels.
3. My channels are blocking and I'm getting deadlocks. I'm going to use buffered channels with *really* big buffers.
4. My channels are still blocking. I'm going to use mutexes.

5. Forget it, I'm giving up on concurrency.

People are attracted to concurrency because they believe concurrent programs run faster. Unfortunately, that's not always the case. More concurrency doesn't automatically make things faster, and it can make code harder to understand. The key is understanding that *concurrency is not parallelism*. Concurrency is a tool to better structure the problem you are trying to solve. Whether or not concurrent code runs in parallel (at the same time) depends on the hardware and if the algorithm allows it. In 1967, Gene Amdahl, one of the pioneers of computer science, derived Amdahl's Law. It is a formula for figuring out how much parallel processing can improve performance, given how much of the work must be performed sequentially. If you want to dive into the details on Amdahl's Law, you can learn more in *The Art of Concurrency* (*https://oreil.ly/HaZQ8*) by Clay Breshears (O'Reilly). For our purposes, all you need to understand is that more concurrency does not mean more speed.

Broadly speaking, all programs follow the same three-step process: they take data, transform it, and then output the result. Whether or not you should use concurrency in your program depends on how data flows through the steps in your program. There are times when two steps can be concurrent because the data from one is not required for the other to proceed, and there are other times when two steps must happen in series because one depends on the other's output. Use concurrency when you want to combine data from multiple operations that can operate independently.

Another important thing to note is that concurrency isn't worth using if the process that's running concurrently doesn't take a lot of time. Concurrency isn't free; many common in-memory algorithms are so fast that the overhead of passing values via concurrency overwhelms any potential time savings you'd gain by running concurrent code in parallel. This is why concurrent operations are often used for I/O; reading or writing to a disk or network is thousands of times slower than all but the most complicated in-memory processes. If you are not sure if concurrency will help, first write your code serially, and then write a benchmark to compare performance with a concurrent implementation. (See "Benchmarks" on page 285 for information on how to benchmark your code.)

Let's consider an example. Say you are writing a web service that calls three other web services. We send data to two of those services, and then take the results of those two calls and send them to the third, returning the result. The entire process must take less than 50 milliseconds, or an error should be returned. This is a good use of concurrency, because there are parts of the code that need to perform I/O that can run without interacting with each other, there's a part where we combine the results, and there's a limit on how long our code needs to run. At the end of this chapter, we'll see how to implement this code.

Goroutines

The goroutine is the core concept in Go's concurrency model. To understand goroutines, let's define a couple of terms. The first is *process*. A process is an instance of a program that's being run by a computer's operating system. The operating system associates some resources, such as memory, with the process and makes sure that other processes can't access them. A process is composed of one or more *threads*. A thread is a unit of execution that is given some time to run by the operating system. Threads within a process share access to resources. A CPU can execute instructions from one or more threads at the same time, depending on the number of cores. One of the jobs of an operating system is to schedule threads on the CPU to make sure that every process (and every thread within a process) gets a chance to run.

Goroutines are lightweight processes managed by the Go runtime. When a Go program starts, the Go runtime creates a number of threads and launches a single goroutine to run your program. All of the goroutines created by your program, including the initial one, are assigned to these threads automatically by the Go runtime scheduler, just as the operating system schedules threads across CPU cores. This might seem like extra work, since the underlying operating system already includes a scheduler that manages threads and processes, but it has several benefits:

- Goroutine creation is faster than thread creation, because you aren't creating an operating system–level resource.

- Goroutine initial stack sizes are smaller than thread stack sizes and can grow as needed. This makes goroutines more memory efficient.

- Switching between goroutines is faster than switching between threads because it happens entirely within the process, avoiding operating system calls that are (relatively) slow.

- The scheduler is able to optimize its decisions because it is part of the Go process. The scheduler works with the network poller, detecting when a goroutine can be unscheduled because it is blocking on I/O. It also integrates with the garbage collector, making sure that work is properly balanced across all of the operating system threads assigned to your Go process.

These advantages allow Go programs to spawn hundreds, thousands, even tens of thousands of simultaneous goroutines. If you try to launch thousands of threads in a language with native threading, your program will slow to a crawl.

 If you are interested in learning more about how the scheduler does its work, listen to the talk Kavya Joshi gave at GopherCon 2018 called The Scheduler Saga (*https://oreil.ly/879mk*).

A goroutine is launched by placing the go keyword before a function invocation. Just like any other function, you can pass it parameters to initialize its state. However, any values returned by the function are ignored.

Any function can be launched as a goroutine. This is different from JavaScript, where a function only runs asynchronously if the author of the function declared it with the async keyword. However, it is customary in Go to launch goroutines with a closure that wraps business logic. The closure takes care of the concurrent bookkeeping. For example, the closure reads values out of channels and passes them to the business logic, which is completely unaware that it is running in a goroutine. The result of the function is then written back to a different channel. (We'll do a brief overview of channels in the next section.) This separation of responsibility makes your code modular, testable, and keeps concurrency out of your APIs:

```go
func process(val int) int {
    // do something with val
}

func runThingConcurrently(in <-chan int, out chan<- int) {
    go func() {
        for val := range in {
            result := process(val)
            out <- result
        }
    }()
}
```

Channels

Goroutines communicate using *channels*. Like slices and maps, channels are a built-in type created using the make function:

```go
ch := make(chan int)
```

Like maps, channels are reference types. When you pass a channel to a function, you are really passing a pointer to the channel. Also like maps and slices, the zero value for a channel is nil.

Reading, Writing, and Buffering

Use the <- operator to interact with a channel. You read from a channel by placing the <- operator to the left of the channel variable, and you write to a channel by placing it to the right:

```go
a := <-ch // reads a value from ch and assigns it to a
ch <- b   // write the value in b to ch
```

Each value written to a channel can only be read once. If multiple goroutines are reading from the same channel, a value written to the channel will only be read by one of them.

It is rare for a goroutine to read and write to the same channel. When assigning a channel to a variable or field, or passing it to a function, use an arrow before the chan keyword (ch <-chan int) to indicate that the goroutine only *reads* from the channel. Use an arrow after the chan keyword (ch chan<- int) to indicate that the goroutine only *writes* to the channel. Doing so allows the Go compiler to ensure that a channel is only read from or written by a function.

By default channels are *unbuffered*. Every write to an open, unbuffered channel causes the writing goroutine to pause until another goroutine reads from the same channel. Likewise, a read from an open, unbuffered channel causes the reading goroutine to pause until another goroutine writes to the same channel. This means you cannot write to or read from an unbuffered channel without at least two concurrently running goroutines.

Go also has *buffered* channels. These channels buffer a limited number of writes without blocking. If the buffer fills before there are any reads from the channel, a subsequent write to the channel pauses the writing goroutine until the channel is read. Just as writing to a channel with a full buffer blocks, reading from a channel with an empty buffer also blocks.

A buffered channel is created by specifying the capacity of the buffer when creating the channel:

```
ch := make(chan int, 10)
```

The built-in functions len and cap return information about a buffered channel. Use len to find out how many values are currently in the buffer and use cap to find out the maximum buffer size. The capacity of the buffer cannot be changed.

 Passing an unbuffered channel to both len and cap returns 0. This makes sense because, by definition, an unbuffered channel doesn't have a buffer to store values.

Most of the time, you should use unbuffered channels. In "When to Use Buffered and Unbuffered Channels" on page 217, we'll talk about the situations where buffered channels are useful.

for-range and Channels

You can also read from a channel using a for-range loop:

```
for v := range ch {
    fmt.Println(v)
}
```

Unlike other for-range loops, there is only a single variable declared for the channel, which is the value. The loop continues until the channel is closed, or until a break or return statement is reached.

Closing a Channel

When you are done writing to a channel, you close it using the built-in close function:

```
close(ch)
```

Once a channel is closed, any attempts to write to the channel or close the channel again will panic. Interestingly, attempting to read from a closed channel always succeeds. If the channel is buffered and there are values that haven't been read yet, they will be returned in order. If the channel is unbuffered or the buffered channel has no more values, the zero value for the channel's type is returned.

This leads to a question that might sound familiar from our experience with maps: when we read from a channel, how do we tell the difference between a zero value that was written and a zero value that was returned because the channel is closed? Since Go tries to be a consistent language, we have a familiar answer: we use the comma ok idiom to detect whether a channel has been closed or not:

```
v, ok := <-ch
```

If ok is set to true, then the channel is open. If it is set to false, the channel is closed.

 Any time you are reading from a channel that might be closed, use the comma ok idiom to ensure that the channel is still open.

The responsibility for closing a channel lies with the goroutine that writes to the channel. Be aware that closing a channel is only required if there is a goroutine waiting for the channel to close (such as one using a for-range loop to read from the channel). Since a channel is just another variable, Go's runtime can detect channels that are no longer used and garbage collect them.

Channels are one of the two things that set apart Go's concurrency model. They guide you into thinking about your code as a series of stages and making data dependencies clear, which makes it easier to reason about concurrency. Other languages rely on global shared state to communicate between threads. This mutable shared state makes it hard to understand how data flows through a program, which in turn makes it difficult to understand whether two threads are actually independent.

How Channels Behave

Channels have many different states, each with a different behavior when reading, writing, or closing. Use Table 10-1 to keep them straight.

Table 10-1. How channels behave

	Unbuffered, open	Unbuffered, closed	Buffered, open	Buffered, closed	Nil
Read	Pause until something is written	Return zero value (use comma ok to see if closed)	Pause if buffer is empty	Return a remaining value in the buffer. If the buffer is empty, return zero value (use comma ok to see if closed)	Hang forever
Write	Pause until something is read	PANIC	Pause if buffer is full	PANIC	Hang forever
Close	Works	PANIC	Works, remaining values still there	PANIC	PANIC

You must avoid situations that cause Go programs to panic. As mentioned earlier, the standard pattern is to make the writing goroutine responsible for closing the channel when there's nothing left to write. When multiple goroutines are writing to the same channel, this becomes more complicated, as calling close twice on the same channel causes a panic. Furthermore, if you close a channel in one goroutine, a write to the channel in another goroutine triggers a panic as well. The way to address this is to use a sync.WaitGroup. We'll see an example in "Using WaitGroups" on page 220.

A nil channel can be dangerous as well, but there are cases where it is useful. We'll learn more about them in "Turning Off a case in a select" on page 219.

select

The select statement is the other thing that sets apart Go's concurrency model. It is the control structure for concurrency in Go, and it elegantly solves a common problem: if you can perform two concurrent operations, which one do you do first? You can't favor one operation over others, or you'll never process some cases. This is called *starvation*.

The select keyword allows a goroutine to read from or write to one of a set of multiple channels. It looks a great deal like a blank switch statement:

```
select {
case v := <-ch:
    fmt.Println(v)
case v := <-ch2:
    fmt.Println(v)
case ch3 <- x:
    fmt.Println("wrote", x)
case <-ch4:
    fmt.Println("got value on ch4, but ignored it")
}
```

Each case in a select is a read or a write to a channel. If a read or write is possible for a case, it is executed along with the body of the case. Like a switch, each case in a select creates its own block.

What happens if multiple cases have channels that can be read or written? The select algorithm is simple: it picks randomly from any of its cases that can go forward; order is unimportant. This is very different from a switch statement, which always chooses the first case that resolves to true. It also cleanly resolves the starvation problem, as no case is favored over another and all are checked at the same time.

Another advantage of select choosing at random is that it prevents one of the most common causes of deadlocks: acquiring locks in an inconsistent order. If you have two goroutines that both access the same two channels, they must be accessed in the same order in both goroutines, or they will *deadlock*. This means that neither one can proceed because they are waiting on each other. If every goroutine in your Go application is deadlocked, the Go runtime kills your program (see Example 10-1).

Example 10-1. Deadlocking goroutines

```
func main() {
    ch1 := make(chan int)
    ch2 := make(chan int)
    go func() {
        v := 1
        ch1 <- v
        v2 := <-ch2
        fmt.Println(v, v2)
    }()
    v := 2
    ch2 <- v
    v2 := <-ch1
    fmt.Println(v, v2)
}
```

If you run this program on The Go Playground (*https://oreil.ly/trOam*), you'll see the following error:

```
fatal error: all goroutines are asleep - deadlock!
```

Remember that our `main` is running on a goroutine that is launched at startup by the Go runtime. The goroutine that we launch cannot proceed until ch1 is read, and the main goroutine cannot proceed until ch2 is read.

If we wrap the channel accesses in the main goroutine in a `select`, we avoid deadlock (see Example 10-2).

Example 10-2. Using `select` to avoid deadlocks

```
func main() {
    ch1 := make(chan int)
    ch2 := make(chan int)
    go func() {
        v := 1
        ch1 <- v
        v2 := <-ch2
        fmt.Println(v, v2)
    }()
    v := 2
    var v2 int
    select {
    case ch2 <- v:
    case v2 = <-ch1:
    }
    fmt.Println(v, v2)
}
```

If you run this program on The Go Playground (*https://oreil.ly/SdQX5*) you'll get the output:

```
2 1
```

Because a `select` checks if any of its cases can proceed, the deadlock is avoided. The goroutine that we launched wrote the value 1 into ch1, so the read from ch1 into v2 in the main goroutine is able to succeed.

Since `select` is responsible for communicating over a number of channels, it is often embedded within a `for` loop:

```
for {
    select {
    case <-done:
        return
    case v := <-ch:
        fmt.Println(v)
    }
}
```

This is so common that the combination is often referred to as a for-select loop. When using a for-select loop, you must include a way to exit the loop. We'll see one way to do this in "The Done Channel Pattern" on page 215.

Just like switch statements, a select statement can have a default clause. Also just like switch, default is selected when there are no cases with channels that can be read or written. If you want to implement a nonblocking read or write on a channel, use a select with a default. The following code does not wait if there's no value to read in ch; it immediately executes the body of the default:

```
select {
case v := <-ch:
    fmt.Println("read from ch:", v)
default:
    fmt.Println("no value written to ch")
}
```

We'll take a look at a use for default in "Backpressure" on page 218.

 Having a default case inside a for-select loop is almost always the wrong thing to do. It will be triggered every time through the loop when there's nothing to read or write for any of the cases. This makes your for loop run constantly, which uses a great deal of CPU.

Concurrency Practices and Patterns

Now that we've covered the basic tools that Go provides for concurrency, let's take a look at some concurrency best practices and patterns.

Keep Your APIs Concurrency-Free

Concurrency is an implementation detail, and good API design should hide implementation details as much as possible. This allows you to change how your code works without changing how your code is invoked.

Practically, this means that you should never expose channels or mutexes in your API's types, functions, and methods (we'll talk about mutexes in "When to Use Mutexes Instead of Channels" on page 227). If you expose a channel, you put the responsibility of channel management on the users of your API. This means that the users now have to worry about concerns like whether or not a channel is buffered or closed or nil. They can also trigger deadlocks by accessing channels or mutexes in an unexpected order.

This doesn't mean that you shouldn't ever have channels as function parameters or struct fields. It means that they shouldn't be exported.

There are some exceptions to this rule. If your API is a library with a concurrency helper function (like time.After, which we'll see in "How to Time Out Code" on page 219), channels are going to be part of its API.

Goroutines, for Loops, and Varying Variables

Most of the time, the closure that you use to launch a goroutine has no parameters. Instead, it captures values from the environment where it was declared. There is one common situation where this doesn't work: when trying to capture the index or value of a for loop. This code contains a subtle bug:

```go
func main() {
    a := []int{2, 4, 6, 8, 10}
    ch := make(chan int, len(a))
    for _, v := range a {
        go func() {
            ch <- v * 2
        }()
    }
    for i := 0; i < len(a); i++ {
        fmt.Println(<-ch)
    }
}
```

We launch one goroutine for each value in a. It looks like we pass a different value in to each goroutine, but running the code shows something different:

```
20
20
20
20
20
```

The reason why every goroutine wrote 20 to ch is that the closure for every goroutine captured the same variable. The index and value variables in a for loop are reused on each iteration. The last value assigned to v was 10. When the goroutines run, that's the value that they see. This problem isn't unique to for loops; any time a goroutine depends on a variable whose value might change, you must pass the value into the goroutine. There are two ways to do this. The first is to shadow the value within the loop:

```go
for _, v := range a {
    v := v
    go func() {
```

```
        ch <- v * 2
    }()
}
```

If you want to avoid shadowing and make the data flow more obvious, you can also pass the value as a parameter to the goroutine:

```
for _, v := range a {
    go func(val int) {
        ch <- val * 2
    }(v)
}
```

 Any time your goroutine uses a variable whose value might change, pass the current value of the variable into the goroutine.

Always Clean Up Your Goroutines

Whenever you launch a goroutine function, you must make sure that it will eventually exit. Unlike variables, the Go runtime can't detect that a goroutine will never be used again. If a goroutine doesn't exit, the scheduler will still periodically give it time to do nothing, which slows down your program. This is called a *goroutine leak*.

It may not be obvious that a goroutine isn't guaranteed to exit. For example, say you used a goroutine as a generator:

```
func countTo(max int) <-chan int {
    ch := make(chan int)
    go func() {
        for i := 0; i < max; i++ {
            ch <- i
        }
        close(ch)
    }()
    return ch
}

func main() {
    for i := range countTo(10) {
        fmt.Println(i)
    }
}
```

 This is just a short example; don't use a goroutine to generate a list of numbers. It's too simple of an operation, which violates one of our "when to use concurrency" guidelines.

In the common case, where you use all of the values, the goroutine exits. However, if we exit the loop early, the goroutine blocks forever, waiting for a value to be read from the channel:

```
func main() {
    for i := range countTo(10) {
        if i > 5 {
            break
        }
        fmt.Println(i)
    }
}
```

The Done Channel Pattern

The *done channel pattern* provides a way to signal a goroutine that it's time to stop processing. It uses a channel to signal that it's time to exit. Let's look at an example where we pass the same data to multiple functions, but only want the result from the fastest function:

```
func searchData(s string, searchers []func(string) []string) []string {
    done := make(chan struct{})
    result := make(chan []string)
    for _, searcher := range searchers {
        go func(searcher func(string) []string) {
            select {
            case result <- searcher(s):
            case <-done:
            }
        }(searcher)
    }
    r := <-result
    close(done)
    return r
}
```

In our function, we declare a channel named done that contains data of type struct{}. We use an empty struct for the type because the value is unimportant; we never write to this channel, only close it. We launch a goroutine for each searcher passed in. The select statements in the worker goroutines wait for either a write on the result channel (when the searcher function returns) or a read on the done channel. Remember that a read on an open channel pauses until there is data available and that a read on a closed channel always returns the zero value for the channel. This means that the case that reads from done will stay paused until done is closed. In searchData, we read the first value written to result, and then we close done. This signals to the goroutines that they should exit, preventing them from leaking.

Sometimes, you want to stop goroutines based on something from an earlier function in the call stack. In "Cancellation" on page 258, we'll see how to use the context to tell one or more goroutines that it is time to shut down.

Using a Cancel Function to Terminate a Goroutine

We can also use the done channel pattern to implement a pattern that we first saw in Chapter 5: return a cancellation function alongside the channel. Let's go back to our previous countTo example to see how this works. The function must be called after the for loop:

```go
func countTo(max int) (<-chan int, func()) {
    ch := make(chan int)
    done := make(chan struct{})
    cancel := func() {
        close(done)
    }
    go func() {
        for i := 0; i < max; i++ {
            select {
            case <-done:
                return
            case ch<-i:

            }
        }
        close(ch)
    }()
    return ch, cancel
}

func main() {
    ch, cancel := countTo(10)
    for i := range ch {
        if i > 5 {
            break
        }
        fmt.Println(i)
    }
    cancel()
}
```

The countTo function creates two channels, one that returns data and another for signaling done. Rather than return the done channel directly, we create a closure that closes the done channel and return the closure instead. Cancelling with a closure allows us to perform additional clean-up work, if needed.

When to Use Buffered and Unbuffered Channels

One of the most complicated techniques to master in Go concurrency is deciding when to use a buffered channel. By default, channels are unbuffered, and they are easy to understand: one goroutine writes and waits for another goroutine to pick up its work, like a baton in a relay race. Buffered channels are much more complicated. You have to pick a size, since buffered channels never have unlimited buffers. Proper use of a buffered channel means that you must handle the case where the buffer is full and your writing goroutine blocks waiting for a reading goroutine. So what is the proper use of a buffered channel?

The case for buffered channels is subtle. To sum it up in a single sentence:

Buffered channels are useful when you know how many goroutines you have launched, want to limit the number of goroutines you will launch, or want to limit the amount of work that is queued up.

Buffered channels work great when you want to either gather data back from a set of goroutines that you have launched or when you want to limit concurrent usage. They are also helpful for managing the amount of work a system has queued up, preventing your services from falling behind and becoming overwhelmed. Here are a couple of examples to show how they can be used.

In our first example, we are processing the first 10 results on a channel. To do this, we launch 10 goroutines, each of which writes its results to a buffered channel:

```
func processChannel(ch chan int) []int {
    const conc = 10
    results := make(chan int, conc)
    for i := 0; i < conc; i++ {
        go func() {
            v := <- ch
            results <- process(v)
        }()
    }
    var out []int
    for i := 0; i < conc; i++ {
        out = append(out, <-results)
    }
    return out
}
```

We know exactly how many goroutines we have launched, and we want each goroutine to exit as soon as it finishes its work. This means we can create a buffered channel with one space for each launched goroutine, and have each goroutine write data to this goroutine without blocking. We can then loop over the buffered channel, reading out the values as they are written. When all of the values have been read, we return the results, knowing that we aren't leaking any goroutines.

Backpressure

Another technique that can be implemented with a buffered channel is *backpressure*. It is counterintuitive, but systems perform better overall when their components limit the amount of work they are willing to perform. We can use a buffered channel and a `select` statement to limit the number of simultaneous requests in a system:

```go
type PressureGauge struct {
    ch chan struct{}
}

func New(limit int) *PressureGauge {
    ch := make(chan struct{}, limit)
    for i := 0; i < limit; i++ {
        ch <- struct{}{}
    }
    return &PressureGauge{
        ch: ch,
    }
}

func (pg *PressureGauge) Process(f func()) error {
    select {
    case <-pg.ch:
        f()
        pg.ch <- struct{}{}
        return nil
    default:
        return errors.New("no more capacity")
    }
}
```

In this code, we create a struct that contains a buffered channel with a number of "tokens" and a function to run. Every time a goroutine wants to use the function, it calls `Process`. The `select` tries to read a token from the channel. If it can, the function runs, and the token is returned to the buffered channel. If it can't read a token, the `default` case runs, and an error is returned instead. Here's a quick example that uses this code with the built-in HTTP server (we'll learn more about working with HTTP in "The Server" on page 249):

```go
func doThingThatShouldBeLimited() string {
    time.Sleep(2 * time.Second)
    return "done"
}

func main() {
    pg := New(10)
    http.HandleFunc("/request", func(w http.ResponseWriter, r *http.Request) {
        err := pg.Process(func() {
            w.Write([]byte(doThingThatShouldBeLimited()))
        })
```

```
            if err != nil {
                w.WriteHeader(http.StatusTooManyRequests)
                w.Write([]byte("Too many requests"))
            }
        })
        http.ListenAndServe(":8080", nil)
    }
```

Turning Off a case in a select

When you need to combine data from multiple concurrent sources, the select keyword is great. However, you need to properly handle closed channels. If one of the cases in a select is reading a closed channel, it will always be successful, returning the zero value. Every time that case is selected, you need to check to make sure that the value is valid and skip the case. If reads are spaced out, your program is going to waste a lot of time reading junk values.

When that happens, we rely on something that looks like an error: reading a nil channel. As we saw earlier, reading from or writing to a nil channel causes your code to hang forever. While that is bad if it is triggered by a bug, you can use a nil channel to disable a case in a select. When you detect that a channel has been closed, set the channel's variable to nil. The associated case will no longer run, because the read from the nil channel never returns a value:

```
// in and in2 are channels, done is a done channel.
for {
    select {
    case v, ok := <-in:
        if !ok {
            in = nil // the case will never succeed again!
            continue
        }
        // process the v that was read from in
    case v, ok := <-in2:
        if !ok {
            in2 = nil // the case will never succeed again!
            continue
        }
        // process the v that was read from in2
    case <-done:
        return
    }
}
```

How to Time Out Code

Most interactive programs have to return a response within a certain amount of time. One of the things that we can do with concurrency in Go is manage how much time a request (or a part of a request) has to run. Other languages introduce additional features on top of promises or futures to add this functionality, but Go's timeout idiom shows how you build complicated features from existing parts. Let's take a look:

```go
func timeLimit() (int, error) {
    var result int
    var err error
    done := make(chan struct{})
    go func() {
        result, err = doSomeWork()
        close(done)
    }()
    select {
    case <-done:
        return result, err
    case <-time.After(2 * time.Second):
        return 0, errors.New("work timed out")
    }
}
```

Any time you need to limit how long an operation takes in Go, you'll see a variation on this pattern. We have a `select` choosing between two cases. The first case takes advantage of the done channel pattern we saw earlier. We use the goroutine closure to assign values to `result` and `err` and to close the done channel. If the done channel closes first, the read from done succeeds and the values are returned.

The second channel is returned by the `After` function in the `time` package. It has a value written to it after the specified `time.Duration` has passed. (We'll talk more about the `time` package in "time" on page 238.) When this value is read before `doSomeWork` finishes, `timeLimit` returns the timeout error.

> If we exit `timeLimit` before the goroutine finishes processing, the goroutine continues to run. We just won't do anything with the result that it (eventually) returns. If you want to stop work in a goroutine when you are no longer waiting for it to complete, use context cancellation, which we'll discuss in "Cancellation" on page 258.

Using WaitGroups

Sometimes one goroutine needs to wait for multiple goroutines to complete their work. If you are waiting for a single goroutine, you can use the done channel pattern that we saw earlier. But if you are waiting on several goroutines, you need to use a `WaitGroup`, which is found in the `sync` package in the standard library. Here is a simple example, which you can run on The Go Playground (*https://oreil.ly/hg7IF*):

```go
func main() {
    var wg sync.WaitGroup
```

```
        wg.Add(3)
        go func() {
            defer wg.Done()
            doThing1()
        }()
        go func() {
            defer wg.Done()
            doThing2()
        }()
        go func() {
            defer wg.Done()
            doThing3()
        }()
        wg.Wait()
    }
```

A sync.WaitGroup doesn't need to be initialized, just declared, as its zero value is useful. There are three methods on sync.WaitGroup: Add, which increments the counter of goroutines to wait for; Done, which decrements the counter and is called by a goroutine when it is finished; and Wait, which pauses its goroutine until the counter hits zero. Add is usually called once, with the number of goroutines that will be launched. Done is called within the goroutine. To ensure that it is called, even if the goroutine panics, we use a defer.

You'll notice that we don't explicitly pass the sync.WaitGroup. There are two reasons. The first is that you must ensure that every place that uses a sync.WaitGroup is using the same instance. If you pass the sync.WaitGroup to the goroutine function and don't use a pointer, then the function has a *copy* and the call to Done won't decrement the original sync.WaitGroup. By using a closure to capture the sync.WaitGroup, we are assured that every goroutine is referring to the same instance.

The second reason is design. Remember, you should keep concurrency out of your API. As we saw with channels earlier, the usual pattern is to launch a goroutine with a closure that wraps the business logic. The closure manages issues around concurrency and the function provides the algorithm.

Let's take a look at a more realistic example. As we mentioned earlier, when you have multiple goroutines writing to the same channel, you need to make sure that the channel being written to is only closed once. A sync.WaitGroup is perfect for this. Let's see how it works in a function that processes the values in a channel concurrently, gathers the results into a slice, and returns the slice:

```
func processAndGather(in <-chan int, processor func(int) int, num int) []int {
    out := make(chan int, num)
    var wg sync.WaitGroup
    wg.Add(num)
    for i := 0; i < num; i++ {
        go func() {
```

```
            defer wg.Done()
            for v := range in {
                out <- processor(v)
            }
        }()
    }
    go func() {
        wg.Wait()
        close(out)
    }()
    var result []int
    for v := range out {
        result = append(result, v)
    }
    return result
}
```

In our example, we launch a monitoring goroutine that waits until all of the process-ing goroutines exit. When they do, the monitoring goroutine calls close on the out-put channel. The for-range channel loop exits when out is closed and the buffer is empty. Finally, the function returns the processed values.

While WaitGroups are handy, they shouldn't be your first choice when coordinating goroutines. Use them only when you have something to clean up (like closing a chan-nel they all write to) after all of your worker goroutines exit.

---

golang.org/x and ErrGroup

The Go authors maintain a set of utilities that supplements the standard library. Col-lectively known as the golang.org/x packages, they include a type called ErrGroup that builds on top of WaitGroup to create a set of goroutines that stop processing when one of them returns an error. Read the ErrGroup documentation (*https:// oreil.ly/_EVsK*) to learn more.

Running Code Exactly Once

As we covered in "The init Function: Avoid if Possible" on page 186, init should be reserved for initialization of effectively immutable package-level state. However, sometimes you want to *lazy load,* or call some initialization code exactly once after program launch time. This is usually because the initialization is relatively slow and may not even be needed every time your program runs. The sync package includes a handy type called Once that enables this functionality. Let's take a quick look at how it works:

```
type SlowComplicatedParser interface {
    Parse(string) string
}
```

```
var parser SlowComplicatedParser
var once sync.Once

func Parse(dataToParse string) string {
    once.Do(func() {
        parser = initParser()
    })
    return parser.Parse(dataToParse)
}

func initParser() SlowComplicatedParser {
    // do all sorts of setup and loading here
}
```

We have declared two package-level variables, parser, which is of type Slow ComplicatedParser, and once, which is of type sync.Once. Like sync.WaitGroup, we do not have to configure an instance of sync.Once (this is called *making the zero value useful*). Also like sync.WaitGroup, we must make sure not to make a copy of an instance of sync.Once, because each copy has its own state to indicate whether or not it has already been used. Declaring a sync.Once instance inside a function is usually the wrong thing to do, as a new instance will be created on every function call and there will be no memory of previous invocations.

In our example, we want to make sure that parser is only initialized once, so we set the value of parser from within a closure that's passed to the Do method on once. If Parse is called more than once, once.Do will not execute the closure again.

Putting Our Concurrent Tools Together

Let's go back to the example from the first section in the chapter. We have a function that calls three web services. We send data to two of those services, and then take the results of those two calls and send them to the third, returning the result. The entire process must take less than 50 milliseconds, or an error is returned.

We'll start with the function we invoke:

```
func GatherAndProcess(ctx context.Context, data Input) (COut, error) {
    ctx, cancel := context.WithTimeout(ctx, 50*time.Millisecond)
    defer cancel()
    p := processor{
        outA: make(chan AOut, 1),
        outB: make(chan BOut, 1),
        inC:  make(chan CIn, 1),
        outC: make(chan COut, 1),
        errs: make(chan error, 2),
    }
    p.launch(ctx, data)
    inputC, err := p.waitForAB(ctx)
```

```
            if err != nil {
                return COut{}, err
            }
            p.inC <- inputC
            out, err := p.waitForC(ctx)
            return out, err
        }
```

The first thing we do is set up a context that times out in 50 milliseconds. When there's a context available, use its timer support rather than calling time.After. One of the advantages of using the context's timer is that it allows us to respect timeouts that are set by the functions that called this function. We talk about the context in Chapter 12 and cover using timeouts in detail in "Timers" on page 262. For now, all you need to know is that reaching the timeout cancels the context. The Done method on the context returns a channel that returns a value when the context is canceled, either by timing out or by calling the context's cancel method explicitly.

After we create the context, we use a defer to make sure the context's cancel function is called. As we'll discuss in "Cancellation" on page 258, you must call this function or resources leak.

We then populate a processor instance with a series of channels that we'll use to communicate with our goroutines. Every channel is buffered, so that the goroutines that write to them can exit after writing without waiting for a read to happen. (The errs channel has a buffer size of two, because it could potentially have two errors written to it.)

The processor struct looks like this:

```
type processor struct {
    outA chan AOut
    outB chan BOut
    outC chan COut
    inC  chan CIn
    errs chan error
}
```

Next, we call the launch method on processor to start three goroutines: one to call getResultA, one to call getResultB, and one to call getResultC:

```
func (p *processor) launch(ctx context.Context, data Input) {
    go func() {
        aOut, err := getResultA(ctx, data.A)
        if err != nil {
            p.errs <- err
            return
        }
        p.outA <- aOut
    }()
    go func() {
```

```
        bOut, err := getResultB(ctx, data.B)
        if err != nil {
            p.errs <- err
            return
        }
        p.outB <- bOut
    }()
    go func() {
        select {
        case <-ctx.Done():
            return
        case inputC := <-p.inC:
            cOut, err := getResultC(ctx, inputC)
            if err != nil {
                p.errs <- err
                return
            }
            p.outC <- cOut
        }
    }()
}
```

The goroutines for getResultA and getResultB are very similar. They call their respective methods. If an error is returned, they write the error to the p.errs channel. If a valid value is returned, they write the value to their channels (p.outA for getResultA and p.outB for getResultB).

Since the call to getResultC only happens if the calls to getResultA and getResultB succeed and happen within 50 milliseconds, the third goroutine is slightly more complicated. It contains a select with two cases. The first is triggered if the context is canceled. The second is triggered if the data for the call to getResultC is available. If the data is available, the function is called, and the logic is similar to the logic for our first two goroutines.

After the goroutines are launched, we call the waitForAB method on processor:

```
func (p *processor) waitForAB(ctx context.Context) (CIn, error) {
    var inputC CIn
    count := 0
    for count < 2 {
        select {
        case a := <-p.outA:
            inputC.A = a
            count++
        case b := <-p.outB:
            inputC.B = b
            count++
        case err := <-p.errs:
            return CIn{}, err
        case <-ctx.Done():
            return CIn{}, ctx.Err()
```

```
        }
    }
    return inputC, nil
}
```

This uses a `for-select` loop to populate `inputC`, an instance of `CIn`, the input parameter for `getResultC`. There are four cases. The first two read from the channels written to by our first two goroutines and populate the fields in `inputC`. If both of these cases execute, we exit the `for-select` loop and return the value of `inputC` and a `nil` error.

The next two cases handle error conditions. If an error was written to the `p.errs` channel, we return the error. If the context has been canceled, we return an error to indicate the request is canceled.

Back in `GatherAndProcess`, we perform a standard `nil` check on the error. If all is well, we write the `inputC` value to the `p.inC` channel and then call the `waitForC` method on `processor`:

```
func (p *processor) waitForC(ctx context.Context) (COut, error) {
    select {
    case out := <-p.outC:
        return out, nil
    case err := <-p.errs:
        return COut{}, err
    case <-ctx.Done():
        return COut{}, ctx.Err()
    }
}
```

This method consists of a single `select`. If `getResultC` completed successfully, we read its output from the `p.outC` channel and return it. If `getResultC` returned an error, we read the error from the `p.errs` channel and return it. Finally, if the context has been canceled, we return an error to indicate that. After `waitForC` completes, `GatherAndProcess` returns the result to its caller.

If you trust the author of `getResultC` to do the right thing, this code can be simplified. Since the context is passed into `getResultC`, the function can be written to respect the timeout and return an error if it was triggered. In that case, we can call `getResultC` directly in `GatherAndProcess`. This eliminates the `inC` and `outC` channels from `processor`, a goroutine from `launch`, and the entire `waitForC` method. The general principle is to use as little concurrency as your program needs to be correct.

By structuring our code with goroutines, channels, and `select` statements, we separate the individual steps, allow independent parts to run and complete in any order, and cleanly exchange data between the dependent parts. In addition, we make sure that no part of the program hangs, and we properly handle timeouts set both within this function and from earlier functions in the call history. If you are not convinced that this is a better method for implementing concurrency, try to implement this in another language. You might be surprised at how difficult it is.

When to Use Mutexes Instead of Channels

If you've had to coordinate access to data across threads in other programming languages, you have probably used a *mutex*. This is short for mutual exclusion, and the job of a mutex is to limit the concurrent execution of some code or access to a shared piece of data. This protected part is called the *critical section*.

There are good reasons why Go's creators designed channels and `select` to manage concurrency. The main problem with mutexes is that they obscure the flow of data through a program. When a value is passed from goroutine to goroutine over a series of channels, the data flow is clear. Access to the value is localized to a single goroutine at a time. When a mutex is used to protect a value, there is nothing to indicate which goroutine currently has ownership of the value, because access to the value is shared by all of the concurrent processes. That makes it hard to understand the order of processing. There is a saying in the Go community to describe this philosophy: "Share memory by communicating; do not communicate by sharing memory."

That said, sometimes it is clearer to use a mutex, and the Go standard library includes mutex implementations for these situations. The most common case is when your goroutines read or write a shared value, but don't process the value. Let's use an in-memory scoreboard for a multiplayer game as an example. We'll first see how we would implement this using channels. Here's a function that we can launch as a goroutine to manage the scoreboard:

```
func scoreboardManager(in <-chan func(map[string]int), done <-chan struct{}) {
    scoreboard := map[string]int{}
    for {
        select {
        case <-done:
            return
        case f := <-in:
            f(scoreboard)
        }
    }
}
```

This function declares a map and then listens on one channel for a function that reads or modifies the map and on a second channel to know when to shut down. Let's create a type with a method to write a value to the map:

```
type ChannelScoreboardManager chan func(map[string]int)

func NewChannelScoreboardManager() (ChannelScoreboardManager, func()) {
    ch := make(ChannelScoreboardManager)
    done := make(chan struct{})
```

```
    go scoreboardManager(ch, done)
    return ch, func() {
        close(done)
    }
}

func (csm ChannelScoreboardManager) Update(name string, val int) {
    csm <- func(m map[string]int) {
        m[name] = val
    }
}
```

The update method is very straightforward: just pass a function that puts a value into the map. But how about reading from the scoreboard? We need to return a value back. That means using the done pattern to wait for the function passed to the ScoreboardManager to finish running:

```
func (csm ChannelScoreboardManager) Read(name string) (int, bool) {
    var out int
    var ok bool
    done := make(chan struct{})
    csm <- func(m map[string]int) {
        out, ok = m[name]
        close(done)
    }
    <-done
    return out, ok
}
```

While this code works, it's cumbersome and only allows a single reader at a time. A better approach is to use a mutex. There are two mutex implementations in the standard library, both in the sync package. The first is called Mutex and has two methods, Lock and Unlock. Calling Lock causes the current goroutine to pause as long as another goroutine is currently in the critical section. When the critical section is clear, the lock is *acquired* by the current goroutine and the code in the critical section is executed. A call to the Unlock method on the Mutex marks the end of the critical section.

The second mutex implementation is called RWMutex and it allows you to have both reader locks and writer locks. While only one writer can be in the critical section at a time, reader locks are shared; multiple readers can be in the critical section at once. The writer lock is managed with the Lock and Unlock methods, while the reader lock is managed with RLock and RUnlock methods.

Any time you acquire a mutex lock, you must make sure that you release the lock. Use a defer statement to call Unlock immediately after calling Lock or RLock:

```
type MutexScoreboardManager struct {
    l         sync.RWMutex
    scoreboard map[string]int
```

```
    }

    func NewMutexScoreboardManager() *MutexScoreboardManager {
        return &MutexScoreboardManager{
            scoreboard: map[string]int{},
        }
    }

    func (msm *MutexScoreboardManager) Update(name string, val int) {
        msm.l.Lock()
        defer msm.l.Unlock()
        msm.scoreboard[name] = val
    }

    func (msm *MutexScoreboardManager) Read(name string) (int, bool) {
        msm.l.RLock()
        defer msm.l.RUnlock()
        val, ok := msm.scoreboard[name]
        return val, ok
    }
```

Now that we've seen an implementation using mutexes, carefully consider your options before using one. Katherine Cox-Buday's excellent book *Concurrency in Go* (*https://oreil.ly/G7bpu*) (O'Reilly) includes a decision tree to help you decide whether to use channels or mutexes:

- If you are coordinating goroutines or tracking a value as it is transformed by a series of goroutines, use channels.

- If you are sharing access to a field in a struct, use mutexes.

- If you discover a critical performance issue when using channels (see "Benchmarks" on page 285 to learn how to do this), and you cannot find any other way to fix the issue, modify your code to use a mutex.

Since our scoreboard is a field in a struct and there's no transfer of the scoreboard, using a mutex makes sense. This is a good use for a mutex only because the data is stored in-memory. When data is stored in external services, like an HTTP server or a database, don't use a mutex to guard access to the system.

Mutexes require you to do more bookkeeping. For example, you must correctly pair locks and unlocks or your programs will likely deadlock. Our example both acquires and releases the locks within the same method. Another issue is that mutexes in Go aren't *reentrant*. If a goroutine tries to acquire the same lock twice, it deadlocks, waiting for itself to release the lock. This is different from languages like Java, where locks are reentrant.

Nonreentrant locks make it tricky to acquire a lock in a function that calls itself recursively. You must release the lock before the recursive function call. In general, be careful when holding a lock while making a function call, because you don't know what locks are going to be acquired in those calls. If your function calls another function that tries to acquire the same mutex lock, the goroutine deadlocks.

Like `sync.WaitGroup` and `sync.Once`, mutexes must never be copied. If they are passed to a function or accessed as a field on a struct, it must be via a pointer. If a mutex is copied, its lock won't be shared.

 Never try to access a variable from multiple goroutines unless you acquire a mutex for that variable first. It can cause odd errors that are hard to trace. See "Finding Concurrency Problems with the Race Checker" on page 297 to learn how to detect these problems.

---

sync.Map—This Is Not the Map You Are Looking For

When looking through the `sync` package, you'll find a type called `Map`. It provides a concurrency-safe version of Go's built-in `map`. Due to trade-offs in its implementation, `sync.Map` is only appropriate in very specific situations:

- When you have a shared map where key/value pairs are inserted once and read many times
- When goroutines share the map, but don't access each other's keys and values

Furthermore, because of the current lack of generics in Go, `sync.Map` uses `interface{}` as the type for its keys and values; the compiler cannot help you ensure that the right data types are used.

Given these limitations, in the rare situations where you need to share a map across multiple goroutines, use a built-in `map` protected by a `sync.RWMutex`.

Atomics—You Probably Don't Need These

In addition to mutexes, Go provides another way to keep data consistent across multiple threads. The `sync/atomic` package provides access to the *atomic variable* operations built into modern CPUs to add, swap, load, store, or compare and swap (CAS) a value that fits into a single register.

If you need to squeeze out every last bit of performance and are an expert on writing concurrent code, you'll be glad that Go includes atomic support. For everyone else, use goroutines and mutexes to manage your concurrency needs.

Where to Learn More About Concurrency

We've covered a few simple concurrency patterns here, but there are many more. In fact, you could write an entire book on how to properly implement various concurrency patterns in Go, and, luckily, Katherine Cox-Buday has. I've already mentioned her book, *Concurrency in Go*, when discussing how to decide between mutexes or channels, but it's an excellent resource on all things involving Go and concurrency. Check out her book if you want to learn more.

Wrapping Up

In this chapter, we've looked at concurrency and learned why Go's approach is simpler than more traditional concurrency mechanisms. In doing so, we've also clarified when you should use concurrency and learned a few concurrency rules and patterns. In the next chapter, we're going to take a quick look at Go's standard library, which embraces a "batteries included" ethos for modern computing.

The Standard Library

One of the best parts of developing with Go is being able to take advantage of its standard library. Like Python, it has a "batteries included" philosophy, providing many of the tools that you need to build an application. Since Go is a relatively new language, it ships with a library that is focused on problems faced in modern programming environments.

We can't cover all of the standard library packages, and luckily, we don't have to, as there are many excellent sources of information on the standard library, starting with the documentation (*https://golang.org/pkg*). Instead, we'll focus on several of the most important packages and how their design and use demonstrate the principles of idiomatic Go. Some packages (errors, sync, context, testing, reflect, and unsafe) are covered in their own chapters. In this chapter, we'll look at Go's built-in support for I/O, time, JSON, and HTTP.

io and Friends

For a program to be useful, it needs to read in and write out data. The heart of Go's input/output philosophy can be found in the io package. In particular, two interfaces defined in this package are probably the second and third most-used interfaces in Go: io.Reader and io.Writer.

What's number one? That'd be error, which we already looked at in Chapter 8.

Both io.Reader and io.Writer define a single method:

```
type Reader interface {
    Read(p []byte) (n int, err error)
}

type Writer interface {
    Write(p []byte) (n int, err error)
}
```

The Write method on the io.Writer interface takes in a slice of bytes, which are written to the interface implementation. It returns the number of bytes written and an error if something went wrong. The Read method on io.Reader is more interesting. Rather than return data through a return parameter, a slice input parameter is passed into the implementation and modified. Up to len(p) bytes will be written into the slice. The method returns the number of bytes written. This might seem a little strange. You might expect this:

```
type NotHowReaderIsDefined interface {
    Read() (p []byte, err error)
}
```

There's a very good reason why io.Reader is defined the way it is. Let's write a function that's representative of how to work with an io.Reader to understand:

```
func countLetters(r io.Reader) (map[string]int, error) {
    buf := make([]byte, 2048)
    out := map[string]int{}
    for {
        n, err := r.Read(buf)
        for _, b := range buf[:n] {
            if (b >= 'A' && b <= 'Z') || (b >= 'a' && b <= 'z') {
                out[string(b)]++
            }
        }
        if err == io.EOF {
            return out, nil
        }
        if err != nil {
            return nil, err
        }
    }
}
```

There are three things to note. First, we create our buffer once and reuse it on every call to r.Read. This allows us to use a single memory allocation to read from a potentially large data source. If the Read method were written to return a []byte, it would require a new allocation on every single call. Each allocation would end up on the heap, which would make quite a lot of work for the garbage collector.

If we want to reduce the allocations further, we could create a pool of buffers when the program launches. We would then take a buffer out of the pool when the function starts, and return it when it ends. By passing in a slice to io.Reader, memory alloca-tion is under the control of the developer.

Second, we use the n value returned from r.Read to know how many bytes were writ-ten to the buffer and iterate over a subslice of our buf slice, processing the data that was read.

Finally, we know that we're done reading from r when the error returned from r.Read is io.EOF. This error is a bit odd, in that it isn't really an error. It indicates that there's nothing left to read from the io.Reader. When io.EOF is returned, we are fin-ished processing and return our result.

There is one unusual thing about the Read method in io.Reader. In most cases when a function or method has an error return value, we check the error before we try to process the nonerror return values. We do the opposite for Read because there might have been bytes returned before an error was triggered by the end of the data stream or by an unexpected condition.

> If you get to the end of an io.Reader unexpectedly, a different sen-tinel error is returned (io.ErrUnexpectedEOF). Note that it starts with the string Err to indicate that it is an unexpected state.

Because io.Reader and io.Writer are such simple interfaces, they can be imple-mented many different ways. We can create an io.Reader from a string using the strings.NewReader function:

```
s := "The quick brown fox jumped over the lazy dog"
sr := strings.NewReader(s)
counts, err := countLetters(sr)
if err != nil {
    return err
}
fmt.Println(counts)
```

As we discussed in "Interfaces Are Type-Safe Duck Typing" on page 142, implemen-tations of io.Reader and io.Writer are often chained together in a decorator pat-tern. Because countLetters depends on an io.Reader, we can use the exact same countLetters function to count English letters in a gzip-compressed file. First we write a function that, when given a filename, returns a *gzip.Reader:

```
func buildGZipReader(fileName string) (*gzip.Reader, func(), error) {
    r, err := os.Open(fileName)
    if err != nil {
        return nil, nil, err
    }
    gr, err := gzip.NewReader(r)
```

```
    if err != nil {
        return nil, nil, err
    }
    return gr, func() {
        gr.Close()
        r.Close()
    }, nil
}
```

This function demonstrates the way to properly wrap types that implement io.Reader. We create an *os.File (which meets the io.Reader interface), and after making sure it's valid, we pass it to the gzip.NewReader function, which returns a *gzip.Reader instance. If it is valid, we return the *gzip.Reader and a closer closure that properly cleans up our resources when it is invoked.

Since *gzip.Reader implements io.Reader, we can use it with countLetters just like we used the *strings.Reader previously:

```
r, closer, err := buildGZipReader("my_data.txt.gz")
if err != nil {
    return err
}
defer closer()
counts, err := countLetters(r)
if err != nil {
    return err
}
fmt.Println(counts)
```

Because we have standard interfaces for reading and writing, there's a standard function in the io package for copying from an io.Reader to an io.Writer, io.Copy. There are other standard functions for adding new functionality to existing io.Reader and io.Writer instances. These include:

io.MultiReader

This returns an io.Reader that reads from multiple io.Reader instances, one after another.

io.LimitReader

This returns an io.Reader that only reads up to a specified number of bytes from the supplied io.Reader.

io.MultiWriter

This returns an io.Writer that writes to multiple io.Writer instances at the same time.

Other packages in the standard library provide their own types and functions to work with io.Reader and io.Writer. We've seen a few of them already, but there are many more. These cover compression algorithms, archives, cryptography, buffers, byte slices, and strings.

There are other one-method interfaces defined in io, such as io.Closer and io.Seeker:

```
type Closer interface {
        Close() error
}

type Seeker interface {
        Seek(offset int64, whence int) (int64, error)
}
```

The io.Closer interface is implemented by types like os.File that need to do cleanup when reading or writing is complete. Usually, Close is called via a defer:

```
f, err := os.Open(fileName)
if err != nil {
    return nil, err
}
defer f.Close()
// use f
```

If you are opening the resource in a loop, do not use defer, as it will not run until the function exits. Instead, you should call Close before the end of the loop iteration. If there are errors that can lead to an exit, you must call Close there, too.

The io.Seeker interface is used for random access to a resource. The valid values for whence are the constants io.SeekStart, io.SeekCurrent, and io.SeekEnd. This should have been made more clear by using a custom type, but in a surprising design oversight, whence is of type int.

The io package defines interfaces that combine these four interfaces in various ways. They include io.ReadCloser, io.ReadSeeker, io.ReadWriteCloser, io.ReadWrite Seeker, io.ReadWriter, io.WriteCloser, and io.WriteSeeker. Use these interfaces to specify what your functions expect to do with the data. For example, rather than just using an os.File as a parameter, use the interfaces to specify exactly what your function will do with the parameter. Not only does it make your functions more general purpose, it also makes your intent clearer. Furthermore, make your code compatible with these interfaces if you are writing your own data sources and sinks. In general, strive to create interfaces as simple and decoupled as the interfaces defined in io. They demonstrate the power of simple abstractions.

The ioutil package provides some simple utilities for things like reading entire io.Reader implementations into byte slices at once, reading and writing files, and working with temporary files. The ioutil.ReadAll, ioutil.ReadFile, and ioutil.WriteFile functions are fine for small data sources, but it's better to use the Reader, Writer, and Scanner in the bufio package to work with larger data sources.

One of the more clever functions in ioutil demonstrates a pattern for adding a method to a Go type. If you have a type that implements io.Reader but not io.Closer (such as strings.Reader) and need to pass it to a function that expects an io.ReadCloser, pass your io.Reader into ioutil.NopCloser and get back a type that implements io.ReadCloser. If you look at the implementation, it's very simple:

```go
type nopCloser struct {
    io.Reader
}

func (nopCloser) Close() error { return nil }

func NopCloser(r io.Reader) io.ReadCloser {
    return nopCloser{r}
}
```

Any time you need to add additional methods to a type so that it can meet an interface, use this embedded type pattern.

 The ioutil.NopCloser function violates the general rule of not returning an interface from a function, but it's a simple adapter for an interface that is guaranteed to stay the same because it is part of the standard library.

time

Like most languages, Go's standard library includes time support, which is found, unsurprisingly, in the time package. There are two main types used to represent time, time.Duration and time.Time.

A period of time is represented with a time.Duration, a type based on an int64. The smallest amount of time that Go can represent is one nanosecond, but the time package defines constants of type time.Duration to represent a nanosecond, microsecond, millisecond, second, minute, and hour. For example, you represent a duration of 2 hours and 30 minutes with:

```go
d := 2 * time.Hour + 30 * time.Minute // d is of type time.Duration
```

These constants make the use of a time.Duration both readable and type-safe. They demonstrate a good use of a typed constant.

Go defines a sensible string format, a series of numbers, that can be parsed into a time.Duration with the time.ParseDuration function. As described in the standard library documentation:

> A duration string is a possibly signed sequence of decimal numbers, each with optional fraction and a unit suffix, such as "300ms", "-1.5h" or "2h45m". Valid time units are "ns", "us" (or "μs"), "ms", "s", "m", "h".
>
> —Go Standard Library Documentation (*https://oreil.ly/wmZdy*)

There are several methods defined on time.Duration. It meets the fmt.Stringer interface and returns a formatted duration string via the String method. It also has methods to get the value as a number of hours, minutes, seconds, milliseconds, microseconds, or nanoseconds. The Truncate and Round methods truncate or round a time.Duration to the units of the specified time.Duration.

A moment of time is represented with the time.Time type, complete with a time zone. You acquire a reference to the current time with the function time.Now. This returns a time.Time instance set to the current local time.

 The fact that a time.Time instance contains a time zone means that you should not use == to check if two time.Time instances refer to the same moment in time. Instead, use the Equal method, which corrects for time zone.

The time.Parse function converts from a string to a time.Time, while the Format method converts a time.Time to a string. While Go usually adopts ideas that worked well in the past, it uses its own date and time formatting language (*https://oreil.ly/yfm_V*). It relies on the idea of formatting the date and time January 2, 2006 at 3:04:05PM MST (Mountain Standard Time) to specify your format.

 Why that date? Because each part of it represents one of the numbers from 1 to 7 in sequence, that is, 01/02 03:04:05PM '06 -0700 (MST is 7 hours before UTC).

For example, the following code:

```
t, err := time.Parse("2006-02-01 15:04:05 -0700", "2016-13-03 00:00:00 +0000")
if err != nil {
    return err
}
fmt.Println(t.Format("January 2, 2006 at 3:04:05PM MST"))
```

prints out:

```
March 13, 2016 at 12:00:00AM UTC
```

While the date and time used for formatting is intended to be a clever mnemonic, I find it hard to remember and have to look it up each time I want to use it. Luckily, the most commonly used date and time formats have been given their own constants in the time package.

Just as there are methods on time.Duration to extract portions of it, there are methods defined on time.Time to do the same, including Day, Month, Year, Hour, Minute, Second, Weekday, Clock (which returns the time portion of a time.Time as separate hour, minute, and second int values), and Date (which returns the year, month, and day as separate int values). You can compare one time.Time instance against another with the After, Before, and Equal methods.

The Sub method returns a time.Duration that represents the elapsed time between two time.Time instances, while the Add method returns a time.Time that is time.Duration later, and the AddDate method returns a new time.Time instance that's incremented by the specified number of years, months, and days. As with time.Duration, there are Truncate and Round methods defined as well. All of these methods are defined on a value receiver, so they do not modify the time.Time instance.

Monotonic Time

Most operating systems keep track of two different sorts of time: the *wall clock*, which corresponds to the current time, and the *monotonic clock* which simply counts up from the time the computer was booted. The reason for tracking two different clocks is that the wall clock doesn't uniformly increase. Daylight Saving Time, leap seconds, and NTP (Network Time Protocol) updates can make the wall clock move unexpectedly forward or backward. This can cause problems when setting a timer or finding the amount of time that's elapsed.

To address this potential problem, Go uses monotonic time to track elapsed time whenever a timer is set or a time.Time instance is created with time.Now. This support is invisible; timers use it automatically. The Sub method uses the monotonic clock to calculate the time.Duration if both of the time.Time instances have it set. If they don't (because one or both of the instances was not created with time.Now), the Sub method uses the time specified in the instances to calculate the time.Duration instead.

If you want to understand the sorts of problems that can occur when not handling monotonic time correctly, take a look at the Cloudflare blog post (*https://oreil.ly/IxS2D*) that detailed a bug caused by the lack of monotonic time support in an earlier version of Go.

Timers and Timeouts

As we covered in "How to Time Out Code" on page 219, the `time` package includes functions that return channels that output values after a specified time. The `time.After` function returns a channel that outputs once, while the channel returned by `time.Tick` returns a new value every time the specified `time.Duration` elapses. These are used with Go's concurrency support to enable timeouts or recurring tasks. You can also trigger a single function to run after a specified `time.Duration` with the `time.AfterFunc` function. Don't use `time.Tick` outside of trivial programs, because the underlying `time.Ticker` cannot be shut down (and therefore cannot be garbage collected). Use the `time.NewTicker` function instead, which returns a `*time.Ticker` that has the channel to listen to, as well as methods to reset and stop the ticker.

encoding/json

REST APIs have enshrined JSON as the standard way to communicate between services, and Go's standard library includes support for converting Go data types to and from JSON. The word *marshaling* means converting from a Go data type to an encoding, and *unmarshaling* means converting to a Go data type.

Use Struct Tags to Add Metadata

Let's say that we are building an order management system and have to read and write the following JSON:

```
{
    "id":"12345",
    "date_ordered":"2020-05-01T13:01:02Z",
    "customer_id":"3",
    "items":[{"id":"xyz123","name":"Thing 1"},{"id":"abc789","name":"Thing 2"}]
}
```

We define types to map this data:

```
type Order struct {
    ID          string    `json:"id"`
    DateOrdered time.Time `json:"date_ordered"`
    CustomerID  string    `json:"customer_id"`
    Items       []Item    `json:"items"`
}
```

```go
type Item struct {
    ID   string `json:"id"`
    Name string `json:"name"`
}
```

We specify the rules for processing our JSON with *struct tags*, strings that are written after the fields in a struct. Even though struct tags are strings marked with backticks, they cannot extend past a single line. Struct tags are composed of one or more tag/value pairs, written as *tagName: "tagValue"* and separated by spaces. Because they are just strings, the compiler cannot validate that they are formatted correctly, but go vet does. Also, note that all of these fields are exported. Like any other package, the code in the encoding/json package cannot access an unexported field on a struct in another package.

For JSON processing, we use the tag name json to specify the name of the JSON field that should be associated with the struct field. If no json tag is provided, the default behavior is to assume that the name of the JSON object field matches the name of the Go struct field. Despite this default behavior, it's best to use the struct tag to specify the name of the field explicitly, even if the field names are identical.

When unmarshaling from JSON into a struct field with no json tag, the name match is case-insensitive. When marshaling a struct field with no json tag back to JSON , the JSON field will always have an uppercase first letter, because the field is exported.

If a field should be ignored when marshaling or unmarshaling, use a dash (-) for the name. If the field should be left out of the output when it is empty, add ,omitempty after the name.

Unfortunately, the definition of "empty" doesn't exactly align with the zero value, as you might expect. The zero value of a struct doesn't count as empty, but a zero-length slice or map does.

Struct tags allow you to use metadata to control how your program behaves. Other languages, most notably Java, encourage developers to place annotations on various program elements to describe *how* they should be processed, without explicitly specifying *what* is going to do the processing. While declarative programming allows for more concise programs, automatic processing of metadata makes it difficult to understand how a program behaves. Anyone who has worked on a large Java project with annotations has had a moment of panic when something goes wrong and they don't understand which code is processing a particular annotation and what changes it made. Go favors explicit code over short code. Struct tags are never evaluated automatically; they are processed when a struct instance is passed into a function.

Unmarshaling and Marshaling

The Unmarshal function in the encoding/json package is used to convert a slice of bytes into a struct. If we have a string named data, this is the code to convert data to a struct of type Order:

```
var o Order
err := json.Unmarshal([]byte(data), &o)
if err != nil {
    return err
}
```

The json.Unmarshal function populates data into an input parameter, just like the implementations of the io.Reader interface. There are two reasons for this. First, just like io.Reader implementations, this allows for efficient reuse of the same struct over and over, giving you control over memory usage. Second, there's simply no other way to do it. Because Go doesn't currently have generics, there's no way to specify what type should be instantiated to store the bytes being read. Even when Go adopts generics, the memory usage advantages will remain.

We use the Marshal function in the encoding/json package to write an Order instance back as JSON, stored in a slice of bytes:

```
out, err := json.Marshal(o)
```

This leads to the question: how are you able to evaluate struct tags? You might also be wondering how json.Marshal and json.Unmarshal are able to read and write a struct of any type. After all, every other method that we've written has only worked with types that were known when the program was compiled (even the types listed in a type switch are enumerated ahead of time). The answer to both questions is reflection. You can find out more about reflection in Chapter 14.

JSON, Readers, and Writers

The json.Marshal and json.Unmarshal functions work on slices of bytes. As we just saw, most data sources and sinks in Go implement the io.Reader and io.Writer interfaces. While you could use ioutil.ReadAll to copy the entire contents of an io.Reader into a byte slice so it can be read by json.Unmarshal, this is inefficient. Similarly, we could write to an in-memory byte slice buffer using json.Marshal and then write that byte slice to the network or disk, but it'd be better if we could write to an io.Writer directly.

The encoding/json package includes two types that allow us to handle these situations. The json.Decoder and json.Encoder types read from and write to anything that meets the io.Reader and io.Writer interfaces, respectively. Let's take a quick look at how they work.

We're going to start with our data in toFile, which implements a simple struct:

```go
type Person struct {
    Name string `json:"name"`
    Age  int    `json:"age"`
}
toFile := Person {
    Name: "Fred",
    Age:  40,
}
```

The os.File type implements both the io.Reader and io.Writer interfaces, so we can use it to demonstrate json.Decoder and json.Encoder. First, we write toFile to a temp file by passing the temp file to json.NewEncoder, which returns a json.Encoder for the temp file. We then pass toFile to the Encode method:

```go
tmpFile, err := ioutil.TempFile(os.TempDir(), "sample-")
if err != nil {
    panic(err)
}
defer os.Remove(tmpFile.Name())
err = json.NewEncoder(tmpFile).Encode(toFile)
if err != nil {
    panic(err)
}
err = tmpFile.Close()
if err != nil {
    panic(err)
}
```

Once toFile is written, we can read the JSON back in by passing a reference to the temp file to json.NewDecoder and then calling the Decode method on the returned json.Decoder with a variable of type Person:

```go
tmpFile2, err := os.Open(tmpFile.Name())
if err != nil {
    panic(err)
}
var fromFile Person
err = json.NewDecoder(tmpFile2).Decode(&fromFile)
if err != nil {
    panic(err)
}
err = tmpFile2.Close()
if err != nil {
    panic(err)
}
fmt.Printf("%+v\n", fromFile)
```

You can see a complete example on The Go Playground (*https://oreil.ly/HU8Ie*).

Encoding and Decoding JSON Streams

What do you do when you have multiple JSON structs to read or write at once? Our friends json.Decoder and json.Encoder can be used for these situations, too.

Assume you have the following data:

```
{"name": "Fred", "age": 40}
{"name": "Mary", "age": 21}
{"name": "Pat", "age": 30}
```

For the sake of our example, we'll assume it's stored in a string called data, but it could be in a file or even an incoming HTTP request (we'll see how HTTP servers work in just a bit).

We're going to store this data into our t variable, one JSON object at a time.

Just like before, we initialize our json.Decoder with the data source, but this time we use the More method on json.Decoder as a for loop condition. This lets us read in the data, one JSON object at a time:

```
var t struct {
    Name string `json:"name"`
    Age  int    `json:"age"`
}

dec := json.NewDecoder(strings.NewReader(data))
for dec.More() {
    err := dec.Decode(&t)
    if err != nil {
        panic(err)
    }
    // process t
}
```

Writing out multiple values with the json.Encoder works just like using it to write out a single value. In this example, we are writing to a bytes.Buffer, but any type that meets the io.Writer interface will work:

```
var b bytes.Buffer
enc := json.NewEncoder(&b)
for _, input := range allInputs {
    t := process(input)
    err = enc.Encode(t)
    if err != nil {
        panic(err)
    }
}
out := b.String()
```

You can run this example on The Go Playground (*https://oreil.ly/gOAnt*).

Our example has multiple JSON objects in the data stream that aren't wrapped in an array, but you can also use the `json.Decoder` to read a single object from an array without loading the entire array into memory at once. This can greatly increase performance and reduce memory usage. An example is in the Go documentation (*https://oreil.ly/_LTZQ*).

Custom JSON Parsing

While the default functionality is often sufficient, there are times you need to override it. While `time.Time` supports JSON fields in RFC 339 format out of the box, you might have to deal with other time formats. We can handle this by creating a new type that implements two interfaces, `json.Marshaler` and `json.Unmarshaler`:

```go
type RFC822ZTime struct {
    time.Time
}

func (rt RFC822ZTime) MarshalJSON() ([]byte, error) {
    out := rt.Time.Format(time.RFC822Z)
    return []byte(`"` + out + `"`), nil
}

func (rt *RFC822ZTime) UnmarshalJSON(b []byte) error {
    if string(b) == "null" {
        return nil
    }
    t, err := time.Parse(`"`+time.RFC822Z+`"`, string(b))
    if err != nil {
        return err
    }
    *rt = RFC822ZTime{t}
    return nil
}
```

We embedded a `time.Time` instance into a new struct called `RFC822ZTime` so that we still have access to the other methods on `time.Time`. As we discussed in "Pointer Receivers and Value Receivers" on page 131, the method that reads the time value is declared on a value receiver, while the method that modifies the time value is declared on a pointer receiver.

We then change the type of our `DateOrdered` field and can work with RFC 822 formatted times instead:

```go
type Order struct {
    ID          string      `json:"id"`
    DateOrdered RFC822ZTime `json:"date_ordered"`
    CustomerID  string      `json:"customer_id"`
```

```
    Items        []Item        `json:"items"`
}
```

You can run this code on The Go Playground (*https://oreil.ly/I_cSY*).

There is a philosophical drawback to this approach: we have allowed the date format of the JSON we are processing to change the types of the fields in our data structure. This is a drawback to the `encoding/json` approach. You could have `Order` implement `json.Marshaler` and `json.Unmarshaler`, but that requires you to write code to handle all of the fields, even the ones that don't require custom support. The struct tag format does not provide a way to specify a function to parse a particular field. That leaves us with creating a custom type for the field.

To limit the amount of code that cares about what your JSON looks like, define two different structs. Use one for converting to and from JSON and the other for data processing. Read in JSON to your JSON-aware type, and then copy it to the other. When you want to write out JSON, do the reverse. This does create some duplication, but it keeps your business logic from depending on wire protocols.

You can pass a `map[string]interface{}` to `json.Marshal` and `json.Unmarshal` to translate back and forth between JSON and Go, but save that for the exploratory phase of your coding and replace it with a concrete type when you understand what you are processing. Go uses types for a reason; they document the expected data and the types of the expected data.

While JSON is probably the most commonly used encoder in the standard library, Go ships with others, including XML and Base64. If you have a data format that you want to encode and you can't find support for it in the standard library or a third-party module, you can write one yourself. We'll learn how to implement our own encoder in "Use Reflection to Write a Data Marshaler" on page 309.

 The standard library includes `encoding/gob`, which is a Go-specific binary representation that is a bit like serialization in Java. Just as Java serialization is the wire protocol for Enterprise Java Beans and Java RMI, the gob protocol is intended as the wire format for a Go-specific RPC (remote procedure call) implementation in the `net/rpc` package. Don't use either `encoding/gob` or `net/rpc`. If you want to do remote method invocation with Go, use a standard protocol like GRPC (*https://grpc.io*) so that you aren't tied to a specific language. No matter how much you love Go, if you want your services to be useful, make them callable by developers using other languages.

net/http

Every language ships with a standard library, but the expectations of what a standard library should include have changed over time. As a language launched in the 2010s, Go's standard library includes something that other language distributions had considered the responsibility of a third party: a production quality HTTP/2 client and server.

The Client

The `net/http` package defines a `Client` type to make HTTP requests and receive HTTP responses. A default client instance (cleverly named `DefaultClient`) is found in the `net/http` package, but you should avoid using it in production applications, because it defaults to having no timeout. Instead, instantiate your own. You only need to create a single `http.Client` for your entire program, as it properly handles multiple simultaneous requests across goroutines:

```
client := &http.Client{
    Timeout: 30 * time.Second,
}
```

When you want to make a request, you create a new `*http.Request` instance with the `http.NewRequestWithContext` function, passing it a context, the method, and URL that you are connecting to. If you are making a `PUT`, `POST`, or `PATCH` request, specify the body of the request with the last parameter as an `io.Reader`. If there is no body, use `nil`:

```
req, err := http.NewRequestWithContext(context.Background(),
    http.MethodGet, "https://jsonplaceholder.typicode.com/todos/1", nil)
if err != nil {
    panic(err)
}
```

 We'll talk about what a context is in Chapter 12.

Once you have an `*http.Request` instance, you can set any headers via the `Headers` field of the instance. Call the `Do` method on the `http.Client` with your `http.Request` and the result is returned in an `http.Response`:

```
req.Header.Add("X-My-Client", "Learning Go")
res, err := client.Do(req)
if err != nil {
```

```
    panic(err)
}
```

The response has several fields with information on the request. The numeric code of the response status is in the StatusCode field, the text of the response code is in the Status field, the response headers are in the Header field, and any returned content is in a Body field of type io.ReadCloser. This allows us to use it with json.Decoder to process REST API responses:

```
defer res.Body.Close()
if res.StatusCode != http.StatusOK {
    panic(fmt.Sprintf("unexpected status: got %v", res.Status))
}
fmt.Println(res.Header.Get("Content-Type"))
var data struct {
    UserID    int    `json:"userId"`
    ID        int    `json:"id"`
    Title     string `json:"title"`
    Completed bool   `json:"completed"`
}
err = json.NewDecoder(res.Body).Decode(&data)
if err != nil {
    panic(err)
}
fmt.Printf("%+v\n", data)
```

There are functions in the net/http package to make GET, HEAD, and POST calls. Avoid using these functions because they use the default client, which means they don't set a request timeout.

The Server

The HTTP Server is built around the concept of an http.Server and the http.Handler interface. Just as the http.Client sends HTTP requests, the http.Server is responsible for listening for HTTP requests. It is a performant HTTP/2 server that supports TLS.

A request to a server is handled by an implementation of the http.Handler interface that's assigned to the Handler field. This interface defines a single method:

```
type Handler interface {
    ServeHTTP(http.ResponseWriter, *http.Request)
}
```

The *http.Request should look familiar, as it's the exact same type that's used to send a request to an HTTP server. The http.ResponseWriter is an interface with three methods:

```
type ResponseWriter interface {
        Header() http.Header
        Write([]byte) (int, error)
        WriteHeader(statusCode int)
}
```

These methods must be called in a specific order. First, call `Header` to get an instance of `http.Header` and set any response headers you need. If you don't need to set any headers, you don't need to call it. Next, call `WriteHeader` with the HTTP status code for your response. (All the status codes are defined as constants in the `net/http` package. This would have been a good place to define a custom type, but that was not done; all status code constants are untyped integers.) If you are sending a response that has a 200 status code, you can skip `WriteHeader`. Finally, call the `Write` method to set the body for the response. Here's what a trivial handler looks like:

```
type HelloHandler struct{}

func (hh HelloHandler) ServeHTTP(w http.ResponseWriter, r *http.Request) {
    w.Write([]byte("Hello!\n"))
}
```

You instantiate a new `http.Server` just like any other struct:

```
s := http.Server{
    Addr:         ":8080",
    ReadTimeout:  30 * time.Second,
    WriteTimeout: 90 * time.Second,
    IdleTimeout:  120 * time.Second,
    Handler:      HelloHandler{},
}
err := s.ListenAndServe()
if err != nil {
    if err != http.ErrServerClosed {
        panic(err)
    }
}
```

The `Addr` field specifies the host and port the server listens on. If you don't specify them, your server defaults to listening on all hosts on the standard HTTP port, 80. You specify timeouts for the server's reads, writes, and idles using `time.Duration` values. Be sure to set these to properly handle malicious or broken HTTP clients, as the default behavior is to not time out at all. Finally, you specify the `http.Handler` for your server with the `Handler` field.

A server that only handles a single request isn't terribly useful, so the Go standard library includes a request router, `*http.ServeMux`. You create an instance with the `http.NewServeMux` function. It meets the `http.Handler` interface, so it can be assigned to the `Handler` field in `http.Server`. It also includes two methods that allow it to dispatch requests. The first method is simply called `Handle` and takes in two parameters, a path and an http.Handler. If the path matches, the http.Handler is invoked.

While you could create implementations of http.Handler, the more common pattern is to use the HandleFunc method on *http.ServeMux:

```
mux.HandleFunc("/hello", func(w http.ResponseWriter, r *http.Request) {
    w.Write([]byte("Hello!\n"))
})
```

This method takes in a function or closure and converts it to a http.HandlerFunc. We already explored the http.HandlerFunc type in "Function Types Are a Bridge to Interfaces" on page 154. For simple handlers, a closure is sufficient. For more complicated handlers that depend on other business logic, use a method on a struct, as demonstrated in "Implicit Interfaces Make Dependency Injection Easier" on page 155.

 There are package-level functions, http.Handle, http.HandleFunc, http.ListenAndServe, and http.ListenAndServeTLS that work with a package-level instance of the *http.ServeMux called http.DefaultServeMux. Don't use them outside of trivial test programs. The http.Server instance is created in the http.ListenAndServe and http.ListenAndServeTLS functions, so you are unable to configure server properties like timeouts. Furthermore, third-party libraries could have registered their own handlers with the http.DefaultServeMux and there's no way to know without scanning through all of your dependencies (both direct and indirect). Keep your application under control by avoiding shared state.

Because an *http.ServeMux dispatches requests to http.Handler instances, and since the *http.ServeMux implements http.Handler, you can create an *http.ServeMux instance with multiple related requests and register it with a parent *http.ServeMux:

```
person := http.NewServeMux()
person.HandleFunc("/greet", func(w http.ResponseWriter, r *http.Request) {
    w.Write([]byte("greetings!\n"))
})
dog := http.NewServeMux()
dog.HandleFunc("/greet", func(w http.ResponseWriter, r *http.Request) {
    w.Write([]byte("good puppy!\n"))
})
mux := http.NewServeMux()
mux.Handle("/person/", http.StripPrefix("/person", person))
mux.Handle("/dog/", http.StripPrefix("/dog", dog))
```

In this example, a request for /person/greet is handled by handlers attached to person, while /dog/greet is handled by handlers attached to dog. When we register person and dog with mux, we use the http.StripPrefix helper function to remove the part of the path that's already been processed by mux.

Middleware

One of the most common requirements of an HTTP server is to perform a set of actions across multiple handlers, such as checking if a user is logged in, timing a request, or checking a request header. Go handles these cross-cutting concerns with the *middleware pattern*. Rather than using a special type, the middleware pattern uses a function that takes in an http.Handler instance and returns an http.Handler. Usually, the returned http.Handler is a closure that is converted to an http.HandlerFunc. Here are two middleware generators, one that provides timing of requests and another that uses perhaps the worst access controls imaginable:

```
func RequestTimer(h http.Handler) http.Handler {
    return http.HandlerFunc(func(w http.ResponseWriter, r *http.Request) {
        start := time.Now()
        h.ServeHTTP(w, r)
        end := time.Now()
        log.Printf("request time for %s: %v", r.URL.Path, end.Sub(start))
    })
}

var securityMsg = []byte("You didn't give the secret password\n")

func TerribleSecurityProvider(password string) func(http.Handler) http.Handler {
    return func(h http.Handler) http.Handler {
        return http.HandlerFunc(func(w http.ResponseWriter, r *http.Request) {
            if r.Header.Get("X-Secret-Password") != password {
                w.WriteHeader(http.StatusUnauthorized)
                w.Write(securityMsg)
                return
            }
            h.ServeHTTP(w, r)
        })
    }
}
```

These two middleware implementations demonstrate what middleware does. First, we do setup operations or checks. If the checks don't pass, we write the output in the middleware (usually with an error code) and return. If all is well, we call the handler's ServeHTTP method. When that returns, we run cleanup operations.

The TerribleSecurityProvider shows how to create configurable middleware. You pass in the configuration information (in this case, the password), and the function returns middleware that uses that configuration information. It is a bit of a mind bender, as it returns a closure that returns a closure.

 You might be wondering how to pass values through the layers of middleware. This is done via the context, which we'll look at in Chapter 12.

We add middleware to our request handlers by chaining them:

```
terribleSecurity := TerribleSecurityProvider("GOPHER")

mux.Handle("/hello", terribleSecurity(RequestTimer(
    http.HandlerFunc(func(w http.ResponseWriter, r *http.Request) {
        w.Write([]byte("Hello!\n"))
    }))))
```

We get back our middleware from the `TerribleSecurityProvider` and then wrap our handler in a series of function calls. This calls the `terribleSecurity` closure first, then calls the `RequestTimer`, which then calls our actual request handler.

Because the `*http.ServeMux` implements the `http.Handler` interface, you can apply a set of middleware to all of the handlers registered with a single request router:

```
terribleSecurity := TerribleSecurityProvider("GOPHER")
wrappedMux := terribleSecurity(RequestTimer(mux))
s := http.Server{
    Addr:    ":8080",
    Handler: wrappedMux,
}
```

Use idiomatic third-party modules to enhance the server

Just because the server is production quality doesn't mean that you shouldn't use third-party modules to improve its functionality. If you don't like the function chains for middleware, you can use a third-party module called `alice` (*https://oreil.ly/_cS1w*), which allows you to use the following syntax:

```
helloHandler := func(w http.ResponseWriter, r *http.Request) {
    w.Write([]byte("Hello!\n"))
}
chain := alice.New(terribleSecurity, RequestTimer).ThenFunc(helloHandler)
mux.Handle("/hello", chain)
```

The biggest weakness in the HTTP support in the standard library is the built-in `*http.ServeMux` request router. It doesn't allow you to specify handlers based on an HTTP verb or header, and it doesn't provide support for variables in the URL path. Nesting `*http.ServeMux` instances is also a bit clunky. There are many, many projects to replace it, but two of the most popular ones are gorilla mux (*https://oreil.ly/CrQ4i*)

and chi (*https://oreil.ly/twYcG*). Both are considered idiomatic because they work with `http.Handler` and `http.HandlerFunc` instances, demonstrating the Go philosophy of using composable libraries that fit together with the standard library. They also work with idiomatic middleware, and both projects provide optional middleware implementations of common concerns.

Wrapping Up

In this chapter, we looked at some of the most commonly used packages in the standard library and demonstrated how they embody best practices that should be emulated in your code. We've also seen other sound software engineering principles: how some decisions might have been made differently given experience, and how to respect backward compatibility so you can build applications on a solid foundation.

In our next chapter, we're going to look at the context, a package and pattern for passing state and timers through Go code.

CHAPTER 12

The Context

Servers need a way to handle metadata on individual requests. This metadata falls into two general categories: metadata that is required to correctly process the request, and metadata on when to stop processing the request. For example, an HTTP server might want to use a tracking ID to identify a chain of requests through a set of micro-services. It also might want to set a timer that ends requests to other microservices if they take too long. Many languages use *threadlocal* variables to store this kind of information, associating data to a specific operating system thread of execution. This does't work in Go because goroutines don't have unique identities that can be used to look up values. More importantly, threadlocals feel like magic; values go in one place and pop up somewhere else.

Go solves the request metadata problem with a construct called the *context*. Let's see how to use it correctly.

What Is the Context?

Rather than add a new feature to the language, a context is simply an instance that meets the Context interface defined in the context package. As you know, idiomatic Go encourages explicit data passing via function parameters. The same is true for the context. It is just another parameter to your function. Just like Go has a convention that the last return value from a function is an error, there is another Go convention that the context is explicitly passed through your program as the first parameter of a function. The usual name for the context parameter is ctx:

```
func logic(ctx context.Context, info string) (string, error) {
    // do some interesting stuff here
    return "", nil
}
```

In addition to defining the Context interface, the context package also contains several factory functions for creating and wrapping contexts. When you don't have an existing context, such as at the entry point to a command-line program, create an empty initial context with the function context.Background. This returns a variable of type context.Context. (Yes, this is an exception to the usual pattern of returning a concrete type from a function call.)

An empty context is a starting point; each time you add metadata to the context, you do so by *wrapping* the existing context using one of the factory functions in the context package:

```
ctx := context.Background()
result, err := logic(ctx, "a string")
```

 There is another function, context.TODO, that also creates an empty context.Context. It is intended for temporary use during development. If you aren't sure where the context is going to come from or how it's going to be used, use context.TODO to put a placeholder in your code. Production code shouldn't include context.TODO.

When writing an HTTP server, you use a slightly different pattern for acquiring and passing the context through layers of middleware to the top-level http.Handler. Unfortunately, context was added to the Go APIs long after the net/http package was created. Due to the compatibility promise, there was no way to change the http.Handler interface to add a context.Context parameter.

The compatibility promise does allow new methods to be added to existing types, and that's what the Go team did. There are two context-related methods on http.Request:

- Context returns the context.Context associated with the request.

- WithContext takes in a context.Context and returns a new http.Request with the old request's state combined with the supplied context.Context.

Here's the general pattern:

```
func Middleware(handler http.Handler) http.Handler {
    return http.HandlerFunc(func(rw http.ResponseWriter, req *http.Request) {
        ctx := req.Context()
        // wrap the context with stuff -- we'll see how soon!
        req = req.WithContext(ctx)
        handler.ServeHTTP(rw, req)
    })
}
```

The first thing we do in our middleware is extract the existing context from the request using the Context method. After we put values into the context, we create a new request based on the old request and the now-populated context using the WithContext method. Finally, we call the handler and pass it our new request and the existing http.ResponseWriter.

When you get to the handler, you extract the context from the request using the Context method and call your business logic with the context as the first parameter, just like we saw previously:

```go
func handler(rw http.ResponseWriter, req *http.Request) {
    ctx := req.Context()
    err := req.ParseForm()
    if err != nil {
        rw.WriteHeader(http.StatusInternalServerError)
        rw.Write([]byte(err.Error()))
        return
    }
    data := req.FormValue("data")
    result, err := logic(ctx, data)
    if err != nil {
        rw.WriteHeader(http.StatusInternalServerError)
        rw.Write([]byte(err.Error()))
        return
    }
    rw.Write([]byte(result))
}
```

There's one more situation where you use the WithContext method: when making an HTTP call from your application to another HTTP service. Just like we did when passing a context through middleware, you set the context on the outgoing request using WithContext:

```go
type ServiceCaller struct {
    client *http.Client
}

func (sc ServiceCaller) callAnotherService(ctx context.Context, data string)
                                          (string, error) {
    req, err := http.NewRequest(http.MethodGet,
                "http://example.com?data="+data, nil)
    if err != nil {
        return "", err
    }
    req = req.WithContext(ctx)
    resp, err := sc.client.Do(req)
    if err != nil {
        return "", err
    }
    defer resp.Body.Close()
    if resp.StatusCode != http.StatusOK {
```

```
            return "", fmt.Errorf("Unexpected status code %d",
                            resp.StatusCode)
    }
    // do the rest of the stuff to process the response
    id, err := processResponse(resp.Body)
    return id, err
}
```

Now that we know how to acquire and pass a context, let's start making them useful. We'll begin with cancellation.

Cancellation

Imagine that you have a request that spawns several goroutines, each one calling a different HTTP service. If one service returns an error that prevents you from returning a valid result, there is no point in continuing to process the other goroutines. In Go, this is called *cancellation* and the context provides the mechanism for implementation.

To create a cancellable context, use the context.WithCancel function. It takes in a context.Context as a parameter and returns a context.Context and a context.CancelFunc. The returned context.Context is not the same context that was passed into the function. Instead, it is a *child* context that *wraps* the passed-in *parent* context.Context. A context.CancelFunc is a function that *cancels* the context, telling all of the code that's listening for potential cancellation that it's time to stop processing.

 We'll see this wrapping pattern several times. A context is treated as an immutable instance. Whenever we add information to a context, we do so by wrapping an existing parent context with a child context. This allows us to use contexts to pass information into deeper layers of the code. The context is never used to pass information out of deeper layers to higher layers.

Let's take a look at how it works. Because this code sets up a server, you can't run it on The Go Playground, but you can download (*https://oreil.ly/qQy5c*) it. First we'll set up two servers in a file called *servers.go*:

```
func slowServer() *httptest.Server {
    s := httptest.NewServer(http.HandlerFunc(func(w http.ResponseWriter,
        r *http.Request) {
        time.Sleep(2 * time.Second)
        w.Write([]byte("Slow response"))
    }))
    return s
}
```

```
func fastServer() *httptest.Server {
    s := httptest.NewServer(http.HandlerFunc(func(w http.ResponseWriter,
        r *http.Request) {
        if r.URL.Query().Get("error") == "true" {
            w.Write([]byte("error"))
            return
        }
        w.Write([]byte("ok"))
    }))
    return s
}
```

These functions launch servers when they are called. One server sleeps for two seconds and then returns the message Slow response. The other checks to see if there is a query parameter error set to true. If there is, it returns the message error. Otherwise, it returns the message ok.

 We are using the httptest.Server, which makes it easier to write unit tests for code that talks to remote servers. It's useful here since both the client and the server are within the same program. We'll learn more about httptest.Server in "httptest" on page 293.

Next, we're going to write the client portion of the code in a file called *client.go*:

```
var client = http.Client{}

func callBoth(ctx context.Context, errVal string, slowURL string,
            fastURL string) {
    ctx, cancel := context.WithCancel(ctx)
    defer cancel()
    var wg sync.WaitGroup
    wg.Add(2)
    go func() {
        defer wg.Done()
        err := callServer(ctx, "slow", slowURL)
        if err != nil {
            cancel()
        }
    }()
    go func() {
        defer wg.Done()
        err := callServer(ctx, "fast", fastURL+"?error="+errVal)
        if err != nil {
            cancel()
        }
    }()
    wg.Wait()
    fmt.Println("done with both")
}
```

```
func callServer(ctx context.Context, label string, url string) error {
    req, err := http.NewRequestWithContext(ctx, http.MethodGet, url, nil)
    if err != nil {
        fmt.Println(label, "request err:", err)
        return err
    }
    resp, err := client.Do(req)
    if err != nil {
        fmt.Println(label, "response err:", err)
        return err
    }
    data, err := ioutil.ReadAll(resp.Body)
    if err != nil {
        fmt.Println(label, "read err:", err)
        return err
    }
    result := string(data)
    if result != "" {
        fmt.Println(label, "result:", result)
    }
    if result == "error" {
        fmt.Println("cancelling from", label)
        return errors.New("error happened")
    }
    return nil
}
```

All of the interesting stuff is in this file. First, our callBoth function creates a cancellable context and a cancellation function from the passed-in context. By convention, this function variable is named cancel. It is important to remember that any time you create a cancellable context, you *must* call the cancel function. It is fine to call it more than once; every invocation after the first is ignored. We use a defer to make sure that it is eventually called. Next, we set up two goroutines and pass the cancellable context, a label, and the URL to callServer, and wait for them both to complete. If either call to callServer returns an error, we call the cancel function.

The callServer function is a simple client. We create our requests with the cancellable context and make a call. If an error happens, or if we get the string error returned, we return the error.

Finally, we have the main function, which kicks off the program, in the file *main.go*:

```
func main() {
    ss := slowServer()
    defer ss.Close()
    fs := fastServer()
    defer fs.Close()

    ctx := context.Background()
    callBoth(ctx, os.Args[1], ss.URL, fs.URL)
}
```

In main, we start the servers, create a context, and then call the clients with the context, the first argument to our program, and the URLs for our servers.

Here's what happens if you run without an error:

```
$ make run-ok
go build
./context_cancel false
fast result: ok
slow result: Slow response
done with both
```

And here's what happens if an error is triggered:

```
$ make run-cancel
go build
./context_cancel true
fast result: error
cancelling from fast
slow response err: Get "http://127.0.0.1:38804": context canceled
done with both
```

 Any time you create a context that has an associated cancel function, you *must* call that cancel function when you are done processing, whether or not your processing ends in an error. If you do not, your program will leak resources (memory and goroutines) and eventually slow down or crash. There is no error if you call the cancel function more than once; any invocation after the first does nothing. The easiest way to make sure you call the cancel function is to use defer to invoke it right after the cancel function is returned.

While manual cancellation is useful, it's not your only option. In the next section, we'll see how to automate cancellation with timeouts.

Handling Server Shutdown

You probably noticed that the program didn't exit immediately when the error is triggered. That's because it's waiting for the slowServer to close. If you lengthen the timeout from 2 seconds to 6 seconds or more, you'll see an error message that starts with httptest.Server blocked in Close after 5 seconds, waiting for connec tions.

If we rewrite slowServer() to properly handle context cancellation, we can shut it down immediately:

```
func slowServer() *httptest.Server {
    s := httptest.NewServer(http.HandlerFunc(func(w http.ResponseWriter,
                                              r *http.Request) {
```

```
        ctx := r.Context()
        select {
        case <-ctx.Done():
            fmt.Println("server shut down")
            return
        case <-time.After(6 * time.Second):
            w.Write([]byte("Slow response"))
        }
    }))
    return s
}
```

Timers

One of the most important jobs for a server is managing requests. A novice programmer often thinks that a server should take as many requests as it possibly can and
work on them for as long as it can until it returns a result for each client.

The problem is that this approach does not scale. A server is a shared resource. Like
all shared resources, each user wants to get as much as they can out of it and isn't
terribly concerned with the needs of other users. It's the responsibility of the shared
resource to manage itself so that it provides a fair amount of time to all of its users.

There are generally four things that a server can do to manage its load:

- Limit simultaneous requests
- Limit how many requests are queued waiting to run
- Limit how long a request can run
- Limit the resources a request can use (such as memory or disk space)

Go provides tools to handle the first three. We saw how to handle the first two when
learning about concurrency in Chapter 10. By limiting the number of goroutines, a
server manages simultaneous load. The size of the waiting queue is handled via buffered channels.

The context provides a way to control how long a request runs. When building an
application, you should have an idea of your performance envelope: how long you
have for your request to complete before the user has an unsatisfactory experience. If
you know the maximum amount of time that a request can run, you can enforce it
using the context.

If you want to limit the memory or disk space that a request uses, you'll have to write the code to manage that yourself. Discussion of this topic is beyond the scope of this book.

You can use one of two different functions to create a time-limited context. The first is context.WithTimeout. It takes two parameters, an existing context and time.Duration that specifies the duration until the context automatically cancels. It returns a context that automatically triggers a cancellation after the specified duration as well as a cancellation function that is invoked to cancel the context immediately.

The second function is context.WithDeadline. This function takes in an existing context and a time.Time that specifies the time when the context is automatically canceled. Like context.WithTimeout, it returns a context that automatically triggers a cancellation after the specified time has elapsed as well as a cancellation function.

If you pass a time in the past to context.WithDeadline, the context is created already canceled.

If you want to find out when a context will automatically cancel, use the Deadline method on context.Context. It returns a time.Time that indicates the time and a bool that indicates if there was a timeout set. This mirrors the comma ok idiom we use when reading from maps or channels.

When you set a time limit for the overall duration of the request, you might want to subdivide that time. And if you call another service from your service, you might want to limit how long you allow the network call to run, reserving some time for the rest of your processing or for other network calls. You control how long an individual call takes by creating a child context that wraps a parent context using context.WithTimeout or context.WithDeadline.

Any timeout that you set on the child context is bounded by the timeout set on the parent context; if a parent context times out in two seconds, you can declare that a child context times out in three seconds, but when the parent context times out after two seconds, so will the child.

We can see this with a simple program:

```
ctx := context.Background()
parent, cancel := context.WithTimeout(ctx, 2*time.Second)
defer cancel()
child, cancel2 := context.WithTimeout(parent, 3*time.Second)
defer cancel2()
```

```
start := time.Now()
<-child.Done()
end := time.Now()
fmt.Println(end.Sub(start))
```

In this sample, we specify a two-second timeout on the parent context and a three-second timeout on the child context. We then wait for the child context to complete by waiting on the channel returned from the Done method on the child context.Context. We'll talk more about the Done method in the next section.

You can run this code on The Go Playground (*https://oreil.ly/FS8h2*) and you'll see the following result:

```
2s
```

Handling Context Cancellation in Your Own Code

Most of the time, you don't need to worry about timeouts or cancellation within your own code; it simply doesn't run for long enough. Whenever you call another HTTP service or the database, you should pass along the context; those libraries properly handle cancellation via the context.

If you do write code that should be interrupted by a context cancellation, you implement the cancellation checks using the concurrency features that we looked at in Chapter 10. The context.Context type has two methods that are used when managing cancellation.

The Done method returns a channel of struct{}. (The reason this is the chosen return type is that an empty struct uses no memory.) The channel is closed when the context is canceled due to a timer or the cancel function being invoked. Remember, a closed channel always immediately returns its zero value when you attempt to read it.

 If you call Done on a context that isn't cancellable, it returns nil. As we covered in Chapter 10, a read from a nil channel never returns. If this is not done inside a case in a select statement, your program will hang.

The Err method returns nil if the context is still active, or it returns one of two sentinel errors if the context has been canceled: context.Canceled and context.DeadlineExceeded. The first is returned after explicit cancellation, and the second is returned when a timeout triggered cancellation.

Here's the pattern for supporting context cancellation in your code:

```
func longRunningThingManager(ctx context.Context, data string) (string, error) {
    type wrapper struct {
        result string
```

```
        err    error
    }
    ch := make(chan wrapper, 1)
    go func() {
        // do the long running thing
        result, err := longRunningThing(ctx, data)
        ch <- wrapper{result, err}
    }()
    select {
    case data := <-ch:
        return data.result, data.err
    case <-ctx.Done():
        return "", ctx.Err()
    }
}
```

In our code, we need to put the data returned from our long-running function into a struct, so we can pass it on a channel. We then create a channel of type wrapper with buffer size 1. By buffering the channel, we allow the goroutine to exit, even if the buffered value is never read due to cancellation.

In the goroutine, we take the output from the long-running function and put it in the buffered channel. We then have a select with two cases. In our first select case, we read the data from the long-running function and return it. This is the case that's triggered if the context isn't canceled due to timeout or invocation of the cancel function. The second select case is triggered if the context is canceled. We return the zero value for the data and the error from the context to tell us why it was canceled.

This looks a lot like the pattern we saw in Chapter 11, when we learned how to use time.After to set a time limit on the execution of code. In this case, the time limit (or the cancellation condition) is specified via context factory methods, but the general implementation is the same.

Values

There is one more use for the context. It also provides a way to pass per-request metadata through your program.

By default, you should prefer to pass data through explicit parameters. As has been mentioned before, idiomatic Go favors the explicit over the implicit, and this includes explicit data passing. If a function depends on some data, it should be clear where it came from.

However, there are some cases where you cannot pass data explicitly. The most common situation is an HTTP request handler and its associated middleware. As we have seen, all HTTP request handlers have two parameters, one for the request and one for the response. If you want to make a value available to your handler in middleware, you need to store it in the context. Some possible situations include extracting a user from a JWT (JSON Web Token) or creating a per-request GUID that is passed through multiple layers of middleware and into your handler and business logic.

Just like there are factory methods in the `context` package to create timed and cancellable contexts, there is a factory method for putting values into the context, `context.WithValue`. It takes in three values: a context to wrap, a key to look up the value, and the value itself. It returns a child context that contains the key-value pair. The type of the key and the value parameters are declared to be empty interfaces (`interface{}`).

To check if a value is in a context or any of its parents, use the `Value` method on `context.Context`. This method takes in a key and returns the value associated with the key. Again, both the key parameter and the value result are declared to be of type `interface{}`. If no value is found for the supplied key, `nil` is returned. Use the comma ok idiom to type assert the returned value to the correct type.

If you are familiar with data structures, you might recognize that searching for values stored in the context chain is a *linear* search. This has no serious performance implications when there are only a few values, but it would perform poorly if you stored dozens of values in the context during a request. That said, if your program is creating a context chain with dozens of values, your program probably needs some refactoring.

While the value stored in the context can be of any type, there is an idiomatic pattern that's used to guarantee the key's uniqueness. Like the key for a `map`, the key for context value must be comparable. Create a new, unexported type for the key, based on an `int`:

```
type userKey int
```

If you use a string or another public type for the type of the key, different packages could create identical keys, resulting in collisions. This causes problems that are hard to debug, such as one package writing data to the context that masks the data written by another package or reading data from the context that was written by another package.

After declaring your unexported key type, you then declare an unexported constant of that type:

```
const key userKey = 1
```

With both the type and the constant of the key being unexported, no code from outside of your package can put data into the context that would cause a collision. If your package needs to put multiple values into the context, define a different key of the same type for each value, using the `iota` pattern we looked at in "iota Is for Enumerations—Sometimes" on page 137. Since we only care about the constant's value as a way to differentiate between multiple keys, this is a perfect use for iota.

Next, build an API to place a value into the context and to read the value from the context. Make these functions public only if code outside your package should be able to read and write your context values. The name of the function that creates a context with the value should start with ContextWith. The function that returns the value from the context should have a name that ends with FromContext. Here are the implementations of our functions to get and read the user from the context:

```
func ContextWithUser(ctx context.Context, user string) context.Context {
    return context.WithValue(ctx, key, user)
}

func UserFromContext(ctx context.Context) (string, bool) {
    user, ok := ctx.Value(key).(string)
    return user, ok
}
```

Now that we've written our user management code, let's see how to use it. We're going to write middleware that extracts a user ID from a cookie:

```
// a real implementation would be signed to make sure
// the user didn't spoof their identity
func extractUser(req *http.Request) (string, error) {
    userCookie, err := req.Cookie("user")
    if err != nil {
        return "", err
    }
    return userCookie.Value, nil
}

func Middleware(h http.Handler) http.Handler {
    return http.HandlerFunc(func(rw http.ResponseWriter, req *http.Request) {
        user, err := extractUser(req)
        if err != nil {
            rw.WriteHeader(http.StatusUnauthorized)
            return
        }
        ctx := req.Context()
        ctx = ContextWithUser(ctx, user)
        req = req.WithContext(ctx)
        h.ServeHTTP(rw, req)
    })
}
```

In the middleware, we first get our user value. Next, we extract the context from the request with the Context method and create a new context that contains the user with our ContextWithUser function. Then we make a new request from the old request and the new context using the WithContext method. Finally, we call the next function in our handler chain with our new request and the supplied http.ResponseWriter.

In most cases, you want to extract the value from the context in your request handler and pass it in to your business logic explicitly. Go functions have explicit parameters and you shouldn't use the context as a way to sneak values past the API:

```go
func (c Controller) handleRequest(rw http.ResponseWriter, req *http.Request) {
    ctx := req.Context()
    user, ok := identity.UserFromContext(ctx)
    if !ok {
        rw.WriteHeader(http.StatusInternalServerError)
        return
    }
    data := req.URL.Query().Get("data")
    result, err := c.Logic.businessLogic(ctx, user, data)
    if err != nil {
        rw.WriteHeader(http.StatusInternalServerError)
        rw.Write([]byte(err.Error()))
        return
    }
    rw.Write([]byte(result))
}
```

Our handler gets the context using the Context method on the request, extracts the user from the context using our UserFromContext function, and then calls the business logic.

There are some situations where it's better to keep a value in the context. The tracking GUID that was mentioned earlier is one. This information is meant for management of your application; it is not part of your business state. Passing it explicitly through your code adds additional parameters and prevents integration with third-party libraries that do not know about your metainformation. By leaving a tracking GUID in the context, it passes invisibly through business logic that doesn't need to know about tracking and is available when your program writes a log message or connects to another server.

Here is a simple context-aware GUID implementation that tracks from service to service and creates logs with the GUID included:

```go
package tracker

import (
    "context"
    "fmt"
    "net/http"
    "github.com/google/uuid"
)

type guidKey int
```

```
const key guidKey = 1

func contextWithGUID(ctx context.Context, guid string) context.Context {
    return context.WithValue(ctx, key, guid)
}

func guidFromContext(ctx context.Context) (string, bool) {
    g, ok := ctx.Value(key).(string)
    return g, ok
}

func Middleware(h http.Handler) http.Handler {
    return http.HandlerFunc(func(rw http.ResponseWriter, req *http.Request) {
        ctx := req.Context()
        if guid := req.Header.Get("X-GUID"); guid != "" {
            ctx = contextWithGUID(ctx, guid)
        } else {
            ctx = contextWithGUID(ctx, uuid.New().String())
        }
        req = req.WithContext(ctx)
        h.ServeHTTP(rw, req)
    })
}

type Logger struct{}

func (Logger) Log(ctx context.Context, message string) {
    if guid, ok := guidFromContext(ctx); ok {
        message = fmt.Sprintf("GUID: %s - %s", guid, message)
    }
    // do logging
    fmt.Println(message)
}

func Request(req *http.Request) *http.Request {
    ctx := req.Context()
    if guid, ok := guidFromContext(ctx); ok {
        req.Header.Add("X-GUID", guid)
    }
    return req
}
```

The Middleware function either extracts the GUID from the incoming request or generates a new GUID. In both cases, it places the GUID into the context, creates a new request with the updated context, and continues the call chain.

Next we see how this GUID is used. The Logger struct provides a generic logging method that takes in a context and a string. If there's a GUID in the context, it appends it to the beginning of the log message and outputs it. The Request function is used when this service makes a call to another service. It takes in an `*http.Request`, adds a header with the GUID if it exists in the context, and returns the `*http.Request`.

Once we have this package, we can use the dependency injection techniques that we discussed in "Implicit Interfaces Make Dependency Injection Easier" on page 155 to create business logic that is completely unaware of any tracking information. First, we declare an interface to represent our logger, a function type to represent a request decorator, and a business logic struct that depends on them:

```
type Logger interface {
    Log(context.Context, string)
}

type RequestDecorator func(*http.Request) *http.Request

type BusinessLogic struct {
    RequestDecorator RequestDecorator
    Logger           Logger
    Remote           string
}
```

Next, we implement our business logic:

```
func (bl BusinessLogic) businessLogic(
    ctx context.Context, user string, data string) (string, error) {
    bl.Logger.Log(ctx, "starting businessLogic for " + user + " with "+ data)
    req, err := http.NewRequestWithContext(ctx,
        http.MethodGet, bl.Remote+"?query="+data, nil)
    if err != nil {
        bl.Logger.Log(ctx, "error building remote request:" + err)
        return "", err
    }
    req = bl.RequestDecorator(req)
    resp, err := http.DefaultClient.Do(req)
    // processing continues
}
```

The GUID is passed through to the logger and the request decorator without the business logic being aware of it, separating the data needed for program logic from the data needed for program management. The only place that's aware of the association is the code in main that wires up our dependencies:

```
bl := BusinessLogic{
    RequestDecorator: tracker.Request,
    Logger:           tracker.Logger{},
    Remote:           "http://www.example.com/query",
}
```

You can find the complete code for the user middleware and the GUID tracker on GitHub (*https://oreil.ly/oyhmP*).

Use the context to pass values through standard APIs. Copy values from the context into explicit parameters when they are needed for processing business logic. System maintenance information can be accessed directly from the context.

Wrapping Up

In this chapter, we learned how to manage request metadata using the context. We can now set timeouts, perform explicit cancellation, pass values through the context, and know when we should do each of these things. In the next chapter, we're going to see Go's built-in testing framework and learn how to use it to find bugs and diagnose performance problems in your programs.

CHAPTER 13

Writing Tests

Over the past two decades, the widespread adoption of automated testing has probably done more to improve code quality than any other software engineering technique. As a language and ecosystem focused on improving software quality, it's not surprising that Go includes testing support as part of its standard library. Go makes it so easy to test your code, there's no excuse to not do it. In this chapter, we'll see how to test our Go code, group our tests into unit and integration tests, examine code coverage, write benchmarks, and learn how to check our code for concurrency issues using the Go race checker. Along the way, we'll discuss how to write code that is testable and why this improves our code quality.

The Basics of Testing

Go's testing support has two parts: libraries and tooling. The `testing` package in the standard library provides the types and functions to write tests, while the `go test` tool that's bundled with Go runs your tests and generates reports. Unlike many other languages, Go tests are placed in the same directory and the same package as the production code. Since tests are located in the same package, they are able to access and test unexported functions and variables. We'll see in a bit how to write tests that ensure that we are only testing a public API.

 Complete code samples for this chapter are found on GitHub (*https://oreil.ly/txE4b*).

Let's write a simple function and then a test to make sure the function works. In the file *adder/adder.go*, we have:

```
func addNumbers(x, y int) int {
    return x + x
}
```

The corresponding test is in *adder/adder_test.go*:

```
func Test_addNumbers(t *testing.T) {
    result := addNumbers(2,3)
    if result != 5 {
        t.Error("incorrect result: expected 5, got", result)
    }
}
```

Every test is written in a file whose name ends with *_test.go*. If you are writing tests against *foo.go*, place your tests in a file named *foo_test.go*.

Test functions start with the word Test and take in a single parameter of type *testing.T. By convention, this parameter is named t. Test functions do not return any values. The name of the test (apart from starting with the word "Test") is meant to document what you are testing, so pick something that explains what you are testing. When writing unit tests for individual functions, the convention is to name the unit test Test followed by the name of the function. When testing unexported functions, some people use an underscore between the word Test and the name of the function.

Also note that we use standard Go code to call the code being tested and to validate if the responses are as expected. When there's an incorrect result, we report the error with the t.Error method, which works like the fmt.Print function. We'll see other error-reporting methods in a bit.

We've just seen the library portion of Go's test support. Now let's take a look at the tooling. Just as go build builds a binary and go run runs a file, the command go test runs the tests in the current directory:

```
$ go test
--- FAIL: Test_addNumbers (0.00s)
    adder_test.go:8: incorrect result: expected 5, got 4
FAIL
exit status 1
FAIL    test_examples/adder     0.006s
```

It looks like we found a bug in our code. Taking a second look at addNumbers, we see that we are adding x to x, not x to y. Let's change the code and rerun our test to verify that the bug is fixed:

```
$ go test
PASS
ok      test_examples/adder     0.006s
```

The `go test` command allows you to specify which packages to test. Using `./...` for the package name specifies that you want to run tests in the current directory and all of the subdirectories of the current directory. Include a `-v` flag to get verbose testing output.

Reporting Test Failures

There are several methods on `*testing.T` for reporting test failures. We've already seen `Error`, which builds a failure description string out of a comma-separated list of values.

If you'd rather use a `Printf`-style formatting string to generate your message, use the `Errorf` method instead:

```
t.Errorf("incorrect result: expected %d, got %d", 5, result)
```

While `Error` and `Errorf` mark a test as failed, the test function continues running. If you think a test function should stop processing as soon as a failure is found, use the `Fatal` and `Fatalf` methods. The `Fatal` method works like `Error`, and the `Fatalf` method works like `Errorf`. The difference is that the test function exits immediately after the test failure message is generated. Note that this doesn't exit *all* tests; any remaining test functions will execute after the current test function exits.

When should you use `Fatal/Fatalf` and when should you use `Error/Errorf`? If the failure of a check in a test means that further checks in the same test function will always fail or cause the test to panic, use `Fatal` or `Fatalf`. If you are testing several independent items (such as validating fields in a struct), then use `Error` or `Errorf` so you can report as many problems at once. This makes it easier to fix multiple problems without rerunning your tests over and over.

Setting Up and Tearing Down

Sometimes you have some common state that you want to set up before any tests run and remove when testing is complete. Use a `TestMain` function to manage this state and run your tests:

```go
var testTime time.Time

func TestMain(m *testing.M) {
    fmt.Println("Set up stuff for tests here")
    testTime = time.Now()
    exitVal := m.Run()
    fmt.Println("Clean up stuff after tests here")
    os.Exit(exitVal)
}

func TestFirst(t *testing.T) {
    fmt.Println("TestFirst uses stuff set up in TestMain", testTime)
```

```
    }

    func TestSecond(t *testing.T) {
        fmt.Println("TestSecond also uses stuff set up in TestMain", testTime)
    }
```

Both `TestFirst` and `TestSecond` refer to the package-level variable `testTime`. We declare a function called `TestMain` with a parameter of type `*testing.M`. Running go `test` on a package with a `TestMain` function calls the function instead of invoking the tests directly. Once the state is configured, call the `Run` method on `*testing.M` to run the test functions. The `Run` method returns the exit code; 0 indicates that all tests passed. Finally, you must call `os.Exit` with the exit code returned from `Run`.

Running go `test` on this produces the output:

```
$ go test
Set up stuff for tests here
TestFirst uses stuff set up in TestMain 2020-09-01 21:42:36.231508 -0400 EDT
    m=+0.000244286
TestSecond also uses stuff set up in TestMain 2020-09-01 21:42:36.231508 -0400
    EDT m=+0.000244286
PASS
Clean up stuff after tests here
ok      test_examples/testmain  0.006s
```

Be aware that `TestMain` is invoked once, not before and after each individual test. Also be aware that you can have only one `TestMain` per package.

There are two common situations where `TestMain` is useful:

- When you need to set up data in an external repository, such as a database
- When the code being tested depends on package-level variables that need to be initialized

As mentioned before (and will be mentioned again!) you should avoid package-level variables in your programs. They make it hard to understand how data flows through your program. If you are using `TestMain` for this reason, consider refactoring your code.

The `Cleanup` method on `*testing.T` is used to clean up temporary resources created for a single test. This method has a single parameter, a function with no input parameters or return values. The function runs when the test completes. For simple tests, you can achieve the same result by using a `defer` statement, but `Cleanup` is useful when tests rely on helper functions to set up sample data, like we see in Example 13-1. It's fine to call `Cleanup` multiple times. Just like `defer`, the functions are invoked in last added, first called order.

Example 13-1. Using t.Cleanup

```go
// createFile is a helper function called from multiple tests
func createFile(t *testing.T) (string, error) {
    f, err := os.Create("tempFile")
    if err != nil {
        return "", err
    }
    // write some data to f
    t.Cleanup(func() {
        os.Remove(f.Name())
    })
    return f.Name(), nil
}

func TestFileProcessing(t *testing.T) {
    fName, err := createFile(t)
    if err != nil {
        t.Fatal(err)
    }
    // do testing, don't worry about cleanup
}
```

Storing Sample Test Data

As go test walks your source code tree, it uses the current package directory as the current working directory. If you want to use sample data to test functions in a package, create a subdirectory named *testdata* to hold your files. Go reserves this directory name as a place to hold test files. When reading from *testdata*, always use a relative file reference. Since go test changes the current working directory to the current package, each package accesses its own *testdata* via a relative file path.

The text package (*https://oreil.ly/nHtrc*) demonstrates how to use *testdata*.

Caching Test Results

Just as we learned in Chapter 9 that Go caches compiled packages if they haven't changed, Go also caches test results when running tests across multiple packages if they have passed and their code hasn't changed. The tests are recompiled and rerun if you change any file in the package or in the *testdata* directory. You can also force tests to always run if you pass the flag -count=1 to go test.

Testing Your Public API

The tests that we've written are in the same package as the production code. This allows us to test both exported and unexported functions.

If you want to test just the public API of your package, Go has a convention for specifying this. You still keep your test source code in the same directory as the production source code, but you use `packagename_test` for the package name. Let's redo our initial test case, using an exported function instead. If we have the following function in the `adder` package:

```
func AddNumbers(x, y int) int {
    return x + y
}
```

then we can test it as public API using the following code in a file in the `adder` package named *adder_public_test.go*:

```
package adder_test

import (
    "testing"
    "test_examples/adder"
)

func TestAddNumbers(t *testing.T) {
    result := adder.AddNumbers(2, 3)
    if result != 5 {
        t.Error("incorrect result: expected 5, got", result)
    }
}
```

Notice that the package name for our test file is `adder_test`. We have to import `test_examples/adder` even though the files are in the same directory. To follow the convention for naming tests, the test function name matches the name of the `AddNumbers` function. Also note that we use `adder.AddNumbers`, since we are calling an exported function in a different package.

Just as you can call exported functions from within a package, you can test your public API from a test that is in the same package as your source code. The advantage of using the `_test` package suffix is that it lets you treat your package as a "black box"; you are forced to interact with it only via its exported functions, methods, types, constants, and variables. Also be aware that you can have test source files with both package names intermixed in the same source directory.

Use go-cmp to Compare Test Results

It can be verbose to write a thorough comparison between two instances of a compound type. While you can use `reflect.DeepEqual` to compare structs, maps, and slices, there's a better way. Google released a third-party module (*https://github.com/google/go-cmp*) called `go-cmp` that does the comparison for you and returns a detailed description of what does not match. Let's see how it works by defining a simple `struct` and a factory function that populates it:

```
type Person struct {
    Name      string
    Age       int
    DateAdded time.Time
}

func CreatePerson(name string, age int) Person {
    return Person{
        Name:      name,
        Age:       age,
        DateAdded: time.Now(),
    }
}
```

In our test file, we need to import `github.com/google/go-cmp/cmp`, and our test function looks like this:

```
func TestCreatePerson(t *testing.T) {
    expected := Person{
        Name: "Dennis",
        Age: 37,
    }
    result := CreatePerson("Dennis", 37)
    if diff := cmp.Diff(expected, result); diff != "" {
        t.Error(diff)
    }
}
```

The `cmp.Diff` function takes in the expected output and the output that was returned by the function that we're testing. It returns a string that describes any mismatches between the two inputs. If the inputs match, it returns an empty string. We assign the output of the `cmp.Diff` function to a variable called `diff` and then check to see if `diff` is an empty string. If it is not, an error occurred.

We'll build and run our test and see the output that `go-cmp` generates when two structs don't match:

```
$ go test
--- FAIL: TestCreatePerson (0.00s)
    ch13_cmp_test.go:16:    ch13_cmp.Person{
            Name:      "Dennis",
            Age:       37,
```

```
-        DateAdded: s"0001-01-01 00:00:00 +0000 UTC",
+        DateAdded: s"2020-03-01 22:53:58.087229 -0500 EST m=+0.001242842",
  }

FAIL
FAIL    ch13_cmp    0.006s
```

The lines with a - and + indicate the fields whose values differ. Our test failed because our dates didn't match. This is a problem because we can't control what date is assigned by the `CreatePerson` function. We have to ignore the `DateAdded` field. You do that by specifying a comparator function. Declare the function as a local variable in your test:

```
comparer := cmp.Comparer(func(x, y Person) bool {
    return x.Name == y.Name && x.Age == y.Age
})
```

Pass a function to the `cmp.Comparer` function to create a customer comparator. The function that's passed in must have two parameters of the same type and return a bool. It also must be symmetric (the order of the parameters doesn't matter), deterministic (it always returns the same value for the same inputs), and pure (it must not modify its parameters). In our implementation, we are comparing the `Name` and `Age` fields and ignoring the `DateAdded` field.

Then change your call to `cmp.Diff` to include `comparer`:

```
if diff := cmp.Diff(expected, result, comparer); diff != "" {
    t.Error(diff)
}
```

This is only a quick preview of the most useful features in `go-cmp`. Check its documentation to learn more about how to control what is compared and the output format.

Table Tests

Most of the time, it takes more than a single test case to validate that a function is working correctly. You could write multiple test functions to validate your function or multiple tests within the same function, but you'll find that a great deal of the testing logic is repetitive. You set up supporting data and functions, specify inputs, check the outputs, and compare to see if they match your expectations. Rather than writing this over and over, you can take advantage of a pattern called *table tests*. Let's take a look at a sample. Assume we have the following function in the `table` package:

```
func DoMath(num1, num2 int, op string) (int, error) {
    switch op {
    case "+":
        return num1 + num2, nil
    case "-":
```

```
            return num1 - num2, nil
        case "*":
            return num1 + num2, nil
        case "/":
            if num2 == 0 {
                return 0, errors.New("division by zero")
            }
            return num1 / num2, nil
        default:
            return 0, fmt.Errorf("unknown operator %s", op)
    }
}
```

To test this function, we need to check the different branches, trying out inputs that return valid results, as well as inputs that trigger errors. We could write code like this, but it's very repetitive:

```
func TestDoMath(t *testing.T) {
    result, err := DoMath(2, 2, "+")
    if result != 4 {
        t.Error("Should have been 4, got", result)
    }
    if err != nil {
        t.Error("Should have been nil error, got", err)
    }
    result2, err2 := DoMath(2, 2, "-")
    if result2 != 0 {
        t.Error("Should have been 0, got", result2)
    }
    if err2 != nil {
        t.Error("Should have been nil error, got", err2)
    }
    // and so on...
}
```

Let's replace this repetition with a table test. First, we declare a slice of anonymous structs. The struct contains fields for the name of the test, the input parameters, and the return values. Each entry in the slice represents another test:

```
data := []struct {
    name     string
    num1     int
    num2     int
    op       string
    expected int
    errMsg   string
}{
    {"addition", 2, 2, "+", 4, ""},
    {"subtraction", 2, 2, "-", 0, ""},
    {"multiplication", 2, 2, "*", 4, ""},
    {"division", 2, 2, "/", 1, ""},
    {"bad_division", 2, 0, "/", 0, `division by zero`},
}
```

Next, we loop over each test case in data, invoking the Run method each time. This is the line that does the magic. We pass two parameters to Run, a name for the subtest and a function with a single parameter of type *testing.T. Inside the function, we call DoMath using the fields of the current entry in data, using the same logic over and over. When you run these tests, you'll see that not only do they pass, but when you use the -v flag, each subtest also now has a name:

```
for _, d := range data {
    t.Run(d.name, func(t *testing.T) {
        result, err := DoMath(d.num1, d.num2, d.op)
        if result != d.expected {
            t.Errorf("Expected %d, got %d", d.expected, result)
        }
        var errMsg string
        if err != nil {
            errMsg = err.Error()
        }
        if errMsg != d.errMsg {
            t.Errorf("Expected error message `%s`, got `%s`",
                d.errMsg, errMsg)
        }
    })
}
```

 Comparing error messages can be fragile, because there may not be any compatibility guarantees on the message text. The function that we are testing uses errors.New and fmt.Errorf to make errors, so the only option is to compare the messages. If an error has a custom type, use errors.Is or errors.As to check that the correct error is returned.

Now that we have a way to run lots of tests, let's learn about code coverage to find out what our tests are testing.

Checking Your Code Coverage

Code coverage is a very useful tool for knowing if you've missed any obvious cases. However, reaching 100% code coverage doesn't guarantee that there aren't bugs in your code for some inputs. First we'll see how go test displays code coverage and then we'll look at the limitations of relying on code coverage alone.

Adding the -cover flag to the go test command calculates coverage information and includes a summary in the test output. If you include a second flag -coverprofile, you can save the coverage information to a file:

```
go test -v -cover -coverprofile=c.out
```

If we run our table test with code coverage, the test output now includes a line that indicates the amount of test code coverage, 87.5%. That's good to know, but it'd be more useful if we could see what we missed. The cover tool included with Go generates an HTML representation of your source code with that information:

```
go tool cover -html=c.out
```

When you run it, your web browser should open and show you a page that looks like Figure 13-1.

```go
package table

import (
        "errors"
        "fmt"
)

func DoMath(num1, num2 int, op string) (int, error) {
        switch op {
        case "+":
                return num1 + num2, nil
        case "-":
                return num1 - num2, nil
        case "*":
                return num1 + num2, nil
        case "/":
                if num2 == 0 {
                        return 0, errors.New("division by zero")
                }
                return num1 / num2, nil
        default:
                return 0, fmt.Errorf("unknown operator %s", op)
        }
}
```

Figure 13-1. Initial code coverage

Every file that's tested appears in the combo box in the upper left. The source code is in one of three colors. Gray is used for lines of code that aren't testable, green is used for code that's been covered by a test, and red is used for code that hasn't been tested. (The reliance on color is unfortunate for readers of the print edition and those who have red-green color blindness. If you are unable to see the colors, the lighter gray is the covered lines.) From looking at this, we can see that we didn't write a test to cover the default case, when a bad operator is passed to our function. Let's add that case to our slice of test cases:

```
{"bad_op", 2, 2, "?", 0, `unknown operator ?`},
```

When we rerun go test -v -cover -coverprofile=c.out and go tool cover
-html=c.out, we see in Figure 13-2 that the final line is covered and we have 100%
test code coverage.

```
test_examples/table/table.go (100.0%)        not tracked   not covered   covered

package table

import (
        "errors"
        "fmt"
)

func DoMath(num1, num2 int, op string) (int, error) {
        switch op {
        case "+":
                return num1 + num2, nil
        case "-":
                return num1 - num2, nil
        case "*":
                return num1 + num2, nil
        case "/":
                if num2 == 0 {
                        return 0, errors.New("division by zero")
                }
                return num1 / num2, nil
        default:
                return 0, fmt.Errorf("unknown operator %s", op)
        }
}
```

Figure 13-2. Final code coverage

Code coverage is a great thing, but it's not enough. There's actually a bug in our code,
even though we have 100% coverage. Have you noticed it? If not, let's add another test
case and rerun our tests:

```
{"another_mult", 2, 3, "*", 6, ""},
```

You should see the error:

```
table_test.go:57: Expected 6, got 5
```

There's a typo in our case for multiplication. It adds the numbers together instead of
multiplying them. (Beware the dangers of copy and paste coding!) Fix the code, rerun
go test -v -cover -coverprofile=c.out and go tool cover -html=c.out, and
you'll see that tests pass again.

Code coverage is necessary, but it's not sufficient. You can have 100% code coverage and still have bugs in your code!

Benchmarks

Determining how fast (or slow) code runs is surprisingly difficult. Rather than trying to figure it out yourself, you should use the benchmarking support that's built into Go's testing framework. Let's explore it with a function in the test_examples/bench package:

```go
func FileLen(f string, bufsize int) (int, error) {
    file, err := os.Open(f)
    if err != nil {
        return 0, err
    }
    defer file.Close()
    count := 0
    for {
        buf := make([]byte, bufsize)
        num, err := file.Read(buf)
        count += num
        if err != nil {
            break
        }
    }
    return count, nil
}
```

This function counts the number of characters in a file. It takes in two parameters, the name of the file and the size of the buffer that we are using to read the file (we'll see the reason for the second parameter in a moment).

Before we see how fast it is, we should test our library to make sure that it works (it does). Here's a simple test:

```go
func TestFileLen(t *testing.T) {
    result, err := FileLen("testdata/data.txt", 1)
    if err != nil {
        t.Fatal(err)
    }
    if result != 65204 {
        t.Error("Expected 65204, got", result)
    }
}
```

Now we can see how long it takes our file length function to run. Our goal is to find out what size buffer we should use to read from the file.

Before you spend time going down an optimization rabbit hole, be sure that you need to optimize. If your program is already fast enough to meet your responsiveness requirements and is using an acceptable amount of memory, then your time is better spent on adding features and fixing bugs. Your business requirements determine what "fast enough" and "acceptable amount of memory" mean.

In Go, benchmarks are functions in your test files that start with the word `Benchmark` and take in a single parameter of type `*testing.B`. This type includes all of the functionality of a `*testing.T` as well as additional support for benchmarking. Let's start by looking at a benchmark that uses a buffer size of 1 byte:

```
var blackhole int

func BenchmarkFileLen1(b *testing.B) {
    for i := 0; i < b.N; i++ {
        result, err := FileLen("testdata/data.txt", 1)
        if err != nil {
            b.Fatal(err)
        }
        blackhole = result
    }
}
```

The `blackhole` package-level variable is interesting. We write the results from `FileLen` to this package-level variable to make sure that the compiler doesn't get too clever and decide to optimize away the call to `FileLen`, ruining our benchmark.

Every Go benchmark must have a loop that iterates from 0 to `b.N`. The testing framework calls our benchmark functions over and over with larger and larger values for N until it is sure that the timing results are accurate. We'll see this in the output in a moment.

We run a benchmark by passing the `-bench` flag to `go test`. This flag expects a regular expression to describe the name of the benchmarks to run. Use `-bench=.` to run all benchmarks. A second flag, `-benchmem`, includes memory allocation information in the benchmark output. All tests are run before the benchmarks, so you can only benchmark code when tests pass.

Here's the output for the benchmark on my computer:

```
BenchmarkFileLen1-12   25   47201025 ns/op   65342 B/op   65208 allocs/op
```

Running a benchmark with memory allocation information produces output with five columns. Here's what each one means:

BenchmarkFileLen1-12

The name of the benchmark, a hyphen, and the value of GOMAXPROCS for the benchmark.

25

The number of times that the test ran to produce a stable result.

47201025 ns/op

How long it took to run a single pass of this benchmark, in nanoseconds (there are 1,000,000,000 nanoseconds in a second).

65342 B/op

The number of bytes allocated during a single pass of the benchmark.

65208 allocs/op

The number of times bytes had to be allocated from the heap during a single pass of the benchmark. This will always be less than or equal to the number of bytes allocated.

Now that we have results for a buffer of 1 byte, let's see what the results look like when we use buffers of different sizes:

```
func BenchmarkFileLen(b *testing.B) {
    for _, v := range []int{1, 10, 100, 1000, 10000, 100000} {
        b.Run(fmt.Sprintf("FileLen-%d", v), func(b *testing.B) {
            for i := 0; i < b.N; i++ {
                result, err := FileLen("testdata/data.txt", v)
                if err != nil {
                    b.Fatal(err)
                }
                blackhole = result
            }
        })
    }
}
```

Just like we launched table tests using t.Run, we're using b.Run to launch benchmarks that only vary based on input. Here are the results of this benchmark on my computer:

```
BenchmarkFileLen/FileLen-1-12           25  47828842 ns/op   65342 B/op  65208 allocs/op
BenchmarkFileLen/FileLen-10-12         230   5136839 ns/op  104488 B/op   6525 allocs/op
BenchmarkFileLen/FileLen-100-12       2246    509619 ns/op   73384 B/op    657 allocs/op
BenchmarkFileLen/FileLen-1000-12     16491     71281 ns/op   68744 B/op     70 allocs/op
BenchmarkFileLen/FileLen-10000-12    42468     26600 ns/op   82056 B/op     11 allocs/op
BenchmarkFileLen/FileLen-100000-12   36700     30473 ns/op  213128 B/op      5 allocs/op
```

These results aren't surprising; as we increase the size of the buffer, we make fewer allocations and our code runs faster, until the buffer is bigger than the file. When the buffer is bigger than the size of the file, there are extra allocations that slow down the output. If we expect files of roughly this size, a buffer of 10,000 bytes would work best.

But there's a change we can make that improves the numbers more. We are reallocating the buffer every time we get the next set of bytes from the file. That's unnecessary. If we move the byte slice allocation before the loop and rerun our benchmark, we see an improvement:

```
BenchmarkFileLen/FileLen-1-12            25   46167597 ns/op      137 B/op   4 allocs/op
BenchmarkFileLen/FileLen-10-12          261    4592019 ns/op      152 B/op   4 allocs/op
BenchmarkFileLen/FileLen-100-12        2518     478838 ns/op      248 B/op   4 allocs/op
BenchmarkFileLen/FileLen-1000-12      20059      60150 ns/op     1160 B/op   4 allocs/op
BenchmarkFileLen/FileLen-10000-12     62992      19000 ns/op    10376 B/op   4 allocs/op
BenchmarkFileLen/FileLen-100000-12    51928      21275 ns/op   106632 B/op   4 allocs/op
```

The number of allocations are now consistent and small, just four allocations for every buffer size. What is interesting is that we now can make trade-offs. If we are tight on memory, we can use a smaller buffer size and save memory at the expense of performance.

> ## Profiling Your Go Code
>
> If benchmarking reveals that you have a performance or memory problem, the next step is figuring out exactly what the problem is. Go includes profiling tools that gather CPU and memory usage data from a running program as well as tools that help you visualize and interpret the generated data. You can even expose a web service endpoint to gather profiling information remotely from a running Go service.
>
> Discussing the profiler is a topic that's beyond the scope of this book. There are many great resources available online with information on it. A good starting point is the blog post Profiling Go programs with pprof (*https://oreil.ly/HHe9c*) by Julia Evans.

Stubs in Go

So far, we've written tests for functions that didn't depend on other code. This is not typical as most code is filled with dependencies. As we saw in Chapter 7, there are two ways that Go allows us to abstract function calls: defining a function type and defining an interface. These abstractions not only help us write modular production code; they also help us write unit tests.

When your code depends on abstractions, it's easier to write unit tests!

Lets take a look at an example in the `test_examples/solver` package. We define a type called `Processor`:

```
type Processor struct {
    Solver MathSolver
}
```

It has a field of type `MathSolver`:

```
type MathSolver interface {
    Resolve(ctx context.Context, expression string) (float64, error)
}
```

We'll implement and test `MathSolver` in a bit.

`Processor` also has a method that reads an expression from an `io.Reader` and returns the calculated value:

```
func (p Processor) ProcessExpression(ctx context.Context, r io.Reader)
                                     (float64, error) {
    curExpression, err := readToNewLine(r)
    if err != nil {
        return 0, err
    }
    if len(curExpression) == 0 {
        return 0, errors.New("no expression to read")
    }
    answer, err := p.Solver.Resolve(ctx, curExpression)
    return answer, err
}
```

Let's write the code to test `ProcessExpression`. First, we need a simple implementation of the `Resolve` method to write our test:

```
type MathSolverStub struct{}

func (ms MathSolverStub) Resolve(ctx context.Context, expr string)
                                 (float64, error) {
    switch expr {
    case "2 + 2 * 10":
        return 22, nil
    case "( 2 + 2 ) * 10":
        return 40, nil
    case "( 2 + 2 * 10":
        return 0, errors.New("invalid expression: ( 2 + 2 * 10")
    }
    return 0, nil
}
```

Next, we write a unit test that uses this stub (production code should test the error messages too, but for the sake of brevity, we'll leave those out):

```
func TestProcessorProcessExpression(t *testing.T) {
    p := Processor{MathSolverStub{}}
```

```
    in := strings.NewReader(`2 + 2 * 10
( 2 + 2 ) * 10
( 2 + 2 * 10`)
    data := []float64{22, 40, 0}
    hasErr := []bool{false, false, true}
    for i, d := range data {
        result, err := p.ProcessExpression(context.Background(), in)
        if err != nil && !hasErr[i] {
            t.Error(err)
        }
        if result != d {
            t.Errorf("Expected result %f, got %f", d, result)
        }
    }
}
```

We can then run our test and see that everything works.

While most Go interfaces only specify one or two methods, this isn't always the case. You sometimes find yourself with an interface that has many methods. Assume you have an interface that looks like this:

```
type Entities interface {
    GetUser(id string) (User, error)
    GetPets(userID string) ([]Pet, error)
    GetChildren(userID string) ([]Person, error)
    GetFriends(userID string) ([]Person, error)
    SaveUser(user User) error
}
```

There are two patterns for testing code that depends on large interfaces. The first is to embed the interface in a struct. Embedding an interface in a struct automatically defines all of the interface's methods on the struct. It doesn't provide any implementations of those methods, so you need to implement the methods that you care about for the current test. Let's assume that `Logic` is a struct that has a field of type `Entities`:

```
type Logic struct {
    Entities Entities
}
```

Assume you want to test this method:

```
func (l Logic) GetPetNames(userId string) ([]string, error) {
    pets, err := l.Entities.GetPets(userId)
    if err != nil {
        return nil, err
    }
    out := make([]string, len(pets))
    for _, p := range pets {
        out = append(out, p.Name)
    }
```

```
    return out, nil
}
```

This method uses only one of the methods declared on `Entities`, `GetPets`. Rather than creating a stub that implements every single method on `Entities` just to test `GetPets`, you can write a stub struct that only implements the method you need to test this method:

```
type GetPetNamesStub struct {
    Entities
}

func (ps GetPetNamesStub) GetPets(userID string) ([]Pet, error) {
    switch userID {
    case "1":
        return []Pet{{Name: "Bubbles"}}, nil
    case "2":
        return []Pet{{Name: "Stampy"}, {Name: "Snowball II"}}, nil
    default:
        return nil, fmt.Errorf("invalid id: %s", userID)
    }
}
```

We then write our unit test, with our stub injected into `Logic`:

```
func TestLogicGetPetNames(t *testing.T) {
    data := []struct {
        name     string
        userID   string
        petNames []string
    }{
        {"case1", "1", []string{"Bubbles"}},
        {"case2", "2", []string{"Stampy", "Snowball II"}},
        {"case3", "3", nil},
    }
    l := Logic{GetPetNamesStub{}}
    for _, d := range data {
        t.Run(d.name, func(t *testing.T) {
            petNames, err := l.GetPetNames(d.userID)
            if err != nil {
                t.Error(err)
            }
            if diff := cmp.Diff(d.petNames, petNames); diff != "" {
                t.Error(diff)
            }
        })
    }
}
```

(By the way, the `GetPetNames` method has a bug. Did you see it? Even simple methods can sometimes have bugs.)

If you embed an interface in a stub struct, make sure you provide an implementation for every method that's called during your test! If you call an unimplemented method, your tests will panic.

If you need to implement only one or two methods in an interface for a single test, this technique works well. The drawback comes when you need to call the same method in different tests with different inputs and outputs. When that happens, you need to either include every possible result for every test within the same implementation or reimplement the struct for each test. This quickly becomes difficult to understand and maintain. A better solution is to create a stub struct that proxies method calls to function fields. For each method defined on `Entities`, we define a function field with a matching signature on our stub struct:

```go
type EntitiesStub struct {
    getUser     func(id string) (User, error)
    getPets     func(userID string) ([]Pet, error)
    getChildren func(userID string) ([]Person, error)
    getFriends  func(userID string) ([]Person, error)
    saveUser    func(user User) error
}
```

We then make `EntitiesStub` meet the `Entities` interface by defining the methods. In each method, we invoke the associated function field. For example:

```go
func (es EntitiesStub) GetUser(id string) (User, error) {
    return es.getUser(id)
}

func (es EntitiesStub) GetPets(userID string) ([]Pet, error) {
    return es.getPets(userID)
}
```

Once you create this stub, you can supply different implementations of different methods in different test cases via the fields in the data struct for a table test:

```go
func TestLogicGetPetNames(t *testing.T) {
    data := []struct {
        name     string
        getPets  func(userID string) ([]Pet, error)
        userID   string
        petNames []string
        errMsg   string
    }{
        {"case1", func(userID string) ([]Pet, error) {
            return []Pet{{Name: "Bubbles"}}, nil
        }, "1", []string{"Bubbles"}, ""},
        {"case2", func(userID string) ([]Pet, error) {
            return nil, errors.New("invalid id: 3")
        }, "3", nil, "invalid id: 3"},
```

```
    }
    l := Logic{}
    for _, d := range data {
        t.Run(d.name, func(t *testing.T) {
            l.Entities = EntitiesStub{getPets: d.getPets}
            petNames, err := l.GetPetNames(d.userID)
            if diff := cmp.Diff(petNames, d.petNames); diff != "" {
                t.Error(diff)
            }
            var errMsg string
            if err != nil {
                errMsg = err.Error()
            }
            if errMsg != d.errMsg {
                t.Errorf("Expected error `%s`, got `%s`", d.errMsg, errMsg)
            }
        })
    }
}
```

We add a field of function type to `data`'s anonymous struct. In each test case, we specify a function that returns the data that `GetPets` would return. When you write your test stubs this way, it's clear what the stubs should return for each test case. As each test runs, we instantiate a new `EntitiesStub` and assign the `getPets` function field in our test data to the `getPets` function field in `EntitiesStub`.

Mocks and Stubs

The terms *mock* and *stub* are often used interchangeably, but they are actually two different concepts. Martin Fowler, a respected voice on all things related to software development, wrote a blog post (*https://oreil.ly/nDkF5*) on mocks that, among other things, covers the difference between mocks and stubs. In short, a stub returns a canned value for a given input, whereas a mock validates that a set of calls happen in the expected order with the expected inputs.

We used stubs in our examples to return canned values to a given response. You can write your own mocks by hand, or you can use a third-party library to generate them. The two most popular options are the gomock (*https://oreil.ly/_EjoS*) library from Google and the testify (*https://oreil.ly/AfDGD*) library from Stretchr, Inc.

---

httptest

It can be difficult to write tests for a function that calls an HTTP service. Traditionally, this became an integration test, requiring you to stand up a test instance of the service that the function calls. The Go standard library includes the net/http/httptest package to make it easier to stub HTTP services. Let's go back to our `test_examples/solver` package and provide an implementation of `MathSolver` that calls an HTTP service to evaluate expressions:

```
type RemoteSolver struct {
    MathServerURL string
    Client        *http.Client
}

func (rs RemoteSolver) Resolve(ctx context.Context, expression string)
                              (float64, error) {
    req, err := http.NewRequestWithContext(ctx, http.MethodGet,
        rs.MathServerURL+"?expression="+url.QueryEscape(expression),
        nil)
    if err != nil {
        return 0, err
    }
    resp, err := rs.Client.Do(req)
    if err != nil {
        return 0, err
    }
    defer resp.Body.Close()
    contents, err := ioutil.ReadAll(resp.Body)
    if err != nil {
        return 0, err
    }
    if resp.StatusCode != http.StatusOK {
        return 0, errors.New(string(contents))
    }
    result, err := strconv.ParseFloat(string(contents), 64)
    if err != nil {
        return 0, err
    }
    return result, nil
}
```

Now let's see how to use the `httptest` library to test this code without standing up a server. The code is in the `TestRemoteSolver_Resolve` in *test_examples/solver/ remote_solver_test.go,* but here are the highlights. First, we want to make sure that the data that's passed into the function arrives on the server. So in our test function, we define a type called `info` to hold our input and output and a variable called `io` that is assigned the current input and output:

```
type info struct {
    expression string
    code       int
    body       string
}
var io info
```

Next, we set up our fake remote server and use it to configure an instance of `RemoteSolver`:

```
server := httptest.NewServer(
    http.HandlerFunc(func(rw http.ResponseWriter, req *http.Request) {
        expression := req.URL.Query().Get("expression")
        if expression != io.expression {
            rw.WriteHeader(http.StatusBadRequest)
            fmt.Fprintf(rw, "expected expression '%s', got '%s'",
                io.expression, expression)
            return
        }
        rw.WriteHeader(io.code)
        rw.Write([]byte(io.body))
    }))
defer server.Close()
rs := RemoteSolver{
    MathServerURL: server.URL,
    Client:        server.Client(),
}
```

The httptest.NewServer function creates and starts an HTTP server on a random unused port. You need to provide an http.Handler implementation to process the request. Since this is a server, you must close it when the test completes. The server instance has its URL specified in the URL field of the server instance and a preconfigured http.Client for communicating with the test server. We pass these into RemoteSolver.

The rest of the function works like every other table test that we've seen:

```
data := []struct {
    name   string
    io     info
    result float64
}{
    {"case1", info{"2 + 2 * 10", http.StatusOK, "22"}, 22},
    // remaining cases
}
for _, d := range data {
    t.Run(d.name, func(t *testing.T) {
        io = d.io
        result, err := rs.Resolve(context.Background(), d.io.expression)
        if result != d.result {
            t.Errorf("io `%f`, got `%f`", d.result, result)
        }
        var errMsg string
        if err != nil {
            errMsg = err.Error()
        }
        if errMsg != d.errMsg {
            t.Errorf("io error `%s`, got `%s`", d.errMsg, errMsg)
        }
    })
}
```

The interesting thing to note is that the variable io has been captured by two different closures: the one for the stub server and the one for running each test. We write to it in one closure and read it in the other. This is a bad idea in production code, but it works well in test code within a single function.

Integration Tests and Build Tags

Even though httptest provides a way to avoid testing against external services, you should still write *integration tests*, automated tests that connect to other services. These validate that your understanding of the service's API is correct. The challenge is figuring out how to group your automated tests; you only want to run integration tests when the support environment is present. Also, integration tests tend to be slower than unit tests, so they are usually run less frequently.

The Go compiler provides *build tags* to control when code is compiled. Build tags are specified on the first line of a file with a magic comment that starts with // +build. The original intent for build tags was to allow different code to be compiled on different platforms, but they are also useful for splitting tests into groups. Tests in files without build tags run all the time. These are the unit tests that don't have dependencies on external resources. Tests in files with a build tag are only run when the supporting resources are available.

Let's try this out with our math solving project. Use Docker to download a server implementation with docker pull jonbodner/math-server and then run the server locally on port 8080 with docker run -p 8080:8080 jonbodner/math-server.

 If you don't have Docker installed or if you want to build the code for yourself, you can find it on GitHub (*https://oreil.ly/yjMzc*).

We need to write an integration test to make sure that our Resolve method properly communicates with the math server. The *test_examples/solver/remote_solver_integration_test.go* file has a complete test in the TestRemoteSolver_ResolveIntegration function. The test looks like every other table test that we've written. The interesting thing is the first line of the file, separated from the package declaration by a newline is:

```
// +build integration
```

To run our integration test alongside the other tests we've written, use:

```
$ go test -tags integration -v ./...
```

Finding Concurrency Problems with the Race Checker

Even with Go's built-in support for concurrency, bugs still happen. It's easy to accidentally reference a variable from two different goroutines without acquiring a lock. The computer science term for this is a *data race*. To help find these sorts of bugs, Go includes a *race checker*. It isn't guaranteed to find every single data race in your code, but if it finds one, you should put proper locks around what it finds.

Let's look at a simple example in *test_examples/race/race.go*:

```
func getCounter() int {
    var counter int
    var wg sync.WaitGroup
    wg.Add(5)
    for i := 0; i < 5; i++ {
        go func() {
            for i := 0; i < 1000; i++ {
                counter++
            }
            wg.Done()
        }()
    }
    wg.Wait()
    return counter
}
```

This code launches five goroutines, has each of them update a shared counter variable 1000 times, and then returns the result. You'd expect it to be 5000, so let's verify this with a unit test in *test_examples/race/race_test.go*:

```go
func TestGetCounter(t *testing.T) {
    counter := getCounter()
    if counter != 5000 {
        t.Error("unexpected counter:", counter)
    }
}
```

If you run go test a few times, you'll see that sometimes it passes, but most of the time it fails with an error message like:

```
unexpected counter: 3673
```

The problem is that there's a data race in the code. In a program this simple, the cause is obvious: multiple goroutines are trying to update counter simultaneously and some of their updates are lost. In more complicated programs, these sorts of races are harder to see. Let's see what the race checker does. Use the flag -race with go test to enable it:

```
$ go test -race
==================
WARNING: DATA RACE
Read at 0x00c000128070 by goroutine 10:
  test_examples/race.getCounter.func1()
      test_examples/race/race.go:12 +0x45

Previous write at 0x00c000128070 by goroutine 8:
  test_examples/race.getCounter.func1()
      test_examples/race/race.go:12 +0x5b
```

The traces make it clear that the line counter++ is the source of our problems.

 Some people try to fix race conditions by inserting "sleeps" into their code, trying to space out access to the variable that's being accessed by multiple goroutines. *This is a bad idea.* Doing so might eliminate the problem in some cases, but the code is still wrong and it will fail in some situations.

You can also use the -race flag when you build your programs. This creates a binary that includes the race checker and that reports any races it finds to the console. This allows you to find data races in code that doesn't have tests.

If the race checker is so useful, why isn't it enabled all the time for testing and production? A binary with -race enabled runs approximately ten times slower than a normal binary. That isn't a problem for test suites that take a second to run, but for large test suites that take several minutes, a 10x slowdown reduces productivity.

Wrapping Up

In this chapter, we've learned how to write tests and improve code quality using Go's built-in support for testing, code coverage, benchmarking, and data race checking. In the next chapter, we're going to explore some Go features that allow you to break the rules: the unsafe package, reflection, and cgo.

CHAPTER 14

Here There Be Dragons: Reflect, Unsafe, and Cgo

The edges of the known world are scary. Ancient maps would fill in the unexplored areas with pictures of dragons and lions. In our previous sections, we have emphasized that Go is a safe language, with typed variables to make clear what sort of data you are using and garbage collection to manage memory. Even the pointers are tame; you can't abuse them in the way that C and C++ do.

All of those things are true, and for the vast majority of the Go code that you'll write, you can be assured that the Go runtime will protect you. But there are escape hatches. Sometimes your Go programs need to venture out into less defined areas. In this chapter, we're going to look at how to handle situations that can't be solved with normal Go code. For example, when the type of the data can't be determined at compile time, you can use the reflection support in the `reflect` package to interact with and even construct data. When you need to take advantage of the memory layout of data types in Go, you can use the `unsafe` package. And if there is functionality that can only be provided by libraries written in C, you can call into C code with `cgo`.

You might be wondering why these advanced concepts appear in a book targeted at those new to Go. There are two reasons. First, developers searching for a solution to a problem sometimes discover (and copy and paste) techniques they don't fully understand. It's best to know a bit about advanced techniques that can cause problems before you add them to your codebase. Second, these tools are fun. Because they allow you to do things that aren't normally possible with Go, it feels a bit exciting to play with them and see what you can do.

Reflection Lets Us Work with Types at Runtime

One of the things that people who use Go like about it is that it is a statically typed language. Most of the time, declaring variables, types, and functions in Go is pretty straightforward. When you need a type, a variable, or a function, you define it:

```
type Foo struct {
  A int
  B string
}

var x Foo

func DoSomething(f Foo) {
  fmt.Println(f.A, f.B)
}
```

We use types to represent the data structures we know we need when we write our programs. Since types are a core part of Go, the compiler uses them to make sure that our code is correct. But sometimes, relying on only compilation-time information is a limitation. You might need to work with variables at runtime using information that didn't exist when the program was written. Maybe you're trying to map data from a file or network request into a variable, or you want to build a single function that works with different types. In those situations, you need to use *reflection*. Reflection allows us to examine types at runtime. It also provides the ability to examine, modify, and create variables, functions, and structs at runtime.

This leads to the question of when we need this functionality. If you look at the Go standard library, you can get an idea. Its uses fall into one of a few general categories:

- Reading and writing from a database. The `database/sql` package uses reflection to send records to databases and read data back.

- Go's built-in templating libraries, `text/template` and `html/template`, use reflection to process the values that are passed to the templates.

- The `fmt` package uses reflection heavily, as all of those calls to `fmt.Println` and friends rely on reflection to detect the type of the provided parameters.

- The `errors` package uses reflection to implement `errors.Is` and `errors.As`.

- The `sort` package uses reflection to implement functions that sort and evaluate slices of any type: `sort.Slice`, `sort.SliceStable`, and `sort.SliceIsSorted`.

- The last main usage of reflection in the Go standard library is for marshaling and unmarshaling data into JSON and XML, along with the other data formats defined in the various `encoding` packages. Struct tags (which we will talk about soon) are accessed via reflection, and the fields in structs are read and written using reflection as well.

Most of these examples have one thing in common: they involve accessing and formatting data that is being imported into or exported out of a Go program. You'll often see reflection used at the boundaries between your program and the outside world.

Another use of the `reflect` package in the Go standard library: testing. In "Slices" on page 37, we mentioned a function that you can find in the `reflect` package called `DeepEqual`. It's in the `reflect` package because it takes advantage of reflection to do its work. The `reflect.DeepEqual` function checks to see if two values are "deeply equal" to each other. This is a more thorough comparison than what you get if you use == to compare two things, and it's used in the standard library as a way to validate test results. It can also compare things that can't be compared using ==, like slices and maps.

Most of the time, you don't need `DeepEqual`, but if you ever wanted to compare two maps to see if all of their keys and values are identical or see if two slices were identical, `DeepEqual` is what you need.

Types, Kinds, and Values

Now that we know what reflection is and when you might need it, let's understand how it all works. The `reflect` package in the standard library is the home for the types and functions that implement reflection in Go. Reflection is built around three core concepts: types, kinds, and values.

First let's look at types. A type in reflection is exactly what it sounds like. It defines the properties of a variable, what it can hold, and how you can interact with it. With reflection, you are able to query a type to find out about these properties using code.

Types and kinds

We get the reflection representation of the type of a variable with the `TypeOf` function in the `reflect` package:

```
vType := reflect.TypeOf(v)
```

The `reflect.TypeOf` function returns a value of type `reflect.Type`, which represents the type of the variable passed into the `TypeOf` function. The `reflect.Type` type defines methods with information about a variable's type. We can't cover all of the methods, but here are a few.

The `Name` method returns, not surprisingly, the name of the type. Let's see a quick example:

```
var x int
xt := reflect.TypeOf(x)
fmt.Println(xt.Name())      // returns int
f := Foo{}
ft := reflect.TypeOf(f)
fmt.Println(ft.Name())      // returns Foo
xpt := reflect.TypeOf(&x)
fmt.Println(xpt.Name())     // returns an empty string
```

We start with a variable x of type `int`. We pass it to `reflect.TypeOf` and get back a `reflect.Type` instance. For primitive types like `int`, `Name()` returns the name of the type, in this case the string "int" for our `int`. For a struct, the name of the struct is returned. Some types, like a slice or a pointer, don't have names; in those cases, `Name` returns an empty string.

The `Kind` method on `reflect.Type` returns a value of type `reflect.Kind`, which is a constant that says what the type is made of—a slice, a map, a pointer, a struct, an interface, a string, an array, a function, an int, or some other primitive type. The difference between the kind and the type can be tricky to understand. Remember this rule: if you define a struct named Foo, the kind is `reflect.Struct` and the type is "Foo".

The kind is very important. One thing to be aware of when using reflection is that everything in the `reflect` package assumes that you know what you are doing. Some of the methods defined on `reflect.Type` and other types in the `reflect` package only make sense for certain kinds. For example, there's a method on `reflect.Type` called `NumIn`. If your `reflect.Type` instance represents a function, it returns the number of input parameters for the function. If your `reflect.Type` instance isn't a function, calling `NumIn` will panic your program.

 In general, if you call a method that doesn't make sense for the kind of the type, the method call panics. Always remember to use the kind of the reflected type to know which methods will work and which ones will panic.

Another important method on `reflect.Type` is `Elem`. Some types in Go have references to other types and `Elem` is how to find out what the contained type is. For example, let's use `reflect.TypeOf` on a pointer to an `int`:

```
var x int
xpt := reflect.TypeOf(&x)
fmt.Println(xpt.Name())       // returns an empty string
fmt.Println(xpt.Kind())       // returns reflect.Ptr
fmt.Println(xpt.Elem().Name()) // returns "int"
fmt.Println(xpt.Elem().Kind()) // returns reflect.Int
```

That gives us a reflect.Type instance with a blank name and a kind of reflect.Ptr, or pointer. When the reflect.Type represents a pointer, Elem returns the reflect.Type for the type the pointer points to. In this case, the Name method returns "int" and Kind returns reflect.Int. The Elem method also works for slices, maps, channels, and arrays.

There are methods on reflect.Type for reflecting on structs. Use the NumField method to get the number of fields in the struct, and get the fields in a struct by index with the Field method. That returns each field's structure described in a reflect.StructField, which has the name, order, type, and struct tags on a field. Let's look at a quick example, which you can run on The Go Playground (https://oreil.ly/Ynv_4):

```
type Foo struct {
    A int    `myTag:"value"`
    B string `myTag:"value2"`
}

var f Foo
ft := reflect.TypeOf(f)
for i := 0; i < ft.NumField(); i++ {
    curField := ft.Field(i)
    fmt.Println(curField.Name, curField.Type.Name(),
        curField.Tag.Get("myTag"))
}
```

We create an instance of type Foo and use reflect.TypeOf to get the reflect.Type for f. Next we use the NumField method to set up a for loop to get the index of each field in f. Then we use the Field method to get the reflect.StructField struct that represents the field, and then we can use the fields on reflect.StructField to get more information about the field. This code prints out:

```
A int value
B string value2
```

There are many more methods in reflect.Type, but they all follow the same pattern, allowing us to access the information that describes the type of a variable. You can look at the reflect.Type documentation (https://oreil.ly/p4AZ6) in the standard library for more information.

Values

In addition to examining the types of variables, you can also use reflection to read a variable's value, set its value, or create a new value from scratch.

We use the `reflect.ValueOf` function to create a `reflect.Value` instance that represents the value of a variable:

```
vValue := reflect.ValueOf(v)
```

Since every variable in Go has a type, `reflect.Value` has a method called `Type` that returns the `reflect.Type` of the `reflect.Value`. There's also a `Kind` method, just as there is on `reflect.Type`.

Just as `reflect.Type` has methods for finding out information about the type of a variable, `reflect.Value` has methods for finding out information about the value of a variable. We're not going to cover all of them, but let's take a look at how we can use a `reflect.Value` to get the value of the variable.

We'll start by looking at how to read our values back out of a `reflect.Value`. The `Interface` method returns the value of the variable as an empty interface. However, the type information is lost; when you put the value returned by `Interface` into a variable, you have to use a type assertion to get back to the right type:

```
s := []string{"a", "b", "c"}
sv := reflect.ValueOf(s)        // sv is of type reflect.Value
s2 := sv.Interface().([]string) // s2 is of type []string
```

While `Interface` can be called for `reflect.Value` instances that contain values of any kind, there are special case methods that you can use if the kind of the variable is one of the built-in, primitive types: `Bool`, `Complex`, `Int`, `Uint`, `Float`, and `String`. There's also a `Bytes` method that works if the type of the variable is a slice of bytes. If you use a method that doesn't match the type of the `reflect.Value`, your code will panic.

We can use reflection to set the value of a variable as well, but it's a three-step process.

First, you pass a pointer to the variable into `reflect.ValueOf`. This returns a `reflect.Value` that represents the pointer:

```
i := 10
iv := reflect.ValueOf(&i)
```

Next, you need to get to the actual value to set it. You use the `Elem` method on `reflect.Value` to get to the value pointed to by the pointer that was passed into `reflect.ValueOf`. Just like `Elem` on `reflect.Type` returns the type that's pointed to by a containing type, `Elem` on `reflect.Value` returns the value that's pointed to by a pointer or the value that's stored in an interface:

```
ivv := iv.Elem()
```

Finally, you get to the actual method that's used to set the value. Just like there are special-case methods for reading primitive types, there are special-case methods for setting primitive types: SetBool, SetInt, SetFloat, SetString, and SetUint. In our example, calling ivv.SetInt(20) changes the value of i. If we print out i now, we will get 20:

```
ivv.SetInt(20)
fmt.Println(i) // prints 20
```

For all other types, you need to use the Set method, which takes a variable of type reflect.Value. The value that you are setting it to doesn't need to be a pointer, because we are just reading this value, not changing it. And just like you can use Interface() to read primitive types, you can use Set to write primitive types.

The reason you need to pass a pointer to reflect.ValueOf to change the value of the input parameter is that it is just like any other function in Go. As we discussed in "Pointers Indicate Mutable Parameters" on page 113, you use a parameter of a pointer type to indicate that you want to modify the value of the parameter. When you modify the value, you dereference the pointer, and then set the value. The following two functions follow the same process:

```
func changeInt(i *int) {
    *i = 20
}

func changeIntReflect(i *int) {
    iv := reflect.ValueOf(i)
    iv.Elem().SetInt(20)
}
```

If you don't pass a pointer to a variable to reflect.ValueOf, you can still read the value of the variable using reflection. But if you try to use any of the methods that can change the value of a variable, the method calls will (not surprisingly) panic.

Making New Values

Before we look at how to best use reflection, there's one more thing to cover: how to create a value. The reflect.New function is the reflection analog of the new function. It takes in a reflect.Type and returns a reflect.Value that's a pointer to a reflect.Value of the specified type. Since it's a pointer, you can modify it and then assign the modified value to a variable using the Interface method.

Just as reflect.New creates a pointer to a scalar type, you can also use reflection to do the same thing as the make keyword with the following functions:

```
func MakeChan(typ Type, buffer int) Value

func MakeMap(typ Type) Value

func MakeMapWithSize(typ Type, n int) Value

func MakeSlice(typ Type, len, cap int) Value
```

Each of these functions takes in a reflect.Type that represents the compound type, not the contained type.

You must always start from a value when constructing a reflect.Type. However, there's a trick that lets you create a variable to represent a reflect.Type if you don't have a value handy:

```
var stringType = reflect.TypeOf((*string)(nil)).Elem()

var stringSliceType = reflect.TypeOf([]string(nil))
```

The variable stringType contains a reflect.Type that represents a string, and the variable stringSliceType contains a reflect.Type that represents a []string. That first line can take a bit of effort to decode. What we are doing is converting nil to a pointer to string, using reflect.TypeOf to make a reflect.Type of that pointer type, and then calling Elem on that pointer's reflect.Type to get the underlying type. We have to put *string in parenthesis because of Go order of operations; without the parenthesis, the compiler thinks that we are converting nil to string, which is illegal.

For the stringSliceType, it's a bit simpler since nil is a valid value for a slice. All we have to do is type conversion of nil to a []string and pass that to reflect.Type.

Now that we have these types, we can see how to use reflect.New and reflect.MakeSlice:

```
ssv := reflect.MakeSlice(stringSliceType, 0, 10)

sv := reflect.New(stringType).Elem()
sv.SetString("hello")

ssv = reflect.Append(ssv, sv)
ss := ssv.Interface().([]string)
fmt.Println(ss) // prints [hello]
```

You can try out this code for yourself on The Go Playground (*https://oreil.ly/ak2PG*).

Use Reflection to Check If an Interface's Value Is nil

As we talked about in "Interfaces and nil" on page 147, if a nil variable of a concrete type is assigned to a variable of an interface type, the variable of the interface type is not nil. This is because there is a type associated with the interface variable. If you want to check if the value associated with an interface is `nil`, you can do so with reflection using two methods: `IsValid` and `IsNil`:

```go
func hasNoValue(i interface{}) bool {
    iv := reflect.ValueOf(i)
    if !iv.IsValid() {
        return true
    }
    switch iv.Kind() {
    case reflect.Ptr, reflect.Slice, reflect.Map, reflect.Func,
        reflect.Interface:
        return iv.IsNil()
    default:
        return false
    }
}
```

The `IsValid` method returns `true` if `reflect.Value` holds anything other than a `nil` interface. We need to check this first because calling any other method on `reflect.Value` will (unsurprisingly) panic if `IsValid` is `false`. The `IsNil` method returns `true` if the value of the `reflect.Value` is `nil`, but it can only be called if the `reflect.Kind` is something that *can* be nil. If you call it on a type whose zero value isn't `nil`, it (you guessed it) panics.

You can see this function in use on The Go Playground (*https://oreil.ly/D-HR9*).

Even though it is possible to detect an interface with a `nil` value, strive to write your code so that it performs correctly even when the value associated with an interface is `nil`. Reserve this code for situations where you have no other options.

Use Reflection to Write a Data Marshaler

As mentioned earlier, reflection is what the standard library uses to implement marshaling and unmarshaling. Let's see how it's done by building a data marshaler for ourselves. Go provides the `csv.NewReader` and `csv.NewWriter` functions to read a CSV file into a slice of slice of strings and to write a slice of slice of strings out to a CSV file, but there's no way to map that data to the fields in a struct. We're going to add that missing functionality.

The examples here have been cut down a bit to fit, reducing the number of supported types. The complete code can be found on The Go Playground (*https://oreil.ly/VDytK*).

We'll start by defining our API. Like other marshalers, we'll define a struct tag that specifies the name of a field in the data to map it to a field in a struct:

```
type MyData struct {
    Name    string `csv:"name"`
    Age     int    `csv:"age"`
    HasPet  bool   `csv:"has_pet"`
}
```

The public API consists of two functions:

```
// Unmarshal maps all of the rows of data in a slice of slice of strings
// into a slice of structs.
// The first row is assumed to be the header with the column names.
func Unmarshal(data [][]string, v interface{}) error

// Marshal maps all of the structs in a slice of structs to a slice of slice
// of strings.
// The first row written is the header with the column names.
func Marshal(v interface{}) ([][]string, error)
```

We'll start with `Marshal`, writing the function and then looking at the two helper functions it uses:

```
func Marshal(v interface{}) ([][]string, error) {
    sliceVal := reflect.ValueOf(v)
    if sliceVal.Kind() != reflect.Slice {
        return nil, errors.New("must be a slice of structs")
    }
    structType := sliceVal.Type().Elem()
    if structType.Kind() != reflect.Struct {
        return nil, errors.New("must be a slice of structs")
    }
    var out [][]string
    header := marshalHeader(structType)
    out = append(out, header)
    for i := 0; i < sliceVal.Len(); i++ {
        row, err := marshalOne(sliceVal.Index(i))
        if err != nil {
            return nil, err
        }
        out = append(out, row)
    }
    return out, nil
}
```

Since we can marshal a struct of any type, we need to use a parameter of type `interface{}`. This isn't a pointer to a slice of structs, because we are only reading from our slice, not modifying it.

The first row of our CSV is going to be the header with the column names, so we get those column names from the struct tags on fields in the struct's type. We use the Type method to get the reflect.Type of the slice from the reflect.Value, and then call the Elem method to get the reflect.Type of the elements of the slice. We then pass this to marshalHeader and append the response to our output.

Next, we iterate through each element in the struct slice using reflection, passing the reflect.Value of each element to marshalOne, appending the result to our output. When we finish iterating, we return our slice of slice of string.

Let's look at the implementation of our first helper function, marshalHeader:

```go
func marshalHeader(vt reflect.Type) []string {
    var row []string
    for i := 0; i < vt.NumField(); i++ {
        field := vt.Field(i)
        if curTag, ok := field.Tag.Lookup("csv"); ok {
            row = append(row, curTag)
        }
    }
    return row
}
```

This function simply loops over the fields of the reflect.Type, reads the csv tag on each field, appends it into a string slice, and returns the slice.

The second helper function is marshalOne:

```go
func marshalOne(vv reflect.Value) ([]string, error) {
    var row []string
    vt := vv.Type()
    for i := 0; i < vv.NumField(); i++ {
        fieldVal := vv.Field(i)
        if _, ok := vt.Field(i).Tag.Lookup("csv"); !ok {
            continue
        }
        switch fieldVal.Kind() {
        case reflect.Int:
            row = append(row, strconv.FormatInt(fieldVal.Int(), 10))
        case reflect.String:
            row = append(row, fieldVal.String())
        case reflect.Bool:
            row = append(row, strconv.FormatBool(fieldVal.Bool()))
        default:
            return nil, fmt.Errorf("cannot handle field of kind %v",
                               fieldVal.Kind())
        }
    }
    return row, nil
}
```

It takes in a reflect.Value and returns a string slice. We create the string slice, and for each field in the struct, we switch on its reflect.Kind to determine how to convert it to a string, and append it to the output.

Our simple marshaler is now complete. Let's see what we have to do to unmarshal:

```go
func Unmarshal(data [][]string, v interface{}) error {
    sliceValPtr := reflect.ValueOf(v)
    if sliceValPtr.Kind() != reflect.Ptr {
        return errors.New("must be a pointer to a slice of structs")
    }
    sliceVal := sliceValPtr.Elem()
    if sliceVal.Kind() != reflect.Slice {
        return errors.New("must be a pointer to a slice of structs")
    }
    structType := sliceVal.Type().Elem()
    if structType.Kind() != reflect.Struct {
        return errors.New("must be a pointer to a slice of structs")
    }

    // assume the first row is a header
    header := data[0]
    namePos := make(map[string]int, len(header))
    for k, v := range header {
        namePos[v] = k
    }

    for _, row := range data[1:] {
        newVal := reflect.New(structType).Elem()
        err := unmarshalOne(row, namePos, newVal)
        if err != nil {
            return err
        }
        sliceVal.Set(reflect.Append(sliceVal, newVal))
    }
    return nil
}
```

Since we are copying data into a slice of any kind of struct, we need to use a parameter of type interface{}. Furthermore, because we are modifying the value stored in this parameter, we *must* pass in a pointer to a slice of structs. The Unmarshal function converts that slice of structs pointer to a reflect.Value, then gets the underlying slice, and then gets the type of the structs in the underlying slice.

As we said earlier, we're assuming that the first row of data is a header with the names of the columns. We use this information to build up a map, so we can associate the csv struct tag value with the correct data element.

We then loop through all of the remaining string slices, creating a new reflect.Value using the reflect.Type of the struct, call unmarshalOne to copy the data in the current string slice into the struct, and then add the struct to our slice. After iterating through all of the rows of data, we return.

All that remains is looking at the implementation of unmarshalOne:

```go
func unmarshalOne(row []string, namePos map[string]int, vv reflect.Value) error {
    vt := vv.Type()
    for i := 0; i < vv.NumField(); i++ {
        typeField := vt.Field(i)
        pos, ok := namePos[typeField.Tag.Get("csv")]
        if !ok {
            continue
        }
        val := row[pos]
        field := vv.Field(i)
        switch field.Kind() {
        case reflect.Int:
            i, err := strconv.ParseInt(val, 10, 64)
            if err != nil {
                return err
            }
            field.SetInt(i)
        case reflect.String:
            field.SetString(val)
        case reflect.Bool:
            b, err := strconv.ParseBool(val)
            if err != nil {
                return err
            }
            field.SetBool(b)
        default:
            return fmt.Errorf("cannot handle field of kind %v",
                            field.Kind())
        }
    }
    return nil
}
```

This function iterates over each field in the newly created reflect.Value, uses the csv struct tag on the current field to find its name, looks up the element in the data slice using the namePos map, converts the value from a string to the correct type, and sets the value on the current field. After all fields have been populated, the function returns.

Now that we have written our marshaler and unmarshaler, we can integrate with the existing CSV support in the Go standard library:

```
data := `name,age,has_pet
Jon,"100",true
"Fred ""The Hammer""" Smith",42,false
Martha,37,"true"
`

r := csv.NewReader(strings.NewReader(data))
allData, err := r.ReadAll()
if err != nil {
    panic(err)
}
var entries []MyData
Unmarshal(allData, &entries)
fmt.Println(entries)

//now to turn entries into output
out, err := Marshal(entries)
if err != nil {
    panic(err)
}
sb := &strings.Builder{}
w := csv.NewWriter(sb)
w.WriteAll(out)
fmt.Println(sb)
```

Build Functions with Reflection to Automate Repetitive Tasks

Another thing that Go lets you do with reflection is create a function. We can use this technique to wrap existing functions with common functionality without writing repetitive code. For example, here's a factory function that adds timing to any function that's passed into it:

```
func MakeTimedFunction(f interface{}) interface{} {
    ft := reflect.TypeOf(f)
    fv := reflect.ValueOf(f)
    wrapperF := reflect.MakeFunc(ft, func(in []reflect.Value) []reflect.Value {
        start := time.Now()
        out := fv.Call(in)
        end := time.Now()
        fmt.Println(end.Sub(start))
        return out
    })
    return wrapperF.Interface()
}
```

This function takes in any function, so the parameter is of type interface{}. It then passes the reflect.Type that represents the function into reflect.MakeFunc, along with a closure that captures the start time, calls the original function using reflection, captures the end time, prints out the difference, and returns the value calculated by the original function. The value returned from reflect.MakeFunc is a reflect.Value, and we call its Interface method to get the value to return. Here's how you use it:

```
func timeMe(a int) int {
    time.Sleep(time.Duration(a) * time.Second)
    result := a * 2
    return result
}

func main() {
    timed:= MakeTimedFunction(timeMe).(func(int) int)
    fmt.Println(timed(2))
}
```

You can run a more complete version of this program on The Go Playground (*https://oreil.ly/NDfp1*).

While generating functions is clever, be careful when using this feature. Make sure that it's clear when you are using a generated function and what functionality it is adding. Otherwise, you will be making it harder to understand the flow of data through your program. Furthermore, as we'll discuss in "Only Use Reflection If It's Worthwhile" on page 316, reflection makes your programs slower, so using it to generate and invoke functions seriously impacts performance unless the code you are generating is already performing a slow operation, like a network call. Remember, reflection works best when it's used to map data in and out of the edge of your programs.

One project that follows these rules for generated functions is my SQL mapping library Proteus. It creates a type-safe database API by generating a function from a SQL query and a function field or variable. You can learn more about Proteus in my GopherCon 2017 talk, "Runtime Generated, Typesafe, and Declarative: Pick Any Three" (*https://oreil.ly/ZUE47*) and you can find the source code on GitHub (*https://oreil.ly/KtFyj*).

You Can Build Structs with Reflection, but Don't

There's one more thing you can make with reflection and it's weird. The reflect.StructOf function takes in a slice of reflect.StructField and returns a reflect.Type that represents a new struct type. These structs can only be assigned to variables of type interface{}, and their fields can only be read and written using reflection.

For the most part, this is a feature of academic interest only. If you want to see a demo of how reflect.StructOf works, look at this memoizer function on The Go Playground (*https://oreil.ly/fXDk2*). It uses dynamically generated structs as the keys to a map that caches the output of a function.

Reflection Can't Make Methods

We've seen all the things that we can do with reflection, but there's one thing we can't make. While we can use reflection to create new functions and new struct types, there's no way to use reflection to add methods to a type. This means you cannot use reflection to create a new type that implements an interface.

Only Use Reflection If It's Worthwhile

While reflection is essential when converting data at the boundaries of Go, be careful using it in other situations. Reflection isn't free. To demonstrate, let's implement Filter using reflection. It's a common function in many languages, which takes in a list of values, tests each item in the list, and returns a list that only contains the items that passed the test. Go doesn't let you write a single type-safe function that works on slices of any type, but you can use reflection to write Filter:

```go
func Filter(slice interface{}, filter interface{}) interface{} {
    sv := reflect.ValueOf(slice)
    fv := reflect.ValueOf(filter)

    sliceLen := sv.Len()
    out := reflect.MakeSlice(sv.Type(), 0, sliceLen)
    for i := 0; i < sliceLen; i++ {
        curVal := sv.Index(i)
        values := fv.Call([]reflect.Value{curVal})
        if values[0].Bool() {
            out = reflect.Append(out, curVal)
        }
    }
    return out.Interface()
}
```

You use it like this:

```go
names := []string{"Andrew", "Bob", "Clara", "Hortense"}
longNames := Filter(names, func(s string) bool {
    return len(s) > 3
}).([]string)
fmt.Println(longNames)

ages := []int{20, 50, 13}
adults := Filter(ages, func(age int) bool {
    return age >= 18
}).([]int)
fmt.Println(adults)
```

This prints out:

```
[Andrew Clara Hortense]
[20 50]
```

Our reflection-using filter function isn't difficult to understand, but it's certainly longer than a custom-written function. Let's see how it performs on my i7-8700 with 32GB of RAM on Go 1.14 when filtering 1,000 element slices of strings and ints, compared to custom-written functions:

```
BenchmarkFilterReflectString-12    4822  229099 ns/op  87361 B/op  2219 allocs/op
BenchmarkFilterString-12         158197    7795 ns/op  16384 B/op     1 allocs/op
BenchmarkFilterReflectInt-12       4962  232885 ns/op  72256 B/op  2503 allocs/op
BenchmarkFilterInt-12            348441    3440 ns/op   8192 B/op     1 allocs/op
```

Sample code can be found on GitHub (*https://oreil.ly/Mj3SR*) so you can run it yourself.

Using reflection is roughly 30 times slower than a custom function for string filtering and nearly 70 times slower for ints. It uses significantly more memory and performs thousands of allocations, which creates additional work for the garbage collector. Depending on your needs, these might be acceptable trade-offs, but you should be hesitant.

A more serious downside is that the compiler can't stop you from passing in a wrong type for either the slice or the filter parameter. You might not mind a few thousand nanoseconds of CPU time, but if someone passes in a function or slice of the wrong type to Filter, your program will crash in production. The maintenance cost might be too high to accept. Writing the same function for multiple types might be repetitive, but saving a few lines of code isn't worth the cost most of the time.

unsafe Is Unsafe

Just as the reflect package allows us to manipulate types and values, the unsafe package allows us to manipulate memory. The unsafe package is very small and very odd. It defines three functions and one type, none of which act like the types and functions found in other packages.

The functions are Sizeof (which takes in a variable of any type and returns how many bytes it uses), Offsetof (which takes in a field of a struct and returns the number of bytes from the start of the struct to the start of the field), and Alignof (which takes in a field or a variable and returns the byte alignment it requires). Unlike every other non-built-in function in Go, these functions can have any value passed into them, and the values returned are constants, so they can be used in constant expressions.

The unsafe.Pointer type is a special type that exists for a single purpose: a pointer of any type can be converted to or from unsafe.Pointer. In addition to pointers, unsafe.Pointer can also be converted to or from a special integer type, called uintptr. Like any other integer type, you can do math with it. This allows you to walk into an instance of a type, extracting individual bytes. You can also perform pointer arithmetic, just like you can with pointers in C and C++. This byte manipulation changes the value of the variable.

There are two common patterns in unsafe code. The first is a conversion between two types of variables that are normally not convertible. This is performed using a series of type conversions with unsafe.Pointer in the middle. The second is reading or modifying the bytes in a variable by converting a variable to an unsafe.Pointer, converting the unsafe.Pointer to a uintptr, and then copying or manipulating the underlying bytes. Let's take a look at when you should do this and when you shouldn't.

Use unsafe to Convert External Binary Data

Given Go's focus on memory safety, you might wonder why unsafe even exists. Just as we used reflect to translate text data between the outside world and Go code, we use unsafe to translate binary data. There are two main reasons for using unsafe. A 2020 paper by Costa, Mujahid, Abdalkareem, and Shihab called "Breaking Type-Safety in Go: An Empirical Study on the Usage of the unsafe Package" (*https://oreil.ly/N_6JX*)[1] surveyed 2,438 popular Go open source projects and found:

- "24% of the studied Go projects use unsafe at least once in their code-base."
- "The majority of unsafe usages were motivated by integration with operating systems and C code (45.7%)."
- "Developers also frequently use unsafe to write more efficient Go code (23.6%)."

The plurality of the uses of unsafe are for system interoperability. The Go standard library uses unsafe to read data from and write data to the operating system. You can see examples in the syscall package in the standard library or in the higher-level sys package (*https://oreil.ly/ueHY3*). You can learn more about how to use unsafe to communicate with the operating system in a great blog post (*https://oreil.ly/VtE1t*) written by Matt Layher.

The second reason that people use unsafe is for performance, especially when reading data from a network. If you want to map the data into or out of a Go data structure, unsafe.Pointer gives you a very fast way to do so. Let's explore this with a contrived example. Let's imagine that we have a wire protocol with the following structure:

---

1 Costa, Diego Elias Damasceno, Suhaib Mujahid, Rabe Abdalkareem and Emad Shihab. "Breaking Type-Safety in Go: An Empirical Study on the Usage of the unsafe Package." ArXiv abs/2006.09973 (2020).

- Value: 4 bytes, representing an unsigned, big-endian 32-bit int
- Label: 10 bytes, ASCII name for the value
- Active: 1 byte, boolean flag to indicate if the field is active
- Padding: 1 byte, because we want everything to fit into 16 bytes

Data sent over a network is usually sent in big-endian (most significant bytes first) format, often called *network byte order*. Since most CPUs in use today are little-endian (or bi-endian running in little-endian mode), you need to be careful when reading or writing data to a network.

We can define a data structure that matches this:

```
type Data struct {
    Value  uint32   // 4 bytes
    Label  [10]byte // 10 bytes
    Active bool     // 1 byte
    // Go padded this with 1 byte to make it align
}
```

Let's say we just read the following bytes off the network:

```
[0 132 95 237 80 104 111 110 101 0 0 0 0 0 1 0]
```

We're going to read these bytes into an array of length 16 and then convert that array into the struct described previously.

Why are we using an array instead of a slice? Remember, arrays, like structs, are value types; the bytes are allocated directly. We'll look at how to use slices with unsafe in the next section.

With safe Go code, we could map it like this:

```
func DataFromBytes(b [16]byte) Data {
    d := Data{}
    d.Value = binary.BigEndian.Uint32(b[:4])
    copy(d.Label[:], b[4:14])
    d.Active = b[14] != 0
    return d
}
```

Or, we could use `unsafe.Pointer` instead:

```
func DataFromBytesUnsafe(b [16]byte) Data {
    data := *(*Data)(unsafe.Pointer(&b))
    if isLE {
        data.Value = bits.ReverseBytes32(data.Value)
    }
    return data
}
```

The first line is a little confusing, but we can take it apart and understand what's going on. First, we take a pointer to our byte array and convert it to an `unsafe.Pointer`. Then we convert the `unsafe.Pointer` to a `(*Data)` (we have to put `(*Data)` in parentheses because of Go's order of operations). We want to return the struct, not a pointer to it, so we dereference the pointer. Next, we check our flag to see if we are on a little-endian platform. If so, we reverse the bytes in the `Value` field. Finally, we return the value.

How do we know if we are on a little-endian platform? Here's the code we're using:

```
var isLE bool

func init() {
    var x uint16 = 0xFF00
    xb := *(*[2]byte)(unsafe.Pointer(&x))
    isLE = (xb[0] == 0x00)
}
```

As we discussed in "The init Function: Avoid if Possible" on page 186, you should avoid using `init` functions, except when initializing a package-level value whose value is effectively immutable. Since the endianness of your processor isn't going to change while your program is running, this is a good use case.

On a little-endian platform, the bytes that represent x will be stored as [00 FF]. On a big-endian platform, x is stored in memory as [FF 00]. We use `unsafe.Pointer` to convert a number to an array of bytes, and we check what the first byte is to determine the value of `isLE`.

Likewise, if we wanted to write our `Data` back to the network, we could use safe Go:

```
func BytesFromData(d Data) [16]byte {
    out := [16]byte{}
    binary.BigEndian.PutUint32(out[:4], d.Value)
    copy(out[4:14], d.Label[:])
    if d.Active {
        out[14] = 1
    }
    return out
}
```

Or we could use `unsafe`:

```
func BytesFromDataUnsafe(d Data) [16]byte {
    if isLE {
        d.Value = bits.ReverseBytes32(d.Value)
    }
    b := *(*[16]byte)(unsafe.Pointer(&d))
    return b
}
```

Is this worth it? On an Intel i7-8700 computer (which is little-endian), using `unsafe.Pointer` is roughly twice as fast:

```
BenchmarkBytesFromData-12        112741796   10.4 ns/op
BenchmarkBytesFromDataUnsafe-12  298846651    4.01 ns/op
BenchmarkDataFromBytes-12        100000000   10.3 ns/op
BenchmarkDataFromBytesUnsafe-12  235992582    5.95 ns/op
```

All of the examples in this section are found on GitHub (*https://oreil.ly/E4MEF*).

If you have a program with many of these kinds of conversions, then it's worth using these low-level techniques. But for the vast majority of programs, stick with the safe code.

unsafe Strings and Slices

We can also use `unsafe` to interact with slices and strings. As we implied in "Strings and Runes and Bytes" on page 48, a `string` is represented in Go as a pointer to a sequence of bytes and a length. There's a type in the `reflect` package called `reflect.StringHeader` that has this structure, and we use it to access and modify the underlying representation of a `string`:

```
s := "hello"
sHdr := (*reflect.StringHeader)(unsafe.Pointer(&s))
fmt.Println(sHdr.Len) // prints 5
```

We can read the bytes in the string using "pointer arithmetic," using the `Data` field in `sHdr`, which is of type `uintptr`:

```
for i := 0; i < sHdr.Len; i++ {
    bp := *(*byte)(unsafe.Pointer(sHdr.Data + uintptr(i)))
    fmt.Print(string(bp))
}
fmt.Println()
runtime.KeepAlive(s)
```

The `Data` field in the `reflect.StringHeader` is of type `uintptr`, and as we've discussed, you can't rely on a `uintptr` to refer to valid memory for longer than a single statement. How do we keep garbage collection from making this reference invalid? We do so by adding a call to `runtime.KeepAlive(s)` at the end of the function. This tells the Go runtime to not garbage collect s until after the call to `KeepAlive`.

If you want to give this code a try, go to The Go Playground (*https://oreil.ly/1DTR5*).

Just as you can get a `reflect.StringHeader` from a string via `unsafe`, you can get a `reflect.SliceHeader` from a slice. It has three fields, `Len`, `Cap`, and `Data`, which represent the length, capacity, and data pointer for the slice, respectively:

```
s := []int{10, 20, 30}
sHdr := (*reflect.SliceHeader)(unsafe.Pointer(&s))
fmt.Println(sHdr.Len) // prints 3
fmt.Println(sHdr.Cap) // prints 3
```

Just like we did for strings, we use a type conversion to convert a pointer to our `int` slice to an `unsafe.Pointer`. We then convert the `unsafe.Pointer` to a pointer to a `reflect.SliceHeader`. We can then access the length and the capacity of the slice via the `Len` and `Cap` fields. Next, we can walk through the slice:

```
intByteSize := unsafe.Sizeof(s[0])
fmt.Println(intByteSize)
for i := 0; i < sHdr.Len; i++ {
    intVal := *(*int)(unsafe.Pointer(sHdr.Data + intByteSize*uintptr(i)))
    fmt.Println(intVal)
}
runtime.KeepAlive(s)
```

Since the size of an `int` can be either 32 or 64 bits, we must use `unsafe.Sizeof` to find out how many bytes each value is in the block of memory that's pointed to by the `Data` field. We then convert `i` to `uintptr`, multiply it by the size of an `int`, add it to the `Data` field, convert from `uintptr` to `unsafe.Pointer`, and then convert to a pointer to an `int`, and then finally dereference the `int` to get the value.

You can run this code on The Go Playground (*https://oreil.ly/u9qB9*).

unsafe Tools

Go is a language that values tooling, and there is a compiler flag to help you find misuse of `uintptr` and `unsafe.Pointer`. Run your code with the flag `-gcflags=-d=checkptr` to add additional checks at runtime. Like the race checker, it's not guaranteed to find every `unsafe` problem and it does slow down your program. However, it's a good practice while testing your code.

If you want to learn more about `unsafe`, read through the package documentation (*https://oreil.ly/xmihF*).

The `unsafe` package is powerful and low-level! Avoid using it unless you know what you are doing and you need the performance improvements that it provides.

Cgo Is for Integration, Not Performance

Just like reflection and `unsafe`, `cgo` is most useful at the border between Go programs and the outside world. Reflection helps integrate with external textual data, `unsafe` is best used with operating system and network data, and `cgo` is best for integrating with C libraries.

Despite being nearly 50 years old, C is still the *lingua franca* of programming languages. All of the major operating systems are primarily written in either C or C++, which means that they are bundled with libraries written in C. It also means that nearly every programming language provides a way to integrate with C libraries. Go calls its FFI (foreign function interface) to C `cgo`.

As we have seen many times, Go is a language that favors explicit specification. Go developers sometimes deride automatic behaviors in other languages as "magic." However, using `cgo` feels a bit like spending time with Merlin. Let's take a look at this magical glue code. You can't run `cgo` code on The Go Playground, so you can find these code samples on GitHub (*https://oreil.ly/ct9xd*). We'll start with a very simple program that calls C code to do some math:

```
package main

import "fmt"

/*
    #cgo LDFLAGS: -lm
    #include <stdio.h>
    #include <math.h>
    #include "mylib.h"

    int add(int a, int b) {
        int sum = a + b;
        printf("a: %d, b: %d, sum %d\n", a, b, sum);
        return sum;
    }
*/
import "C"

func main() {
    sum := C.add(3, 2)
    fmt.Println(sum)
    fmt.Println(C.sqrt(100))
```

```
        fmt.Println(C.multiply(10, 20))
}
```

The *mylib.h* header is in the same directory as our *main.go*, along with *mylib.c*:

```
int multiply(int a, int b);

#include "mylib.h"

int multiply(int a, int b) {
    return a * b;
}
```

Assuming you have a C compiler installed on your computer, all you need to do is compile your program with go build:

```
$ go build
$ ./example1
a: 3, b: 2, sum 5
5
10
200
```

What's going on here? There isn't a real package in the standard library named C. Instead, C is an automatically generated package whose identifiers mostly come from the C code embedded in the comments that immediately proceed it. In our example, we declare a C function called add and cgo makes it available to your Go program as the name C.add. We can also invoke functions or global variables that are imported into the comment block from libraries via header files, as you can see when we call C.sqrt from main (imported from *math.h*) or C.multiply (imported from *mylib.h*).

In addition to the identifier names that appear in the comment block (or are imported into the comment block), the C pseudopackage also defines types like C.int and C.char to represent the built-in C types and functions, such as C.CString to convert a Go string to a C string.

You can use more magic to call Go functions from C functions. Go function can be exposed to C code by putting an //export comment before the function:

```
//export doubler
func doubler(i int) int {
    return i * 2
}
```

If you do this, you can no longer declare C code directly in the comment before the import "C" statement. You can only declare functions, not define them:

```
/*
    extern int add(int a, int b);
*/
import "C"
```

You then have to place your C code into a *.c* file in the same directory as your Go code and include the magic header "_cgo_export.h":

```
#include "_cgo_export.h"

int add(int a, int b) {
    int doubleA = doubler(a);
    int sum = doubleA + b;
    return sum;
}
```

So far, this seems pretty simple, but there's one stumbling block when using cgo: Go is a garbage-collected language and C is not. This makes it difficult to integrate non-trivial Go code with C. While you can pass a pointer into C code, you cannot pass something that contains a pointer. This is very limiting, as things like strings, slices, and functions are implemented with pointers and therefore cannot be contained in a struct passed into a C function. That's not all: a C function cannot store a copy of a Go pointer that lasts after the function returns. If you break these rules, your program will compile and run, but it may crash or behave incorrectly at runtime when the memory pointed to by the pointer is garbage collected.

There are other limitations. For example, you cannot use cgo to call a variadic C function (such as printf). Union types in C are converted into byte arrays. And you cannot invoke a C function pointer (but you can assign it to a Go variable and pass it back into a C function).

These rules make using cgo nontrivial. If you have a background in Python or Ruby, you might think that using cgo is worth it for performance reasons. Those developers write the performance-critical parts of their programs in C. The speed of NumPy is due to the C libraries that are wrapped by Python code.

In most cases, Go code is many times faster than Python or Ruby, so the need to rewrite algorithms in a lower-level language is greatly reduced. You might think that you could save cgo for those situations when you do need additional performance gains, but unfortunately, it's very difficult to make your code faster using cgo. Due to the mismatches in the processing and memory models, calling a C function from Go is roughly 29 times slower than a C function calling another C function. At CapitalGo 2018, Filippo Valsorda gave a talk, called "Why cgo is slow." Unfortunately, the talk wasn't recorded, but slides are available (*https://oreil.ly/MLRFY*). They explain why cgo is slow and why it will not be made appreciably faster in the future.

Since cgo isn't fast, and it isn't easy to use for nontrivial programs, the only reason to use cgo is if there is a C library that you must use and there is no suitable Go replacement. Rather than writing cgo yourself, see if there's already a third-party module that provides the wrapper. For example, if you want to embed SQLite in a Go application, look at GitHub (*https://oreil.ly/IEskN*). For ImageMagick, check out this repository (*https://oreil.ly/l58-1*).

If you find yourself needing to use an internal C library or third-party library that doesn't have a wrapper, you can find additional details (*https://oreil.ly/9JvNI*) on how to write your integration in the Go documentation. For information on the sorts of performance and design trade-offs that you are likely to encounter when using cgo, read Tobias Grieger's blog post called "The Cost and Complexity of Cgo" (*https://oreil.ly/Oj9Tw*).

Wrapping Up

In this chapter, we've covered reflection, unsafe, and cgo. These features are probably the most exciting parts of Go because they allow you to break the rules that make Go a boring, type-safe, memory-safe language. More importantly, we've learned *why* you would want to break the rules and why you should avoid doing so most of the time.

In the next chapter, we're taking a look at a feature that's coming soon: Go is adding generics.

CHAPTER 15

Welcome to the Future: Generics in Go

Despite the lower priority placed on features, Go isn't a static, unchanging language. New features are adopted slowly, after much discussion and experimentation. Since the initial release of Go 1.0, there have been significant changes to the patterns that define idiomatic Go. The first was the adoption of the context in Go 1.7. This was followed by the adoption of modules in Go 1.11 and error wrapping in Go 1.13.

The next big change has arrived. Version 1.18 of Go includes an implementation of type parameters, which are colloquially referred to as generics. In this chapter we'll explore why people want generics, what Go's implementation of generics can do, what generics can't do, and how they might change idiomatic patterns.

Generics Reduce Repetitive Code and Increase Type Safety

Go is a statically typed language, which means that the types of variables and parameters are checked when the code is compiled. Built-in types (maps, slices, channels) and functions (such as len, cap, or make) are able to accept and return values of different concrete types, but until Go 1.18, user-defined Go types and functions could not.

If you are familiar with dynamically typed languages, where types are not evaluated until the code runs, you might not understand what the fuss is about generics, and you might be a bit unclear on what they are. It helps if you think of them as "type parameters." We are used to writing functions that take in parameters whose values are specified when the function is called. In this code, we specify that Min takes in two parameters of type float64 and returns a float64:

```
func Min(v1, v2 float64) float64 {
    if v1 < v2 {
        return v1
    }
```

```
        return v2
    }
```

Similarly, we create structs where the type for the fields is specified when the struct is declared. Here, Node has a field of type int and another field of type *Node.

```
type Node struct {
    val int
    next *Node
}
```

There are, however, situations where it's useful to write functions or structs where the specific *type* of a parameter or field is left unspecified until it is used.

The case for generic types is easy to understand. In "Code Your Methods for nil Instances" on page 133, we looked at a binary tree for ints. If we want a binary tree for strings or float64s and we wanted type safety, there are a few options. The first possibility is writing a custom tree for each type, but having that much duplicated code is verbose and error-prone.

Before Go added generics, the only way to avoid duplicated code would be to modify our tree implementation so that it uses an interface to specify how to order values. The interface would look like this:

```
type Orderable interface {
    // Order returns:
    // a value < 0 when the Orderable is less than the supplied value,
    // a value > 0 when the Orderable is greater than the supplied value,
    // and 0 when the two values are equal.
    Order(interface{}) int
}
```

Now that we have Orderable, we can modify our Tree implementation to support it:

```
type Tree struct {
    val         Orderable
    left, right *Tree
}

func (t *Tree) Insert(val Orderable) *Tree {
    if t == nil {
        return &Tree{val: val}
    }

    switch comp := val.Order(t.val); {
    case comp < 0:
        t.left = t.left.Insert(val)
    case comp > 0:
        t.right = t.right.Insert(val)
    }
    return t
}
```

With an `OrderableInt` type, we can then insert `int` values:

```
type OrderableInt int

func (oi OrderableInt) Order(val interface{}) int {
    return int(oi - val.(OrderableInt))
}

func main() {
    var it *Tree
    it = it.Insert(OrderableInt(5))
    it = it.Insert(OrderableInt(3))
    // etc...
}
```

While this code works correctly, it doesn't allow the compiler to validate that the values inserted into our data structure are all the same. If we also had an `Orderable String` type:

```
type OrderableString string

func (os OrderableString) Order(val interface{}) int {
    return strings.Compare(string(os), val.(string))
}
```

The following code compiles:

```
var it *Tree
it = it.Insert(OrderableInt(5))
it = it.Insert(OrderableString("nope"))
```

The `Order` function uses `interface{}` to represent the value that's passed in. This effectively short-circuits one of Go's primary advantages, compile-time type safety checking. When we compile code that attempts to insert an `OrderableString` into a `Tree` that already contains an `OrderableInt`, the compiler accepts the code. However, the program panics when run:

```
panic: interface conversion: interface {} is main.OrderableInt, not string
```

Now that Go has added generics, there's a way to implement a data structure once for multiple types and detect incompatible data at compile-time. We'll see how to properly use them in just a bit.

While data structures without generics are inconvenient, the real limitation is in writing functions. Several implementation decisions in Go's standard library were made because generics weren't originally part of the language. For example, rather than write multiple functions to handle different numeric types, Go implements functions like `math.Max`, `math.Min`, and `math.Mod` using `float64` parameters, which have a range big enough to represent nearly every other numeric type exactly. (The exceptions are an `int`, `int64`, or `uint` with a value greater than $2^{53} - 1$ or less than $-2^{53} - 1$.)

There are other things that are impossible without generics. You cannot create a new instance of a variable that's specified by interface, nor can you specify that two parameters that are of the same interface type are also of the same concrete type. Without generics, you cannot write a function to process a slice of any type without resorting to reflection and giving up some performance along with compile-time type safety (this is how sort.Slice works). This meant that historically, functions that operate on slices would be repeated for each type of slice.

In 2017, I wrote a blog post called *Closures Are the Generics for Go* (*https://oreil.ly/2pKYt*) that explored using closures to work around some of these issues. However, the closure approach has several drawbacks. It is far less readable, forces values to escape to the heap, and simply doesn't work in many common situations.

The result is that many common algorithms, such as map, reduce, and filter, end up being reimplemented for different types. While simple algorithms are easy enough to copy, many (if not most) software engineers find it grating to duplicate code simply because the compiler isn't smart enough to do it automatically.

Introducing Generics in Go

Since the first announcement of Go, there have been calls for generics to be added to the language. Russ Cox, the development lead for Go, wrote a blog post (*https://oreil.ly/U4huA*) in 2009 to explain why generics weren't initially included. Go emphasizes a fast compiler, readable code, and good execution time, and none of the generics implementations that they were aware of would allow them to include all three. After a decade studying the problem, the Go team has a workable approach, which is outlined in the Type Parameters Proposal (*https://oreil.ly/31ay7*).

We'll see how generics work in Go by looking at a stack. If you don't have a computer science background, a stack is a data type where values are added and removed in last in-first out (LIFO) order. It's like a pile of dishes waiting to be washed; the ones that were placed first are at the bottom, and you only get to them by working through the ones that were added later. Let's see how to make a stack using generics:

```go
type Stack[T any] struct {
    vals []T
}

func (s *Stack[T]) Push(val T) {
    s.vals = append(s.vals, val)
}

func (s *Stack[T]) Pop() (T, bool) {
    if len(s.vals) == 0 {
        var zero T
        return zero, false
    }
```

```
        top := s.vals[len(s.vals)-1]
        s.vals = s.vals[:len(s.vals)-1]
        return top, true
    }
```

There are a few things to note. First, we have [T any] after the type declaration. Type parameters are placed within brackets. They are written just like variable parameters, with the type name first and the type constraint second. You can pick any name for the type parameter, but it is customary to use capital letters for them. Go uses interfaces to specify which types can be used. If any type is usable, this is specified with the new universe block identifier any, which is exactly equivalent to interface{}. (starting with Go 1.18 and later, you can use any anywhere in your code where you would have used interface{}, but be aware that your code will not compile with versions of Go before 1.18.) Inside the Stack declaration, we declare vals to be of type []T.

Next, we look at our method declarations. Just like we used T in our vals declaration, we do the same here. We also refer to the type in the receiver section with Stack[T] instead of Stack.

Finally, generics make zero value handling a little interesting. In Pop, we can't just return nil, because that's not a valid value for a value type, like int. The easiest way to get a zero value for a generic is to simply declare a variable with var and return it, since by definition, var always initializes its variable to the zero value if no other value is assigned.

Using a generic type is very similar to using a nongeneric one:

```
func main() {
    var intStack Stack[int]
    intStack.Push(10)
    intStack.Push(20)
    intStack.Push(30)
    v, ok := intStack.Pop()
    fmt.Println(v, ok)
}
```

The only difference is that when we declare our variable, we include the type that we want to use with our Stack, in this case int. If you try to push a string onto our stack, the compiler will catch it. Adding the line:

```
intStack.Push("nope")
```

produces the compiler error:

```
cannot use "nope" (untyped string constant) as int value
    in argument to intStack.Push
```

You can try out our generic stack on The Go Playground (*https://oreil.ly/9vzHB*) .

Let's add another method to our stack to tell us if the stack contains a value:

```go
func (s Stack[T]) Contains(val T) bool {
    for _, v := range s.vals {
        if v == val {
            return true
        }
    }
    return false
}
```

Unfortunately, this does not compile. It gives the error:

```
invalid operation: v == val (type parameter T is not comparable with ==)
```

Just as `interface{}` doesn't say anything, neither does any. We can only store values of any type and retrieve them. To use `==`, we need a different type. Since nearly all Go types can be compared with `==` and `!=`, a new built-in interface called `comparable` is defined in the universe block. If we change our definition of `Stack` to use `comparable`:

```go
type Stack[T comparable] struct {
    vals []T
}
```

we can then use our new method:

```go
func main() {
    var s Stack[int]
    s.Push(10)
    s.Push(20)
    s.Push(30)
    fmt.Println(s.Contains(10))
    fmt.Println(s.Contains(5))
}
```

This prints out:

```
true
false
```

You can try out this updated stack (*https://oreil.ly/Qc4J3*) as well.

Later on, we'll see how to make a generic binary tree. Before we do so, we're going to cover some additional concepts: *generic functions*, how generics work with interfaces, and *type terms*.

Generic Functions Abstract Algorithms

As we have hinted, you can also write generic functions. Earlier we mentioned that not having generics made it difficult to write map, reduce, and filter implementations that work for all types. Generics make it easy. Here are implementations from the type parameters proposal:

```
// Map turns a []T1 to a []T2 using a mapping function.
// This function has two type parameters, T1 and T2.
// This works with slices of any type.
func Map[T1, T2 any](s []T1, f func(T1) T2) []T2 {
    r := make([]T2, len(s))
    for i, v := range s {
        r[i] = f(v)
    }
    return r
}

// Reduce reduces a []T1 to a single value using a reduction function.
func Reduce[T1, T2 any](s []T1, initializer T2, f func(T2, T1) T2) T2 {
    r := initializer
    for _, v := range s {
        r = f(r, v)
    }
    return r
}

// Filter filters values from a slice using a filter function.
// It returns a new slice with only the elements of s
// for which f returned true.
func Filter[T any](s []T, f func(T) bool) []T {
    var r []T
    for _, v := range s {
        if f(v) {
            r = append(r, v)
        }
    }
    return r
}
```

Functions place their type parameters after the function name and before the variable parameters. Map and Reduce have two type parameters, both of any type, while Filter has one. When we run the code:

```
words := []string{"One", "Potato", "Two", "Potato"}
filtered := Filter(words, func(s string) bool {
    return s != "Potato"
})
fmt.Println(filtered)
lengths := Map(filtered, func(s string) int {
    return len(s)
})
fmt.Println(lengths)
sum := Reduce(lengths, 0, func(acc int, val int) int {
    return acc + val
})
fmt.Println(sum)
```

we get the output:

```
[One Two]
[3 3]
6
```

Try it (*https://oreil.ly/Ahf2b*) for yourself.

Generics and Interfaces

You can use any interface as a type constraint, not just any and comparable. For example, say you wanted to make a type that holds any two values of the same type, as long as the type implements fmt.Stringer. Generics make it possible to enforce this at compile-time:

```
type Pair[T fmt.Stringer] struct {
    Val1 T
    Val2 T
}
```

You can also create interfaces that have type parameters. For example, here's an interface with a method that compares against a value of the specified type and returns a float64. It also embeds fmt.Stringer:

```
type Differ[T any] interface {
    fmt.Stringer
    Diff(T) float64
}
```

We'll use these two types to create a comparison function. The function takes in two Pair instances that have fields of type Differ, and returns the Pair with the closer values:

```
func FindCloser[T Differ[T]](pair1, pair2 Pair[T]) Pair[T] {
    d1 := pair1.Val1.Diff(pair1.Val2)
    d2 := pair2.Val1.Diff(pair2.Val2)
    if d1 < d2 {
        return pair1
    }
    return pair2
}
```

Note that FindCloser takes in Pair instances that have fields that meet the Differ interface. Pair requires that its fields are both of the same type and that the type meets the fmt.Stringer interface; this function is more selective. If the fields in a Pair instance don't meet Differ, the compiler will prevent you from using that Pair instance with FindCloser.

We now define a couple of types that meet the Differ interface:

```
type Point2D struct {
    X, Y int
}
```

```go
func (p2 Point2D) String() string {
    return fmt.Sprintf("{%d,%d}", p2.X, p2.Y)
}

func (p2 Point2D) Diff(from Point2D) float64 {
    x := p2.X - from.X
    y := p2.Y - from.Y
    return math.Sqrt(float64(x*x) + float64(y*y))
}

type Point3D struct {
    X, Y, Z int
}

func (p3 Point3D) String() string {
    return fmt.Sprintf("{%d,%d,%d}", p3.X, p3.Y, p3.Z)
}

func (p3 Point3D) Diff(from Point3D) float64 {
    x := p3.X - from.X
    y := p3.Y - from.Y
    z := p3.Z - from.Z
    return math.Sqrt(float64(x*x) + float64(y*y) + float64(z*z))
}
```

And here's what it looks like to use this code:

```go
func main() {
    pair2Da := Pair[Point2D]{Point2D{1, 1}, Point2D{5, 5}}
    pair2Db := Pair[Point2D]{Point2D{10, 10}, Point2D{15, 5}}
    closer := FindCloser(pair2Da, pair2Db)
    fmt.Println(closer)

    pair3Da := Pair[Point3D]{Point3D{1, 1, 10}, Point3D{5, 5, 0}}
    pair3Db := Pair[Point3D]{Point3D{10, 10, 10}, Point3D{11, 5, 0}}
    closer2 := FindCloser(pair3Da, pair3Db)
    fmt.Println(closer2)
}
```

Run it for yourself on The Go Playground (*https://oreil.ly/rnKj9*).

Use Type Terms to Specify Operators

There's one more thing that we need to represent with generics: operators. If we want to write a generic version of Min, we need a way to specify that we can use comparison operators, like < and >. Go generics do that with a *type element*, which is composed of one or more *type terms* within an interface:

```go
type BuiltInOrdered interface {
    string | int | int8 | int16 | int32 | int64 | float32 | float64 |
```

```
                uint | uint8 | uint16 | uint32 | uint64 | uintptr
    }
```

We've already seen interfaces that have type elements in "Embedding and Interfaces" on page 146 . In that situation, we were embedding another interface to indicate that the method set of the containing interface includes the methods of the embedded interface. Here, we are listing concrete types separated by |. This specifies which types can be assigned to a type parameter and which operators are supported. The allowed operators are the ones that are valid for *all* of the listed types. In this case, those are the operators ==, !=, >, <, >=, <=, and +. Be aware that interfaces with concrete type terms in a type element are only valid as type parameter bounds. It is a compile-time error to use them as the type for a variable, field, return value, or parameter.

Now we can write our generic version of Min and use it with the built-in int type (or any of the other types listed in BuiltInOrdered):

```
func Min[T BuiltInOrdered](v1, v2 T) T {
    if v1 < v2 {
        return v1
    }
    return v2
}

func main() {
    a := 10
    b := 20
    fmt.Println(Min(a, b))
}
```

By default, type terms match exactly. If we try to use Min with a user-defined type whose underlying type is one of the types listed in BuiltInOrdered, we'll get an error. This code:

```
type MyInt int
var myA MyInt = 10
var myB MyInt = 20
fmt.Println(Min(myA, myB))
```

Produces the error:

```
MyInt does not implement BuiltInOrdered (possibly missing ~ for
int in constraint BuiltInOrdered)
```

The error text gives a hint for how to solve this problem. If you want a type term to be valid for any type that has the type term as its underlying type, put a ~ before the type term. This changes our definition of BuiltInOrdered to:

```
type BuiltInOrdered interface {
    ~string | ~int | ~int8 | ~int16 | ~int32 | ~int64 | ~float32 | ~float64 |
```

```
        ~uint | ~uint8 | ~uint16 | ~uint32 | ~uint64 | ~uintptr
}
```

You can look at this Min function on The Go Playground (*https://oreil.ly/1Cwq8*).

It is legal to have both type elements and method elements in an interface used for a type parameter. For example, you could specify that a type must have an underlying type of int and a String() string method:

```
type PrintableInt interface {
    ~int
    String() string
}
```

Be aware that Go will let you declare a type parameter interface that is impossible to actually instantiate. If we had used int instead of ~int in PrintableInt, there would be no valid type that meets it, since int has no methods. This might seem bad, but the compiler still comes to your rescue. If you declare a type or function with an impossible type parameter, any attempt to use it causes a compiler error. Assume we declare these types:

```
type ImpossiblePrintableInt interface {
    int
    String() string
}

type ImpossibleStruct[T ImpossiblePrintableInt] struct {
    val T
}

type MyInt int

func (mi MyInt) String() string {
    return fmt.Sprint(mi)
}
```

Even though we cannot instantiate ImpossibleStruct, the compiler has no problem with any of these declarations. However, once we try using ImpossibleStruct, the compiler complains. This code:

```
s := ImpossibleStruct[int]{10}
s2 := ImpossibleStruct[MyInt]{10}
```

Produces the compile-time errors:

```
int does not implement ImpossiblePrintableInt (missing String method)
MyInt does not implement ImpossiblePrintableInt (possibly missing ~ for
int in constraint ImpossiblePrintableInt)
```

Try this out on The Go Playground (*https://oreil.ly/eFx6t*).

In addition to built-in primitive types, type terms can also be slices, maps, arrays, channels, structs, or even functions. They are most useful when you want to ensure that a type parameter has a specific underlying type and one or more methods.

Type Inference and Generics

Just as Go supports type inference when using the := operator, it also supports type inference to simplify calls to generic functions. You can see this in the calls to Map, Filter, and Reduce above. In some situations, type inference isn't possible (for example, when a type parameter is only used as a return value). When that happens, all type arguments must be specified. Here's a slightly silly bit of code that demonstrates a situation where type inference doesn't work:

```
type Integer interface {
    int | int8 | int16 | int32 | int64 | uint | uint8 | uint16 | uint32 | uint64
}

func Convert[T1, T2 Integer](in T1) T2 {
    return T2(in)
}

func main() {
    var a int = 10
    b := Convert[int, int64](a) // can't infer the return type
    fmt.Println(b)
}
```

Try it out (*https://oreil.ly/tWsu3*) on The Go Playground.

Type Elements Limit Constants

Type elements also specify which constants can be assigned to variables of the generic type. Like operators, the constants need to be valid for all the type terms in the type element. There are no constants that can be assigned to every listed type in BuiltInOrdered, so you cannot assign a constant to a variable of that generic type. If you use the Integer interface, the following code will not compile, because you cannot assign 1,000 to an 8-bit integer:

```
// INVALID!
func PlusOneThousand[T Integer](in T) T {
    return in + 1_000
}
```

However, this is valid:

```
// VALID
func PlusOneHundred[T Integer](in T) T {
    return in + 100
}
```

Combining Generic Functions with Generic Data Structures

Let's return to our binary tree example and see how to combine everything we've learned to make a single tree that works for any concrete type.

The secret is to realize that what our tree needs is a single generic function that compares two values and tells us their order:

```
type OrderableFunc [T any] func(t1, t2 T) int
```

Now that we have OrderableFunc, we can modify our tree implementation slightly. First, we're going to split it into two types, Tree and Node :

```
type Tree[T any] struct {
    f    OrderableFunc[T]
    root *Node[T]
}

type Node[T any] struct {
    val        T
    left, right *Node[T]
}
```

We construct a new Tree with a constructor function:

```
func NewTree[T any](f OrderableFunc[T]) *Tree[T] {
    return &Tree[T]{
        f: f,
    }
}
```

Tree 's methods are very simple, because they just call Node to do all the real work:

```
func (t *Tree[T]) Add(v T) {
    t.root = t.root.Add(t.f, v)
}

func (t *Tree[T]) Contains(v T) bool {
    return t.root.Contains(t.f, v)
}
```

The Add and Contains methods on Node are very similar to what we've seen before. The only difference is that the function we are using to order our elements is passed in:

```
func (n *Node[T]) Add(f OrderableFunc[T], v T) *Node[T] {
    if n == nil {
        return &Node[T]{val: v}
    }
    switch r := f(v, n.val); {
    case r <= -1:
```

```
            n.left = n.left.Add(f, v)
        case r >= 1:
            n.right = n.right.Add(f, v)
        }
        return n
    }

    func (n *Node[T]) Contains(f OrderableFunc[T], v T) bool {
        if n == nil {
            return false
        }
        switch r := f(v, n.val); {
        case r <= -1:
            return n.left.Contains(f, v)
        case r >= 1:
            return n.right.Contains(f, v)
        }
        return true
    }
```

Now we need a function that matches the OrderedFunc definition. By taking advantage of BuiltInOrdered, we can write a single function that supports any primitive type:

```
    func BuiltInOrderable[T BuiltInOrdered](t1, t2 T) int {
        if t1 < t2 {
            return -1
        }
        if t1 > t2 {
            return 1
        }
        return 0
    }
```

When we use BuiltInOrderable with our Tree, it looks like this:

```
    t1 := NewTree(BuiltInOrderable[int])
    t1.Add(10)
    t1.Add(30)
    t1.Add(15)
    fmt.Println(t1.Contains(15))
    fmt.Println(t1.Contains(40))
```

For structs, we have two options. We can write a function:

```
    type Person struct {
        Name string
        Age  int
    }

    func OrderPeople(p1, p2 Person) int {
        out := strings.Compare(p1.Name, p2.Name)
        if out == 0 {
```

```
        out = p1.Age - p2.Age
    }
    return out
}
```

Then we can pass that function in when we create our tree:

```
t2 := NewTree(OrderPeople)
t2.Add(Person{"Bob", 30})
t2.Add(Person{"Maria", 35})
t2.Add(Person{"Bob", 50})
fmt.Println(t2.Contains(Person{"Bob", 30}))
fmt.Println(t2.Contains(Person{"Fred", 25}))
```

Instead of using a function, we can also supply a method to NewTree. As we talked about in "Methods Are Functions Too" on page 134, you can use a method expression to treat a method like a function. Let's do that here. First we write the method:

```
func (p Person)Order(other Person) int {
    out := strings.Compare(p.Name, other.Name)
    if out == 0 {
        out = p.Age - other.Age
    }
    return out
}
```

And then we use it:

```
t3 := NewTree(Person.Order)
t3.Add(Person{"Bob", 30})
t3.Add(Person{"Maria", 35})
t3.Add(Person{"Bob", 50})
fmt.Println(t3.Contains(Person{"Bob", 30}))
fmt.Println(t3.Contains(Person{"Fred", 25}))
```

You can find the code for this tree on The Go Playground (*https://oreil.ly/7KhTT*).

Things That Are Left Out

Go remains a small, focused language, and the generics implementation for Go doesn't include many features that are found in generics implementations in other languages. Here are some of the features that are not in the initial implementation of Go generics.

While we can build a single tree that works with both user-defined and built-in types, languages like Python, Ruby, and C++ solve this problem in a different way. They include *operator overloading*, which allows user-defined types to specify implementations for operators. Go will not be adding this feature. This means that you can't use range to iterate over user-defined container types or [ ] to index into them.

There are good reasons for leaving out operator overloading. For one thing, there are a surprisingly large number of operators in Go. Go also doesn't have function or method overloading, and you'd need a way to specify different operator functionality for different types. Furthermore, operator overloading can lead to code that's harder to follow as developers invent clever meanings for symbols (in C++, << means "shift bits left" for some types and "write the value on the right to the value on the left" for others). These are the sorts of readability issues that Go tries to avoid.

Another useful feature that's been left out of the initial Go generics implementation is additional type parameters on methods. Looking back on the Map/Reduce/Filter functions, you might think they'd be useful as methods, like this:

```
type functionalSlice[T any] []T

// THIS DOES NOT WORK
func (fs functionalSlice[T]) Map[E any](f func(T) E) functionalSlice[E] {
    out := make(functionalSlice[E], len(fs))
    for i, v := range fs {
        out[i] = f(v)
    }
    return out
}

// THIS DOES NOT WORK
func (fs functionalSlice[T]) Reduce[E any](start E, f func(E, T) E) E {
    out := start
    for _, v := range fs {
        out = f(out, v)
    }
    return out
}
```

which you could use like this:

```
var numStrings = functionalSlice[string]{"1", "2", "3"}
sum := numStrings.Map(func(s string) int {
    v, _ := strconv.Atoi(s)
    return v
}).Reduce(0, func(acc int, cur int) int {
    return acc + cur
})
```

Unfortunately for fans of functional programming, this does not work. Rather than chaining method calls together, you need to either nest function calls or use the much more readable approach of invoking the functions one at a time and assigning the intermediate values to variables. The type parameter proposal goes into detail on the reasons for excluding parameterized methods.

There are also no variadic type parameters. In "Build Functions with Reflection to Automate Repetitive Tasks" on page 314, we wrote a wrapper function using reflection to time any existing function. Those must still be handled via reflection as there's no way to do this with generics. Any time you use type parameters, you must explicitly provide a name for each type you need, so you cannot represent a function with any number of parameters of different types.

Other features left out of Go generics are more esoteric. These include:

Specialization
A function or method can be overloaded with one or more type-specific versions in addition to the generic version. Since Go doesn't have overloading, this feature is not under consideration.

Currying
Allows you to partially instantiate a function or type based on another generic function or type by specifying some of the type parameters.

Metaprogramming
Allows you to specify code that runs at compile-time to produce code that runs at runtime.

Idiomatic Go and Generics

Adding generics clearly changes some of the advice for how to use Go idiomatically. The use of `float64` to represent any numeric type will end. You should use `any` instead of `interface{}` to represent an unspecified type in a data structure or function parameter. You can handle different slice types with a single function. But don't feel the need to switch all of your code over to using type parameters immediately. Your old code will still work as new design patterns are invented and refined.

It's still too early to judge the long-term impact of generics on performance. The compiler in Go 1.18 is slower than in previous versions, but this is expected to be addressed in future releases. There has already been some research on the current runtime impact. Vicent Marti wrote a detailed blog post (*https://oreil.ly/YK4HT*) where he explores cases where generics result in slower code and the implementation details that explain why this is so. Conversely, Eli Bendersky wrote a blog post (*https://oreil.ly/2Mqms*) that shows that generics make sorting algorithms faster. Again, as the generics implementation matures in future versions of Go, expect runtime performance to improve.

As always, the goal is to write maintainable programs that are fast enough to meet your needs. Use the benchmarking and profiling tools we discussed in "Benchmarks" on page 285 to measure and improve.

Further Futures Unlocked

The initial release of generics in Go 1.18 was very conservative. It added the new interfaces any and comparable to the universe block, but there were no API changes in the standard library to support generics. A stylistic change has been made; virtually all uses of interface{} in the standard library were replaced with any.

It is likely that future versions of the standard library will include new interface definitions to represent common cases (like Orderable), new types (like a set, tree, or ordered map), and new functions. Feel free to write your own in the meantime, but consider replacing them once the standard library is updated.

Generics might be the basis for other future features. One possibility is *sum types*. Just as type elements are used to specify the types that can be substituted for a type parameter, they could also be used for interfaces in variable parameters. This would enable some interesting features. Today, Go has a problem with a common situation in JSON: a field that can be a single value or a list of values. Even with generics, the only way to handle this is with a field of type any. Adding sum types would allow you to create an interface that specifies that a field could be a string, a slice of strings, and nothing else. A type switch could then completely enumerate every valid type, improving type safety. This ability to specify a bounded set of types allows many modern languages (including Rust and Swift) to use sum types to represent enums. Given the weakness of Go's current enum features, this might be an attractive solution, but it will take time for these ideas to be evaluated and explored.

Wrapping Up

In this chapter, we took a look at generics and how to use them to simplify our code. It's still early days for generics in Go. It will be exciting to see how they help grow the language while still maintaining the spirit that make Go special.

We've completed our journey through Go and how to use it idiomatically. Like any graduation ceremony, it's time for a few closing words. Let's look back at what was said in the preface. "[P]roperly written, Go is boring....Well-written Go programs tend to be straightforward and sometimes a bit repetitive." I hope you can now see why this leads to better software engineering. Idiomatic Go is a set of tools, practices, and patterns that makes it easier to maintain software across time and changing teams. That's not to say the cultures around other languages don't value maintainability; it just may not be their highest priority. Instead, they emphasize things like performance, new features, or concise syntax. There is a place for these trade-offs, but in the long run, I suspect Go's focus on crafting software that lasts will win out.

I wish you the best as you create the software for the next 50 years of computing.

Index

I

identifiers, exporting, 178, 189
IEEE 754 specification, 23
if statements, 65-67, 83
imag function, 24
immutable values, 29, 187
implicit interfaces, 142, 155-159
import paths, 180, 199
import statement, 61, 178, 187
increment operator (++), 54
index expression, 48
indirection operator (*), 109
inheritance, 135, 140
init function, 186, 320
int32 type, 26
integer literals, 18
integer operators, 22
integer types, 20
integration, 26, 323
integration tests, 296
interfaces
    accept interfaces, return structs, 146
    declaring, 141
    embedding and, 146
    function types as a bridge to, 154
    implicit interfaces, 155-159
    naming, 142
    nil (zero value)
        empty interfaces, 148
        nil versus non-nil, 147
        type assertions and type switches,
            150-154
    optional interfaces, 152
    purpose of, 142
    sharing, 144
    as type-safe duck typing, 142-145
internal package, 185
interoperability, 318
interpreted string literals, 18
io package, 233-238
    io.Closer, 237
    io.Copy, 236
    io.LimitReader, 236
    io.MultiReader, 236
    io.MultiWriter, 236
    io.ReadCloser, 237
    io.Reader, 233
    io.ReadSeeker, 237
    io.ReadWriteCloser, 237

io.ReadWriter, 237
io.ReadWriteSeeker, 237
io.SeekCurrent, 237
io.SeekEnd, 237
io.Seeker, 237
io.SeekStart, 237
io.WriteCloser, 237
io.Writer, 233
io.WriteSeeker, 237
ioutil package
    ioutil.NopCloser, 238
    ioutil.ReadAll, 237
    ioutil.ReadFile, 237
    ioutil.WriteFile, 237
Is function, 170-173

J

JSON, 241
    (see also encoding/json package)

K

keywords
    break, 69
    case, 79, 210
    chan, 207
    const, 29-31
    continue, 70
    default, 78
    defer, 100-104, 173
    do (simulation of), 70
    else, 65
    fallthrough, 80
    for, 67
    func, 87, 130
    go, 206
    goto, 83
    if, 65
    import, 178
    interface, 141
    looping keywords, 67
    map, 51
    package, 179
    versus predeclared identifiers, 65
    range, 71
    return, 88
    select, 209-212, 219
    struct, 56
    switch, 78, 150
    type, 56, 188

working with, 192-194
vetting, 8, 64
Visual Studio Code, 9

W

WaitGroups, 220-222
wall clock, 240
Wire, 159

wrapping pattern, 258

X

XML encoding, 247

Z

zero value, 17, 118

About the Author

Jon Bodner has been a software engineer, lead developer, and architect for over 20 years. In that time, he has worked on software across many fields, including education, finance, commerce, healthcare, law, government, and internet infrastructure.

Jon is a Distinguished Engineer at Capital One, where he has contributed to the company's development and testing workflow, developed patented techniques for web payment page detection and population, and coauthored tools for finding and managing software development issues.

Jon is a frequent speaker at Go conferences, and his blog posts on Go and software engineering have been viewed more than 300,000 times. He is the creator of the Proteus data access library (*https://github.com/jonbodner/proteus*) and codeveloper of checks-out (*https://github.com/capitalone/checks-out*), a fork of the LGTM project.

Colophon

The animal on the cover of *Learning Go* is a plains pocket gopher (*Geomys bursarius*), a burrowing mammal found across the Great Plains of North America. These rodents are highly adapted to digging and live primarily underground.

Plains pocket gophers are covered in brown fur and have a nearly naked tail. Physical adaptations to digging include small eyes, short ears, and large, clawed front feet. They also have a tolerance for low oxygen and high carbon dioxide levels. The gophers are named for their external cheek pouches, which can be used for carrying food.

The gophers are territorial and aggressive, and will rarely enter another's burrow. They spend nearly three-quarters of their time in their own burrows, which contain their nests and food caches of roots and grasses. They go above ground to search for food and mates.

The plains pocket gopher's conservation status is of least concern. Many of the animals on O'Reilly covers are endangered; all of them are important to the world.

The cover illustration is by Susan Thompson, based on an antique black and white engraving from an unknown source. The cover fonts are Gilroy Semibold and Guardian Sans. The text font is Adobe Minion Pro; the heading font is Adobe Myriad Condensed; and the code font is Dalton Maag's Ubuntu Mono.

O'REILLY®

Learn from experts.
Become one yourself.

Books | Live online courses
Instant Answers | Virtual events
Videos | Interactive learning

Get started at oreilly.com.

CPSIA information can be obtained
at www.ICGtesting.com
Printed in the USA
JSHW050714160223
37786JS00009B/629